EYES AND EARS.

BY

HENRY WARD BEECHER.

BOSTON:
TICKNOR AND FIELDS.
1862.

UNIVERSITY PRESS:
WELCH, BIGELOW, AND COMPANY,
CAMBRIDGE.

HE papers in this volume are reprinted, with a few exceptions, from the New York Ledger, where they appeared, under the title of "Thoughts as they Occur, by one who keeps his Eyes and Ears open." Besides these, a few have been taken from the New York Independent.

Nothing could be less studied or pretentious than these papers, thrown off almost as rapidly as a photograph is printed, and representing the impressions of happy hours, or the moods and musings of the moment. They are fragmentary, and as careless as even a newspaper style will permit.

If they serve to inspire a love of Nature, or an enjoyment of rural occupations, or to form a kindly habit of judging men and events, or if they even serve only to enliven the tedium of sickness, or while away a summer hour with innocent amusement, they will answer the author's utmost expectations.

H. W. B.

CONTENTS.

EYES AND EARS.

MODERN CONVENIENCES AND FIRST-CLASS HOUSES.

THERE are many persons who suppose that people who live in first-class houses, with all the modern improvements, must of course be much puffed up, and that they become quite grand in their own eyes. It is true, sometimes, that fine houses have proud people in them. We can imagine a pride so reluctant of discipline, and so indocile, as to survive in spite of the experience of a first-class house. But we suspect the same of very poor tenements.

When we moved into a capacious brown-stone dwelling, our better nature, with great simplicity, whispered, "Beware of temptation." And, with an ignorance quite as simple, we supposed that the thieves of grace would be found lurking in large rooms, at ambush behind cornices reproduced from old Rome, or in stately appearances! How little did we suspect that these were harmless, and that very different elements were to moth our patience!

But let a little preliminary exultation of a new man in a new place be forgiven, ye who are now established! Remember your own household fervor on first setting up, while we recount our economic joy, and anticipations of modern conveniences that would take away all human care, and speed life upon a down-hill path, where it was to be easier to move than to stand still! Everything was admirable! The attic had within it a tank so large as better to be called a reservoir. Down from it ran the serviceable pipes to every part of the dwelling. Each chamber had its invisible water-maid in the wall, ready to spring the floods upon you by the mere turn of your hand; then the bath-room, with tub, douche, shower, and indeed various and universal squirt, — up, down, and promiscuous. The kitchen, too, — the tubs with water waiting to leap into them, the long cylinder by the side of the fire, as if the range had its baby wrapped up, and set perpendicular in the corner to nurse. But greatest of all admirations was the furnace! This, too, was interframed with the attic tank; for it was a hot-water furnace. For a time this was our peculiar pride. The water flowed down into a system of coiled tubes, which were connected with the boiler surrounding the furnace fire. The idea was, when the water got as hot as it could well bear, that it should frisk out of one end of the boiler into the pipes, and round through the whole system, and come back into the other end cooled off. Thus a complete arterial system was established, — the boiler being the heart, the water the blood, the pipes at the hot end the arteries, and the return pipes at the cool end the veins; — the whole enclosed in a brick chamber, from which the air warmed by this liquid heat was given off to the dwelling. It was a day of great glory when we thought the chill in the air required a fire in the furnace. The fact was that we wanted to play with our pet, and were half vexed with the old conservative thermometer, that would not come down, and admit that it was cold enough for a fire. However, we do not recollect ever afterwards to have been so eager.

In the first place, we never could raise enough heat to change the air in the house more than from cold to chill. We piled in the coal, and watched the thermometer; ran down for coal again, and ran back to watch the thermometer. We brought home coal, exchanged glances over the bill with the consulting partner, and made silent estimates of the expenses of the whole winter, if this were but the beginning. But there was the old red dragon in the cellar devouring coal remorselessly, with his long iron tail folded and coiled in the furnace chamber without heat. Thus, for a series of weeks, we fired off the furnace in the cellar at the thermometer in the parlor, and never hit. But we did accomplish other things. Once the fire was driven so hard that steam began to form and rumble and blow off, very innocently; but the girls did not know that, and took to their heels for fear of being blown up. When the cause was discovered, the remedy was not easy, for the furnace bottom was immovable, and the fire could not be let down. But our Joan of Arc assailed the enemy in his own camp, and threw a bucket of water into the fire. This produced several effects; it put out the fire, it also put out so much gas, steam, and ashes that the maiden was quite put out also. And more than all, it cracked the boiler. But this we did not know till some time afterwards. There were a few days of comparative rest. The weather was mild out of doors, and cold within. It was soon reported that one of the pipes was stopped up in the chamber, for the water would not flow. The plumber was sent for. He was already well acquainted with the way to the house. He brought upon himself a laugh of ridicule by suggesting that the water had given out in the tank! Water given out? We turned inwardly pale behind the outward red of laughing. We thought we had a pocket-ocean up stairs. Up we marched, climbed up the sides, peered down to the dirty bottom of an emptied tank! Alas! the whole house was symmetrically connected. Everything depended upon this tank; the furnace in the cellar, the range in the kitchen, the laundry department, all the washing apparatus of the chambers, the convenient china-closet sink, where things were to be washed without going down stairs, the entry closets, and almost everything else, except the door-bell, were made to go by water, and now the universal motive power was gone! A new system of conveniences was now developed. We stationed an Irish engine at the force-pump to throw up water into the tank from the street cistern. Blessings be on that cistern in the street! No man knew how deep that was. Like the pond in every village, nobody had ever found bottom. And so we limped along for a few days. Meanwhile, the furnace having been examined, the secret of all this trouble was detected. The life-blood of the house had been oozing and flowing away through this furnace! How much would it cost to repair it? More money than a hot-air furnace would cost, and half more than that! So we determined to clear out the pet. Alas, (again,) how we fondled the favorite at first, and how contemptuously we kicked it at last! It is said that no one is a whole man; we have partial gifts. In our own case, the gift of buying was liberally bestowed, but the talent for selling was either withheld or lay an undeveloped embryo. How to sell the old furnace and to get a new one! There is a great psychological experience there. We aroused ourselves, gave several days to contemplation, laid aside all other cares, ran from furnace to furnace, saw six or eight patterns, each one of which was better than all the others, and all of them were able to evolve vast quantities of heat, with an imaginary amount of fuel. But fortune, that had so long persecuted us, did not presume to destroy us yet, and, as a cat with a rat, let us out of its paws for a moment's ease. In other words, we arranged with Messrs. Richardson & Boynton to put their furnace in the place of the hot-air gentleman in black. And to this hour we have been glad of it. A winter and a half on Brooklyn Heights will put any furnace to proof. And we are prepared to defy the north wind, the west, or the boisterous southwest. They may heap winter as high as they please without, we have summer within.

But O the changing! It was mid-winter. The mild weather took this chance to go South, and got in its place the niggardliest fellow that ever stood sentinel in Kamtschatka. The cellar was divided from the kitchen in part by this furnace. For two or three weeks they were chiselling the tubes apart, and getting the rubbish out of the way; — masons, tenders, ironmen, old iron and new iron, tin pipes, carpenters, and new air-boxes, girls and dinner, the Irishman wheezing at the pump, — all mixed in such confusion, that language under the tower of Babel was a euphonious literature in comparison. Sometimes, as we walked out, our good and loving deacons, in a delicate way, would warn us of the danger of being puffed up with the pride of a stylish house!

At length, after nearly six weeks of the coldest weather of the season, the new furnace took charge of the house. Water returned to the attic. The girls no longer dreaded being blown up by the boiler at the range. But the report came up that the sinks were stopped. After investigation, the kitchen floor must be ripped up, the great waste-pipe reached by digging, and laid open. Broken tumblers, plates, and cups stopped up the pipes. Another week for this. Just as we were sitting down to a dangerous peace, we walked to the window one morning, to see that our yard had disappeared! The roof of the store on which it was laid had given way, and carried down all the earth, crashing through the four stories to the ground! Just one thing more was needed, — that the house itself should slide off bodily, and dump itself into the East River! Yet the misfortune was not without comfort. The store was used for grinding drugs. Ten thousand pounds of salts, ipecac, rhubarb, strychnine, and such like delicacies, were hidden beneath a hundred tons of earth, — the medicine being, where many people for whom it was destined would have been, buried under ground. For several weeks afterwards, I think the bills of mortality improved in the region around.

There were a great number of other things exceedingly convenient in our house. The water-pipe from the roof to the front cistern was carried down *within* the wall to the ground. The bitter cold froze it up. Nobody could get at it. We salted it, we poked hot irons into the tap, we took counsel, and finally let it alone. The cornice leaked, the walls were damp, the ceiling threatened to come off; our neighbor's pipe discharged so much of its contents on the ground as to saturate the wall in our basement entry, the area overflowed into the cellar, we dug a cess-pool to let it off, and cut through the cistern pipe leading to the kitchen pump. It could not be soldered with water in it, and the cistern must be run dry before that could be fixed. The attic tank gave out again. No water!

> "Water, water everywhere,
> And not a drop" —

to wash with. Then came on a system of begging. We took the neighborhood in order, and went from house to house, till we exhausted the patience and the cisterns of every friend within reach. Then we betook ourselves to the street pump, and for two months we and the milkman subsisted upon that.

There was a grand arrangement of bells at our front door which seldom failed to make everybody outside mad because they would not ring, or everybody inside mad because they rang so furiously. The contrivance was, that two bells should be rung by one wire; a common bell in the servants' entry, and a gong in the upper entry. The bell-train was so heavy to draw, that it never operated till the man got angry and pulled with the strength of an ox. But *then* it went off with such a crash and jingle, that one would think a band of music with all its cymbals had fallen through the sky-light down into the entry. Thus, women, children, and modest men seldom got in, and sturdy beggars had it all their own way. It was quite edifying to see experiments performed on that bell. A man would first give a modest pull, — and then reflect what he was about to say. No one coming, he gave a longer pull, and returned to waiting and meditation. A third pull was the preface to stepping back, surveying the windows, looking into the area, when, seeing signs of unquestionable habitation, he returns with flushed face to the bell; — now for it! He pulls as if he held a line by the side of a river with a thirty-pound salmon on it; while all the bells go off, up and down, till the house seemed full of bells. Things are not mended when he finds the gentleman of the house is not at home! We fear that much grace has been lost at that front door.

In the midst of these luxuries of a first-class house, we sometimes would look wistfully out of the window, tempted to envy the unconscious happiness of our two-story neighbors. They had no *conveniences*, and were at peace; while we had all manner of conveniences, that drove us up and down stairs; — now to keep the flood out, and then to bring it in; now to raise a heat, then to keep off a conflagration, so that we were but little better off at home than are those innocently insane people who leave home every summer, and go into the country to take care of twenty trunks for two months. But the cruellest thing of all, as we stood at the window, was the pious looks of passers-by, who seemed to say with their eyes, "A man cannot expect much grace that lives in such a fine house."

It has certainly been a means of grace to us! Never such a field for patience, such humbling of expectations and high looks. If it would not seem like trifling with serious subjects, when asked how one might attain to perfection, we should advise him to buy a first-class house with modern improvements, and live in it for a year. If that did not fit him for translation, he might well despair of any chance.

Ye who envy us, will you exchange with us? Ye who laugh sarcastically at ministerial luxury, will you lend us your sackcloth and take our conveniences? But those who do live in houses full of conveniences will henceforth be our fast friends. They will say, What if he is abolitionist, and we pro-slavery? What if he is radical, and we conservative? The poor fellow lives in a first-class house, and is punished enough without our adding to his misfortunes!

Meanwhile we practise the same charity. We rail no more at Fifth Avenue, and admire what saintly virtue enables so many to carry cheerful faces, who live in houses with even more conveniences than ours. We are grateful for our happier lot. Though we are worse off than people in two-story houses, how much better are we placed than if we lived in Fifth Avenue!

We bear our burden patiently, knowing that in the very moment of despair persons are at the very point of deliverance. Who knows but he may have a fire as well as his neighbors? One hour would suffice to set a man free from all his troubles, and permit him to walk the streets at liberty, unharassed by plumbers, carpenters, tinners, glaziers, gas-fixers, carpet-fitters, bell-hangers, and the whole tribe of bell-pullers!

We are now living at peace. We are in a plain two-story country house, without "conveniences." We are recruiting. Nothing gets out of order. We do not wake to hear water trickling from bursted pipes; we have no chandelier to fall down; the gas never leaks; we are not afraid to use our furniture; our chairs have no linen clothes on; the carpets are without drugget. The children bless the country and a country house, in which they are not always scratching something, or hitting something with shoe, or button, or finger-nails. And we already feel that a few weeks more will so far invigorate us that we shall be able to return for a ten months' life in a *modern house with conveniences.*

*

THE DOG NOBLE, AND THE EMPTY HOLE.

August 7, 1856.

HE first summer which we spent in Lenox, we had along a very intelligent dog, named Noble. He was learned in many things, and by his dog-lore excited the undying admiration of all the children. But there were some things which Noble could never learn. Having on one occasion seen a red squirrel run into a hole in a stone wall, he could not be persuaded that he was not there forevermore.

Several red squirrels lived close to the house, and

had become familiar, but not tame. They kept up a regular romp with Noble. They would come down from the maple-trees with provoking coolness; they would run along the fence almost within reach; they would cock their tails and sail across the road to the barn; and yet there was such a well-timed calculation under all this apparent rashness, that Noble invariably arrived at the critical spot just as the squirrel left it.

On one occasion Noble was so close upon his red-backed friend that, unable to get up the maple-tree, he dodged into a hole in the wall, ran through the chinks, emerged at a little distance, and sprung into the tree. The intense enthusiasm of the dog at that hole can hardly be described. He filled it full of barking. He pawed and scratched as if undermining a bastion. Standing off at a little distance, he would pierce the hole with a gaze as intense and fixed as if he were trying magnetism on it. Then, with tail extended, and, every hair thereon electrified, he would rush at the empty hole with a prodigious onslaught.

This imaginary squirrel haunted Noble night and day. The very squirrel himself would run up before his face into the tree, and, crouched in a crotch, would sit silently watching the whole process of bombarding the empty hole, with great sobriety and relish. But Noble would allow of no doubts. His conviction that that hole had a squirrel in it continued unshaken for six weeks. When all other occupations failed, this hole remained to him. When there were no more chickens to harry, no pigs to bite, no cattle to chase, no children to romp with, no expeditions to make with the grown folks, and when he had slept all that his dog-skin would hold, he would walk out of the yard, yawn and stretch himself, and then look wistfully at the hole, as if thinking to himself, "Well, as there is nothing else to do, I may as well try that hole again!"

We had almost forgotten this little trait, until the conduct of the *New York Express*, in respect to Colonel Fremont's religion, brought it ludicrously to mind again. Colonel Fremont is, and always has been, as sound a Protestant as John Knox ever was. He was bred in the Protestant faith, and has never changed. He is unacquainted with the doctrines and ceremonies of the Catholic Church, and has never attended the services of that Church, with two or three exceptions, when curiosity, or some extrinsic reason, led him as a witness. We do not state this upon vague belief. We know what we say. We say it upon our own personal honor and proper knowledge. Colonel Fremont never was, and is not now, a Roman Catholic. He has never been wont to attend that Church. Nor has he in any way, directly or indirectly, given occasion for this report.

It is a gratuitous falsehood, — utter, barren, absolute, and unqualified. The story has been got up for political effect. It is still circulated for that reason, and, like other political lies, it is a sheer, unscrupulous falsehood, from top to bottom, from the core to the skin, and from the skin back to the core again. In all its parts, in pulp, tegument, rind, cell, and seed, it is a thorough and total untruth, and they who spread it bear false witness. And as to all the stories of the Fulmer, etc., as to supposed conversations with Fremont, in which he defended the mass, and what not, they are pure fictions. They never happened. The authors of them are slanderers; the men to believe them are dupes; the men who spread them become indorsers of wilful and corrupt libellers.

But the *Express*, like Noble, has opened on this hole in the wall, and can never be done barking at it. Day after day it resorts to this empty hole. When everything else fails, this resource remains. There they are, indefatigably, — the *Express* and Noble, — a church without a Fremont, and a hole without a squirrel in it!

In some respects, however, the dog had the advantage. Sometimes we thought that he really believed that there was a squirrel there. But at other times he apparently had an inkling of the ridiculousness of his conduct, for he would drop his tail, and walk towards us with his tongue out, and his eyes a little aslant, seeming to say: "My dear sir, you don't understand a dog's feelings. I should of course much prefer a squirrel, but if I can't have that, an empty hole is better than nothing. I imagine how I would catch him if he *was* there. Besides, people who pass by don't know the facts. They think that I have got something. It is needful to keep up my reputation for sagacity. Besides, to tell the truth, I have looked into that hole so long that I have half persuaded myself that there is a squirrel there, or will be, if I keep on."

Well, every dog must have his day, and every dog must have his way. No doubt if we were to bring back Noble now, after two summers' absence, he would make straight for that hole in the wall with just as much zeal as ever.

We never read the *Express*, now-a-days, without thinking involuntarily, "Goodness! the dog is letting off at that hole again."

*

LITCHFIELD REVISITED.

THE progression of life is so simple, and, in the greatest number of persons, so quiet, that men only know, at length, that they are changed, but seldom perceive the process of changing. We know that we are no longer boys, but cannot tell when we crossed the line. We are conscious that we have reached manhood, and that youth has departed. But so gently did it go, that we are as those who listen to a bird singing in a tree. After it has flown, they listen still, and only know its flight because it no longer sings.

But now and then we are turned back, and brought face to face with the past, in such a way that two lives gaze at each other; and we walk as if one identity had two expressions.

The recollections of the past beat upon the heart, and we stood in its door, as a parent to whom comes back the child not seen for scores of years, uncertain whether to doubt or to accept the familiar strangeness. After long absence, let any one revisit the scenes of his childhood home, and see whether these things be not so. There will be a soft bewilderment, a sad joy of excitement, which, perhaps, one may not be able to analyze, but which is, in fact, the flowing together of the two great streams of life, the past and the present.

Surely, Old Litchfield was a blessed place for one's birth and childhood. Although there were no mountains, there were hills, — the oldest-born of mountains; high, round, and innumerable. Great trees there were; full of confidences with the wind that chastised them in winter, and kissed and caressed them all the summer. The roar of winter winds to our young ears was terrible as the thunder of waves or the noise of battle. All night long the cold, shelterless trees moaned. Their strong crying penetrated our sleep, and shaped our dreams. At every waking, the air was full of mighty winds. The house creaked and strained, and, at some more furious gust, shuddered and trembled all over. Then the windows rattled, the cracks and crevices whistled each its own distinctive note, and the chimneys, like diapasons in an organ, had their deep and hollow rumble. Each room had its own note, and, if carried blindfold, we could have told the rooms over all the house by the peculiar wind-sound which each had.

Next to the winds, our night-experiences in early boyhood were much affected by rats. The old house seems to have been a favorite of this curious vermin. There is something in the short, hot glitter of a rat's eye that has never ceased to affect us unpleasantly. We could not help imagining them to be the mere receptacles of mischievous spirits, and their keen eyes had always a kind of mocking expression, as if they said, "You think we are rats, but if we get hold of you, you will know that we are a good deal more than that." We never could estimate how many populated our old house. The walls seemed like city thoroughfares, and the ceiling like a Forum or a Roman theatre. We used to lie in bed and marvel at what was going on. Sometimes there would be a great stillness, as if they had all gone to meeting. Then again they would troop about with such a swell of liberty and gladness, that it was quite plain that the meeting was out. But nothing ever scared and amused us so much as their way of going up and down the partitions. At first, up would come one, then another, and finally quite a bevy, squeaking and frolicking, as if they were schoolboys going up stairs, nipping each other and cutting up all manner of pranks. Then came a stillness. Next, a premonitory rat would rush down, evidently full of news, and immediately down would pour after him a stream of rats, rushing like mad, and apparently tumbling heels over head. By and by, some old sawyer would commence where he left off the night before, cutting the same partition. To this must be added nibblings, rat-nestled paper, an occasional race of rats across the bed, the manipulation of corn in the garret, the forays with cats and kittens, the rat-engines, — "steel-traps," "box-traps," "figure-fours," and all manner of devices, — in spite of which the rats held their own, and, if allowed suffrage, would have out-voted the whole family, dog and cats to boot, four to one.

The morning after our arrival in Litchfield we sallied forth alone. The day was high and wide, full of stillness, and serenely radiant. As we carried our present life up the North Street, we met at every step our boyhood life coming down. There were the old trees, but looking not so large as to our young eyes. The stately road had, however, been bereaved of the button-ball trees, which had been crippled by disease. But the old elms retained a habit peculiar to Litchfield. There seems to be a current of wind which at times passes high up in the air over the town, and which moves the tops of the trees, while on the ground there is no movement of wind. How vividly did that sound from above bring back early days, when for hours we lay upon the windless grass, and watched the top leaves flutter, and marked how still were the under leaves of the same trees!

One by one came the old houses. On the corner stood and stands the jail, — awful building to young sinners! We never passed its grated windows without a salutary chill. The old store, and the same old name, Buell, on it; the bank, and its long, lean legs spindling up to hold the shelf up under the roof! The Colonel Tallmadge house, that used to seem so grand that it was cold, but whose cherry-trees in the front-yard seemed warm enough and attractive to our longing lips and watery mouth. How well do we remember the stately gait of the venerable Colonel of Revolutionary memory! We do not recollect that he ever spoke to us or greeted us. Not because he was austere or unkind, but from a kind of military reserve. We thought him good and polite, but should as soon have thought of climbing the church steeple as of speaking to one living so high and venerable above all boys!

Then came Judge Gould's! Did we not remember that, and the faces that used to illumine it? The polished and polite judge, the sons and daughters, the little office in the yard, the successive classes of law students that received here that teaching which has since so often honored both bar and bench. Here, too, and we stopped to retrace the very place, being set on by a fiery young Southern blood, without any cause that we knew of then or can remember now, we undertook to whip one of Judge Gould's sons, and did not do it. We never were satisfied with the result, and think if the thing could be reviewed now it might turn out differently.

There, too, stood Dr. Catlin's house, looking as if the rubs of time had polished it, instead of injuring. Next there seemed to our puzzled memory a vacancy. Ought there not to be about there a Holmes house, — to which we used to go and get baskets of Virgaloo pears, and were inwardly filled, as a satisfying method of keeping us honest toward the pears in the basket?

But Dr. Sheldon's house is all right. Dear old Dr. Sheldon! We began to get well as soon as he came into the house. Or if the evil spirit delayed, a little "cream o' tartar, with hot water poured upon it, and sweetened," finished the work. He had learned, long before the days of homœopathy, that a doctor's chief business is to keep parents from giving their children medicine, so that Nature may have a fair chance at the disease, without having its attention divided or diverted.

But now we stop before Miss Pierce's, — a name known in thousands of families, when gray-haired mothers remember the soft and gentle days of Litchfield schooling! The fine residence is well preserved, and time hath been gentle within likewise. But the school-house is gone, and she that for so many years kept it busy is gone, and the throng that have crossed its threshold brood the whole globe with offices of maternal love. The Litchfield Law School, in the days of Judge Tapping Reeve and Judge Gould, and Miss Pierce's Female School, were, in their day, two very memorable institutions; and, though since supplanted by others upon a larger scale, there are few that will have performed so much, if we take into account the earliness of the times, and the fact that they were pioneers and parents of those that have supplanted them. But they are gone, the buildings moved off, and the ground smoothed, and soft to the foot with green grass. No more shall the setting sun see Litchfield streets thronged with young gentlemen and ladies, and filling the golden air with laughter, or low converse which, un-laughing then, made life musical forever after!

But where is the Brace house? An old red house,—red once, but picked at by winds, and washed by rains, till the color was neutral. Thanks to the elements, the old elm-trees guard the spot, a brotherhood as noble as these eyes have ever seen, lifted high up, and in the part nearest heaven locking their arms together, and casting back upon their separate trunks and bole an undivided shade. So are many, separate in root and trunk, united far up by their heaven-touching thoughts and affections.

Mrs. Lord's house is the only one now before we reach our own native spot. This, too, holds its own, and is fertile in memories. Across the way lived Sheriff Landon, famous for dry wit and strong politics. A thread there spun has stretched far down into later time, and been woven in the light and dark of after-figures in the fabric of life. But south of him lived the greatest man in town, Mr. Parkes, that owned the stages! and the wittiest man in town with us boys was Hiram Barnes, that drove stage for him! To be sure, neither of them were eminent for learning or civil influence. But in that temple which boys' imaginations make, a stage-proprietor and a stage-driver stand forth as grand as Minerva in the Parthenon!

But there are houses on the other side. The eastern side of Litchfield North Street, like the eastern side of Broadway, was never so acceptable to fashion, albeit some memorable names lived there. It was our good fortune to be born on the west side of the street. We know not what blessings must have descended upon us from having been born on the fashionable side of the street. One shudders to think how near he escaped being born on the other side, — the east side of the street.

But there is our own old home! Of this we must not speak at the end of a long article.

*

—♦—

PHRENOLOGY.

How to make Preaching Hit.

THE Rev. Henry Ward Beecher is quoted as having said in a sermon that he believed Phrenology, and owed to the "practical knowledge of the human soul" thence acquired whatever success he had had "in bringing the truths of the Gospel to bear practically upon the minds of men." The *Catholic Herald* thinks there is something in this, but suggests to Mr. Beecher that there is a lack of desirable certainty in this process of gathering the character of one's congregation by surveying the cranial developments, and that they have something far better.

"Now, just where Phrenology fails, the *confessional* succeeds. No bumps are studied, and no characteristic is guessed at. The penitent says plainly and distinctly, 'Thus and thus I thought, and thus and thus I did.' 'So I acted, and so I failed to act.'

"If he says, 'I took that wrongfully which was another's,' it is not necessary that the confessor should know that there is a bump of accretiveness. If he say, 'I have been violent, and struck my associate,' what is the need of knowing that he has a development of the organ of 'combativeness.' If he is sinful in thought, and not in act, the tendency is better manifested by confession than by physical development; and in all cases the teacher in the confessional is close to him, and ready to give the advice, adminster the commonition or discipline, or offer consolation and encouragement, that the whole circumstances of the case demand.

"Mr. Beecher asks the *head* of his hearers, that he may deal with the concerns of their souls, while a Catholic priest says, 'My son, give me thy heart.'"

The *Examiner*, a Baptist paper of New York, adds: "It may be allowed a third party to suggest, that both methods have some defect. The phrenological inference is not infallible; the 'penitent' may not tell the full and exact truth. What then?"

In regard to this matter of Phrenology, a few words may not be amiss.

1. When *we* employ the term Phrenology, it conveys to our mind no such idea as a science of *bumps*, as it is vulgarly called: nor is it Craniology, or a science of the skull. It is the *science of the mind*. It includes within its circle the nature, conditions,

and habits of the human mind, as far as they are known.

The only thing which many people suppose Phrenology to teach is, that mental traits can be discovered by the conformation of the head. But this is its least value. It is not unimportant. It has a degree of use in practical life. But, in the nature of the case, it alone will be serviceable principally in exaggerated and imperfect heads, and doubtful and difficult in proportion as one's mind is generally and evenly developed. Phrenology assumes the brain to be the organ of the mind. It teaches that the brain is not a simple unity, but a congeries of organs; that special faculties employ several special portions of the brain for their manifestation; that the skull, in general, conforms to the brain, and indicates the size of its different parts. But, then, what is the *quality* of the substance of the brain? is it fine and healthy? or is it coarse and flabby? This must be known, also; and it is to be judged by the general appearance of the man, his temperament, skin, muscle, etc. In like manner, the quantity and quality of blood which flows upon the brain and stimulates it, determine the power of action to a certain degree, and this must be judged by the size of the organs of digestion, of aeration, and of propulsion, or, in other words, by the form and perfection of the organs of the *trunk*. The head alone does not indicate character. But the head, the texture of the skin and muscle, the build of the body, and, lastly, the expression of the face, posture, gesture. It takes the whole man to be the proper index of man. And Phrenology, as the science of *the mind*, includes in its circuit whatever the mind uses, and whatever in the human body aids, modifies, or influences the mind. Of course, Physiognomy, Physiology, etc., are, to a degree, included in its limits.

We are far from regarding Phrenology as a completed science. Indeed, we believe that more yet remains to be done than has been done. But adolescent and undeveloped as it yet is, we regard it as incomparably beyond anything which has been regarded as a science of mind.

2. Although a knowledge of Organology, and a certain facility of judging men's nature from the structure, is desirable, yet, if one did not know a single *external* phase of Phrenology, if he accepted its classification and division of faculties, and its laws of combination and activity, he would derive from these more advantage in the use of himself, and in his judgment of others, than could be had from all other systems. And this, chiefly, because the faculties are precise and specific, discriminated one from another, and consonant with the experiences and observations of men in daily life.

We do not say, that to a Phrenologist the human soul becomes clear as crystal; that he can walk about and read men like large printed placards. No such thing! There is great skill required, much experience, careful observation, and even then there will be many mistakes made, and much found that will baffle the most penetrating. All that can be said properly is, that practical Phrenology adds very largely to our stock of knowledge, that it simplifies many things which in other systems are obscure, that it very materially helps us even when it does not give us the whole, and especially, that it gives us the *right direction* of research, and the right *method*, so that whatever we do read is more likely to be sober truth, than the results of the spider-systems of philosophy, in which each philosopher spun his theory in some corner, from the web-bag of his own personal consciousness, and left his starved disciples to hang upon it like flies upon cobwebs.

3. The usefulness of Phrenology to a minister of the Gospel is to be settled by asking the question, *Is it beneficial to a teacher and healer of the mind to know what the human mind is, and what are the laws of its action?*

It is a mere impertinence to say that the knowledge of the human mind, or of Phrenology or the science of mind, will not secure a man from mistakes. Nothing will secure a man from mistakes but Death. That settles everything very accurately.

Are not the sciences of Anatomy and Physiology to be studied? and yet the most skilful physician blunders every day of his life. Is there no use in mechanics, because the artisan commits mistakes? Ought not an artist to dissect and study the human structure, because the best-instructed students err in drawing?

No man will ever know the human soul so well as to be able to judge rightly, trace skilfully and aim accurately, every time. Man is too vast an organization to be judged as we would a fly. Men, acting in masses, played upon by a thousand diverse influences, changing their fancies every hour, yet under all changes true to some certain ruling impulses; strangely blended with good and evil, — good and evil that come and go as the shadows of wind-shaken leaves do upon the tremulous waters, — are not to be known with the same precision as we know inanimate things, or the simple and constant laws of nature.

But there is a great difference between knowing nothing and knowing something. There is a great benefit, in practical affairs, in a degree of knowledge which is altogether too vague for scientific uses; and no minister of the Gospel can afford to be without a practical knowledge of men, and in gaining that, nothing will aid him more than a use of the materials afforded by Phrenology. And if, when he has done all that he can, he finds that he is far from a perfect understanding of man in all the mazes of his daily activities, he will still know vastly more than if he had not at all explored the springs of action and the laws of activity.

Our Roman Catholic friend must be simple indeed, if he thinks that the Confessional is the grand means of knowledge. A few overt actions may be found out there. But what does it reveal of the inward states, the multitude of fancies, the swarm of thoughts that spring and spread themselves in an instant the world over, like the rosy flushes of sunset rays, spread through half a hemisphere in a moment, and in a moment retracted and vanished, — of all those dark passions that lurk, but never appear, — of those moods of mind that have no language, that never form themselves into ideas, and that yet do fever the whole being and change the complexion of thought and purpose?

One might as well suppose that he could learn the whole mystery of generation and life, because he heard the hen cackle when she laid her egg, as to suppose that the priest knows the human soul, because the thief told his theft and the murderer his crime.

LETTERS FROM THE COUNTRY.

Mountain Rest, Matteawan, August, 1857.

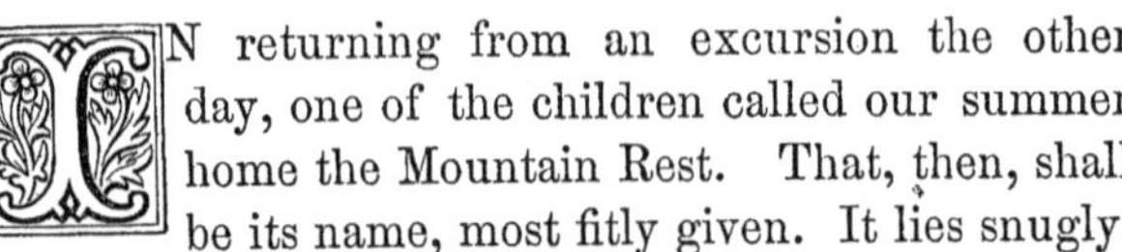

IN returning from an excursion the other day, one of the children called our summer home the Mountain Rest. That, then, shall be its name, most fitly given. It lies snugly, close up under the North Beacon. The North and South Beacons form the two sides of an immense mountain bowl, and the highest point is marked upon local maps as 1,650 feet high. If we were any nearer to the mountain, we should be *on* it. We touch the hem of its garment. We are adopted into its favor. Every day it breathes a blessing upon us. All the loose winds that fly about without anybody to take care of them in the high pastures of the upper realm, it collects in its shepherd bosom, and, feeding them with moistness and the balsamic odors of pine-leaves and other evergreens, it sends them down upon us in refreshing draughts and puffs. Yonder, in parcels, lies the Hudson; beyond it the sparkling city of Newburg, most beautiful in the distance. At night its windows, star-like, speak through the dark air of hundreds of families gathered for the evening. And Powell's factory, close upon the water's edge, with its lines of brilliant lights, is like a fiery-eyed battalion watching the ford, or ferry rather. Farther back swells up a young mountain, behind Newburg, just large enough to hang clouds on for splendid sunsets; and farthest of all, the long blue horizon line made by the Shawangunk mountains, the bound of our sight, to whose level summits the sun attracts our evening eyes, and rewards them by ten thousand valiant feats of clouds and colors. South of us are the Storm King mountains, and the pass of the Hudson through the Highlands.

There is nothing so simple and apparently unchanging as are mountains. And yet there is no variety in tree, in plain, in river or lake, that can be compared to mountain variations. Upon nothing else does the atmosphere work such wonderful effects. We do not refer to those vast heights whose snow and ice-clad summits play with such witching effects with light and color; but to our lower and home-bred mountains. This one behind us, not two thousand feet high, is a solemn necromancer, forever putting forth new fancies.

It wears one face in the morning; it changes its countenance at noon; it surprises you with still another at night. It has one face for heat, and one for the cold. It shags and beards itself with mists, looking down upon you venerable as a hoary seer. Then it drives away every vestige of cloud, and reveals to the eye each line, every depression, every crease and crevice, with such plainness that it changes the whole mountain expression, and you doubt whether you have ever before seen it. A new picture stands before you every day, and yet its identity is preserved, so that it maintains its old associations with new sites of beauty. Not a cloud can come near without paying some tribute. Sometimes you shall see a vast range of white, glistering clouds piled up in banks and brilliant boulders, one upon another silently rising up behind the green mountain, that thus appears but a foreground figured upon this magnificent range of air-mountains.

At other times, fleets of clouds are seen piloting their way quietly through the air, and letting down their shadows upon the mountain-side, as if to anchor there. But both cloud-ship and cloud-anchor move on, dark below and white above! It would seem as if the smile of the cloud was the frown of the mountain.

But all these are mere fancies compared with the grandeur of mountains when storms make them their walking-ground. After long heat and dryness, the mountains seem to shrink back, lose distinctness, and become almost insignificant. The summer, which shrivels vegetation with long droughts, seems to parch and shrink the very rocks. But, suddenly, from the South there come up the tokens of a thunder-storm. Storms especially love mountain highways, and walk upon their summits with a majesty unknown in lowlands. Upon such a theatre the spectacle, lifted up above you, exhibits itself with a grandeur that recalls the noble old conception, that God rides upon storms, and tabernacles himself in clouds upon mountain-tops. Indeed, we never see that half-scared motion of cloud-folds rolling out from the interior, as if there were an inner presence which drove forth the terrified mists, and justified their fear by headlong thunderbolts and fierce lightning-flashes, without an irresistible impression of a real living agency at work within the storm; and that clouds are but the hiding of the Divine Presence!

Nor is the imagination lessened when the murky splendor passes on, and the mountain lifts up its cleansed head and sides with such vivid green, and in such clearness and exquisite beauty, that you feel as if they had been in communion with superior influence, and had received a baptism from on high. This never seemed more striking than yesterday. While in church, in the morning, there came on a sudden dash of rain and hail. We rode home with the mountains before us wearing robes of clouds, and grand with flying storm. To look at these tops, and to recall all the passages of the Old Testament which speak divinely of mountains, would be a sermon more impressive than any from the living voice.

By the way, yesterday morning I was at the Methodist church here. A very pleasant room it is, and I am told that a very worthy society occupy it. But I have a most weighty charge to bring against the good people, of musical apostasy. I had expected a treat of good hearty singing. There were Charles Wesley's hymns, and there were the good old Methodist tunes that ancient piety loved and modern conceit laughs at! Imagine my chagrin when, after reading the hymn, up rose a choir from the shelf at the other end of the church, and began to sing a monotonous tune of the modern music-book style. The patient congregation stood up meekly to be sung to, as men stand under rain when there is no shelter. Scarcely a lip moved. No one seemed to hear the hymn, or to care for the music. How I longed for the good old Methodist thunder! One good burst of old-fashioned music would have blown this modern singing out of the windows like wadding from a gun! Men may call this an improvement, and genteel! Gentility has nearly killed our churches, and it will kill Methodist churches if they give way to its false and pernicious ambition. We know very well what good old-fashioned Methodist music was. It had faults enough, doubtless, against taste. But it had an *inward purpose and a religious earnestness* which enabled it to carry all its faults, and to triumph in spite of them! It *was* worship. Yesterday's music was tolerable singing, but very poor worship. We are sorry that just as our churches are beginning to imitate the former example of Methodist churches, and to introduce melodies that the people love, and to encourage universal singing in the congregation, our Methodist brethren should pick up our cast-off formalism in church music. It will be worse with them than with us. It will mark a greater length of decline. We could hardly believe our eyes and ears yesterday. We could not persuade ourselves that we stood before a Methodist church. We should have supposed it to be a good solid Presbyterian or Congregational church, in which the choir and pulpit performed everything, and the people did nothing.

Our brethren in this church must not take these remarks unkindly. They are presented in all kindness and affection. The choir sung better than many choirs in city churches, but no one sung with them. The people were mute. They used their ears, and not their mouths! But alas! we missed the old fervor,—the good old-fashioned Methodist fire. We have seen the time when one of Charles Wesley's hymns, taking the congregation by the hand, would have led them up to the gate of heaven. But yesterday it only led them up as far as the choir, about ten feet above the pews. This will never do. Methodists will make magnificent worshipping Christians if they are not ashamed of their own ways, but very poor ones if they are. Brethren! you are in the wrong way. It will never do for you to silence the people. Your fire will go out if you rake it up under the ashes of a false refinement. Let an outsider, but a well-wisher, say these plain words to you without offence. The Methodist Church has laid the Christian world under a great debt by its service in the cause of Christ, and we have a right in it, and an interest in it, as common Christians, too great to suffer us to see signs of degeneracy in it without sorrow and alarm. We hope God means to do great things by it yet, for our land. But it will not be by giving up heart and soul, zeal and popular enthusiasm in worship, for the sake of sham propriety and tasteful formalism, that the Methodist Church will become yet further efficient. We hope to see such a revival of religion among them as shall come like a freshet upon their churches, and sweep out the channels of song, and carry away the dead wood and trash which has already dammed up the current of song, and made the congregation stagnant. O that there may be a rain of righteousness upon them, which shall swell their hearts to overflowing, and cleanse their sanctuary from all formalism, and especially from the formalism of pedantic music!

*

HOURS OF EXALTATION.

Matteawan, N. Y., August 17, 1857.

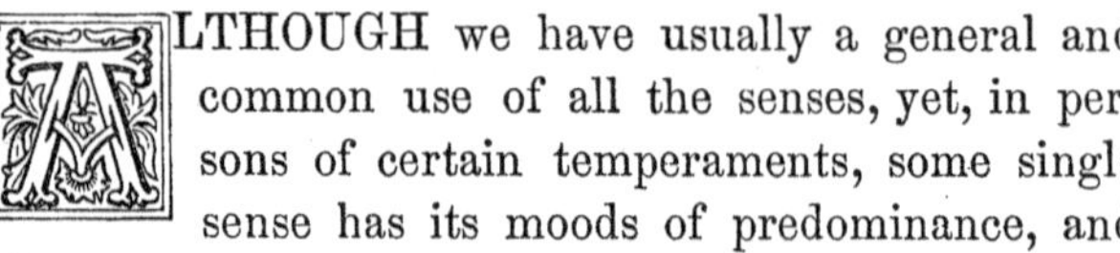

ALTHOUGH we have usually a general and common use of all the senses, yet, in persons of certain temperaments, some single sense has its moods of predominance, and all the others subside and accompany it, as a low and pleasant harmony in music. We have compared it to the habit of a band, in which the French horn seems to rise at times above all others, and to float upon the harmony like a yacht upon the sea; then subsiding, the clarinets emerge and shout above all other instruments, but only for a moment, and then mingling again with their companions, they send forth the bugle, or other instrument. Some such change as this is going on in every one who carries all his senses into Nature for the enjoyment of her melodies and harmonies.

Some days seem to be characterized by some single sense. There are head-days, heart-days, there are eye-days and ear-days, and promiscuous days in which delicious sensations of pleasure at life in general predominate. These last are transcendent. It would seem as if each faculty, every sense, and all the nerves, had come to an agreement, and were sensitively submissive to all the effects of nature and society. In such transfigurations it scarcely matters what happens. Nothing can be amiss. All sounds, all colors, all movements, all conditions of cloud, air, temperature; all things, — grass, rock, or wood, are not only satisfying, but blissful. We seem to hang like a harp in the air, and all things reach forth to touch the strings for joy. And the sense of perfect rejoicing is so unconnected with any apparent cause, or else so far beyond their ordinary effects, that the mind is in a gentle wondering, all the time, as to what can be the cause of such satisfaction. Thus it is that consciousness is reversed; and whereas commonly we feel that happiness is an effect *within* us, that its seat is in our own mind, upon these rare days of ubiquitous and general gladness it seems as if the happiness lay *without* us, and we were voyagers sailing through it, and it lapped and murmured upon us from without, as waves and ripples do upon the summer sides of tranquil ships. The air seems made up of happiness, the clouds, the trees, the grass, the pathless birds, land and water, — all seem to pulsate happiness, to emit it, to breathe it forth upon us; and it falls upon us as dew upon flowers, as serenades rising into the moonlit air seem to rain down on every roof and every casement through the whole town. It is a rare and gracious treat when, in these moods, Nature, like some magnificent Handel, seems to rest from her graver labors and exercises, and to run her fingers, in wild caprices of fancy and joy, over the keys of her organ; exercising herself upon every stop, and filling the whole air and world with delights innumerable! We are filled with the very affluence of peacefulness and joy. There is neither sorrow, nor want, nor madness, nor trouble in the wide world! The glory of the Lord, that at other times hangs upon the horizon, like embattled clouds, — full, gorgeous with the sun, — on such days as we have described descends and fills the whole earth. The impassioned language of the Psalmist and prophets, which, on other days, is lifted up so high above our imagination that we can scarcely hear it, now comes down and sounds all its grandeur in our ears. The mountains praise the Lord. The trees clap their hands. The clouds are his chariot, and bear him through the air, leaving brightness and joy along the path. The birds know their King. The flowers lift up their heads, and with the silent tongue of perfume praise God with choice of odors! The whole earth doth praise thee!

In these transcendent moods each sense radiates a glory upon whatever it perceives. Sounds are magical. That which we usually notice with no favor becomes sweet. Even discordant sounds are smoothed and softened. The eye detects new lines, new symmetries, more beautiful forms, and more exquisite colors, than it is wont to do. The memories that come up from the past bring joys even greater for the moment than the reality. Friends and friendships are glorified. And over against the past stands the future, full of dim joys that hourly increase. These joys of the past and of the future may be likened to that hour, at certain conjunctions of the sun and moon, when one has just left the horizon, but suffuses it yet with his trail of light, while the other, dim in the east, is advancing every moment with growing brightness to rule the hour!

But such days have no art to perpetuate themselves. To-morrow will sweep you to the opposite pole. Yet they are of great use. They exalt an ideal of life. Subjects held up in their light will never be as low and ignoble as they may have been before. And the light in which Duty, Love, and Labor shine in these lucid days will give us exaltation for many days after.

The roots of Nature are in the human mind. The life and meaning of the outward world is not in itself, but in us. And when we have taken in all that the eye can gather, the ear, the hand, and the other senses, we have but the *body;* we do not yet read and know the spirit and truth, which cannot be received by the senses, but by the soul. And Nature comprises in herself all the effects which she causes upon the *senses*, and all that she causes upon the *mind*. He will see the most without who has the most within; and he who only sees with his bodily organs sees but the surface. He who paints or describes with the senses alone is but a surface artist. This superficial reading of Nature is as if one had been taught, like Milton's daughters, to read the Greek language fluently without understanding any part of its meaning. The sound is sweet, the reading is fluent. But all the life and contents are wanting. And he that reads Nature reads God's language. He only pronounces the words, without the meanings, who sees the natural world by his senses only, and not also by his feelings. The bell from yonder steeple sounds out suddenly through the storm-washed air. What does that sound mean? To the bell, rattling. To the mechanical philosopher it means the vibration produced upon the air. To the watchmaker it means twelve o'clock, — noon. To the laborer it means rest and food. To the schoolboy it means release from a living tomb. To the nurse it is the hour for appointed medicine. To the impatient bridegroom it is the hour of wedding. It is the funeral hour also, and the sexton cracks his whip. It means separation and heart-pangs to those aboard the cars. That bell-stroke means all that it can make a man feel and think. It bears back the thought on its waves, and strands us upon the shores of childhood. It opens the door of tears or of smiles, of joyful remembrances or of sad ones. It reaches toward the feelings. Those pulsations beat upon the gate of Eternity. Lying upon the warm and fragrant grass, flecked all over with the golden-spotted shadow of an elm, that deep, solitary, single stroke of the bell, lifted high above the ground, that does not sound out one note and cease, as a trumpet does, but moves and warbles; that pulses again and again, going and coming, as if it were beckoning and soliciting us to follow; — upon that sound we do ride bravely heavenward, and in its dying cadences hear a hundred voices, speaking things to the feeling unutterable in human language. And that single sound *is* all that it can *do*. It is a cause that includes in itself all the effects it is capable of producing.

Nature, likewise, implants her spirit in the human soul. Her shape is without us. Her meaning is within us.

This great mountain behind me is not simply granite lifted up against the eastern sky, as a bulwark against the morning sun, which it hinders from my windows a full morning hour. It is a silent prophet of God, that reveals both ways, past and future, backward and forward; and all that I think when I gaze upon it, and all that I feel, and all that airy middle-experience of deliquescing thought resolving itself into emotion, tenuous and misty; and all that it suggests by association, — all belong to it.

What a man sees in Nature will therefore depend upon what he has to see with. Deprived of four senses, a man would perceive only sounds; deprived of but three senses, he would perceive only sounds and sights. If he have all his physical senses, and nothing more, he will see the rind and husk of Nature. If he bring reason along, he will perceive the connections and homogeneities of natural objects, their relations to each other and to us. If he add imagination, he will find yet deeper insight; if feeling, deeper yet; if religious feeling, more profoundly; and if he hold all these up against the background of the Infinite, then indeed, to his unspeakable satisfaction, the heavens declare the *glory of God*, and the firmament showeth his handiwork. Then day unto day uttereth speech, and night unto night showeth knowledge.

In this view is revealed the difference between one man and another in the enjoyment of Nature. One man communes with natural objects by many more faculties than another. One artist represents Nature seen with the *eyes* simply; another, as seen with the *soul.* And though we cannot by form and color represent all or the chief part of that which the mind perceives, yet what we do picture will be very different if seen only superficially or likewise with feeling.

The augmentations of pleasure in this way are wonderful. The least things and the most obscure become ministers of rare delight. The hands of a giant upon the keys of an organ make no more music than the hands of a common man, for the sound is in the instrument, not in the hand that touches it. And the fingers of Nature, touching the faculties of the human soul, produce effects, not by the magnitude of the thing acting, but by the music within the instrument touched.

Nevertheless, there is a great difference between one thing and another in Nature. All things are not just alike, and the seeming difference of outward things is not altogether in us. It is not to obliterate or confuse a well-known truth that we write, but to make plainer a truth not so well known, — that is, it requires foresight, an object to project its image, and an eye to receive it; — so, on a larger sphere, an outward world is required to produce an effect, and an inward nature to receive it; and both of these working together are required before either of them is clearly developed.

*

FIRST SUMMER LETTER.

Matteawan, July 19, 1857.

HE summer has broken forth. The earth is filled with heat, and the whole heaven is hot! The morning greedily drinks up the dew. The plump stems by noon lose their tenseness, and wilt down. The afternoon rides over the subdued flowers. We all seek the shade, and hold our open necks to the winds, meanwhile greatly

admiring the insects on every side, that grow more nimble with every degree of heat. With the thermometer at 60°, flies are quite sedate and thoughtful; at 75° they grow gay and musical; but at 85° or 90° they become wild with excitement, and whirl and dance through the quivering air as if heat were wine to them.

But we have taken to ourselves the friendship of mountains, and made league with them against the summer fervor. They lift up their great orb as a shield against the morning sun, and when, turning their flank, the sun comes down from the south, they breathe forth a cool wind from their hidden places, and we defy the heat!

Every summer has its own portrait and peculiar individualism. This summer has brought around us multitudes of birds beyond any former one. We are living in a pleasant old house, around which fruit-trees have grown in which birds have bred and lived unmolested from year to year. It is but a dozen wing-beats from the house to the mountain woods. Nothing can please a meditative bird better than to have domestic scenes on one side and the seclusion of the wilderness on the other. A bird loves a kind of shy familiarity. Here we have a garden, a door-yard, an orchard, a barn, grouped together,—and then, on the other hand, the young forests of scooped mountain-side. So the birds come down here for fun, and go up there for reflection. This is their world; that is their cathedral. I notice that they are fond of congregational singing; not only, but every one sings his own tune, in his own time, and to his own words. Nevertheless their singing sounds well. They begin when the stars fade in the morning, and not an hour till star-time again do they leave untremulous with music. The sweetest of them all is the song-sparrow or song-finch ; and it is most numerous and most constant in its music. Two or three pairs seem to have nests in the yard, and apparently many neighbors come to visit and have a chat with them over a social worm.

The bobolink has ceased his song. This fantastic fellow only sings during his love season. Then he takes to the duties of life with great sobriety. He goes through his season, and flies off to the South to become a rice-bird. The song of these birds sounds to me as if they were trying to laugh and sing at the same time. Their song is in snatches, like an old harper's preliminary touches before he sounds forth the real tune ; only they are *always* preluding, and never come to the real subject-matter! Then we have goldfinches, or "yellow-birds," the egotistic "phebes," that sit and call their own name for amusement; the pert and springy wren, barn-swallows and martins, robins, larks, and, at night, *whippowills*. Blessed be the whippowill! that opens up so many volumes in the mind, and sets one thinking backward, — if, as I did, one ever heard them in their youth, waking in the moonlit chamber to hear them sound their notes, bold and plaintive, upon the rock that stood in the edge of the wheat-field! From that day to this the whippowill has had the luck to gather about him fond associations. How little he knows, as he sings, unconscious messenger, what he is saying to me!

Unnamed birds there are, I know not how many.

But I have my books. I shall find you out, every one of you, whose names are there written; and if there be anything worth imparting, our readers shall have the benefit thereof.

*

SECOND SUMMER LETTER.

Matteawan, July 27, 1857.

NOBODY has any business to expect satisfaction in a pure country life, for two months, unless he has a decided genius for *leisure.* If a man expects to live in the country, to gain and spend his means there, of course he must have something to do, and do it all the while. So, too, those who have a *tramp* on hand, — who make a pedestrian tour or a fishing excursion, — must needs stir about. Likewise must they have something to do who go into the country to see city people in the country. Such I take to be all loungers and visitors at fashionable country resorts. This lunacy, however, is modest. It pretends to nothing but what it is. But to gather up yourself and kindred, and sit down in a plain country house, without bears or lions about it, without anything to do but to rest, with no marvels or phenomena, but only the good, real, common country; — if you mean to be happy in this, I repeat, you should have the element of leisure fully developed in you. You cannot be happy if you are in a hurry. You must not be in a hurry to get up or to sit down. You must not be in a hurry to get up in the morning or to retire at night. You must regard it as quite the same, whether you look at a tree ten minutes or thirty. If you walk out, never must you look at your watch; go till you return. If you sit down upon a breezy fence or wall, it should be a matter of indifference to you whether it be four o'clock, or five, or six. There can be no greater impertinence than to say, "It is time to go!" There is no such thing as time to a man in a summer vacation.

When you come into a new scene, you must not expect to be at home in a moment. Nature may say to you, very kindly, "Make yourself at home"; but Nature says it just as any other sensible personage does, not with the expectation that you will do it, but only to show a spirit of hospitality. For it is quite impossible that you should be acquainted with scenery in a moment. Nature is both frank and shy. Like well-bred people, she receives you graciously in all common intercourse, but confidentially only after she has found you out, and knows you to be worthy. Sudden intimacies are always shallow. Wells quickly dug are quickly dry. We have never been able to force matters in thus growing acquainted with new scenery. We never can get along but only just so fast. Things must begin to be familiar before we feel their full meaning; and familiarity comes not by dunning and questioning, not by putting at things, as a burglar would at a lock, punching and screwing, but by a natural and gradual opening of things to us, by a growing sensibility in us to them. For there is always to be an education. Man is forever a disciple, and not a master, before nature. He that knows more than nature does about beauty will get very little help from her.

The eye is a daguerrotype-plate. It is set to receive pictures, not compose or paint them. The art of seeing well is not to think about seeing. Let your eye alone. Let it go as clouds go, floating hither and thither at their will. Things will come to you if you are patient and receptive. No man knows what he sees, but only what he has seen. One looks at a great many things, but sees only a few; and those things which come back to him spontaneously, which rise up as pictures, afterwards, are the things which he really saw.

There is a time for exact study, and sharp examination, and all that; but it is not in summer vacations, of which I am speaking, when a man is looking at nature for no other purpose than rich, ripe enjoyment.

Yet, amid this tranquil, dreaming, gazing life, one cannot always be quite as serene as he would. For example, this morning, while the dew was yet on the grass, word came that "Charley had got away." Now Charley is a most important member of the family, and as shrewd a horse as ever need be. Lately he had found out the difference between being harnessed by a boy and a man. Accordingly, on several occasions, as soon as the halter dropped from his head, and before the bridle could take its place, he proceeded to back boldly out of the stable, in spite of the stout boy pulling with all his might at his mane and ears. This particular morning, we were to put a passenger friend on board the cars at 8.10, — it was now 7.30. Out popped Charley from his stall like a cork from a bottle, and lo! some fifty acres there were in which to exercise his legs and ours, to say nothing of temper and ingenuity. First, the lady with a measure of oats attempted to do the thing by bribing him genteelly. Not he! He had no objection to the oats, none to the hand, until it came near his head, then off he sprang. After one or two trials, we dropped the oats, and went at it in good earnest, — called all the boys, headed him off this way, ran him out of the growing oats, drove him into the upper lot, and out of it again. We got him into a corner with great pains, and he got himself out of it without the least trouble. He would dash through a line of six or eight whooping boys, with as little resistance as if they had been so many mosquitos! Down he ran to the lower side of the lot, and down we all walked after him. Up he ran to the upper end of the lot, and up we all walked after him, — too tired to run. O, it was glorious fun — to him! The sun was hot. The cars were coming, and we had two miles to ride to the depot! He *did* enjoy it, and we did *not*. We resorted to expedients, — opened wide the great gate of the barnyard, and essayed to drive him in, and we did it too — almost; for he ran close up to it, — and just sailed past, with a laugh as plain on his face as ever horse had! Man is vastly superior to a horse in many respects. But running, on a hot summer day, in a twenty-acre lot, is not one of them! We got him by the brook, and, while he drank, O how leisurely! we started up and succeeded in just missing our grab at his mane! Now comes another splendid run. His head was up, his eye flashing, his tail streamed out like a banner, and glancing his head this way and that, right and left, he allowed us to come on to the brush corner; from whence, in a few moments, he allowed us to emerge, and come afoot after him down to the barn again. But luck will not hold forever, even with horses. He dashed down a lane, and we had him! But as soon as he saw the gate closed, and perceived the state of the case, how charmingly he behaved; allowed us to come up and bridle him without a movement of resistance, and affirmed by his whole conduct that it was the merest sport in the world, all this seeming disobedience; and to him we have no doubt it was! We had but seventeen minutes before car time. But we made the best use of it that we could.

The very best method of catching a nimble and roguish horse in a twenty or fifty acre lot is — not to let him get away from you! As to the tranquil and leisurely method of examining nature, we shall defer further remarks until we are cool.

*

SNOW POWER.

IS there anything in the world so devoid of all power as a snow-flake? It has no life. It is not organized. It is not even a positive thing, but is formed negatively, by the withdrawal of heat from moisture. It forms in silence and in the obscurity of the radiant ether, far up above eyesight or hand-reach. It starts earthward so thin, so filmy and unsubstantial, that gravitation itself seems at a loss to know how to get a hold upon it. Therefore it comes down with a wavering motion, half attracted and half let alone. We have sat and watched the fall of snow until our head grew dizzy, for it is a bewitching sight to persons speculatively inclined. There is an aimless way of riding down, a simple, careless, thoughtless motion, that leads you to think that nothing can be more *nonchalant* than snow. And then it rests upon a leaf, or alights upon the ground, with such a dainty step, so softly, so quietly, that you almost pity its virgin helplessness. If you reach out your hand to help it, your very touch destroys it. It dies in your palm, and departs as a tear. Thus, the ancients feigned that— let me see, what was it that they feigned? Lot's spouse went into salt. That was not it. Niobe to stone, several into vegetables, some into deer; but was nobody changed to a fountain? Ah yes, it was Arethusa. But now that we have hit the thing that dimly floated in our memory, it is not a case to the point, so we will let Arethusa flow (slide), and return to our snow.

If any one should ask what is the most harmless and innocent thing on earth, he might be answered, A snow-flake. And yet, in its own way of exerting itself, it stands among the foremost powers on earth. When it fills the air, the sun cannot shine, the eye becomes powerless; neither hunter nor pilot, guide nor watchman, is any better than a blind man. The eagle and the mole are on a level of vision. All the kings of the earth could not send forth an edict to mankind, saying, "Let labor cease." But this white-plumed light-infantry clears out the fields, drives men home from the highway, and puts half a continent under ban. It is a despiser of old landmarks, and very quietly unites all properties, covering up fences, hiding paths and roads, and doing in one day a work which the engineers and laborers of the whole earth could not do in years!

But let the wind arise, (itself but the movement of soft, invisible particles of air,) and how is this peaceful seeming of snow-flakes changed! In an instant the air raves. There is fury and spite in the atmosphere. It pelts you, and searches you out in every fold and seam of your garments. It comes without search-warrant through each crack and crevice of your house. It pours over the hills, and lurks down in valleys, or roads, or cuts, until in a night it has entrenched itself formidably against the most expert human strength; for now, lying in drifts huge and wide, it bids defiance to engine and engineer.

All these thoughts, and a great many others, we had leisure to spin, last night, while we lay within two miles of Morristown, N. J., beating away at a half-mile inclined plane heaped with snow. We look upon the engine as the symbol of human skill and power. In its summer rush along a dry track it would seem literally invincible. It comes roaring up towards you, it sweeps gigantically past you, with the wild scream of its whistle, waving the bushes and rustling the grass and flowers on either side, and filling the air with clouds of smoke and dust, and you look upon its roaring course gradually dying out of sight and hearing as if some supernatural development of Might had passed by you in a vision. But now this wonderful thing is as tame as a wounded bird; all its spirit is gone. No blow is .struck. The snow puts forth no power. It simply lies still. That is enough. The laboring engine groans and pushes; backs out, and plunges in again; retreats, and rushes again.

It becomes entangled. The snow is everywhere. It is before it and behind it. It penetrates the whole engine, is sucked up in the draft, whirls in sheets into the engine-room; torments the cumbered wheels, clogs the joints, and, packing down under the drivers, it fairly lifts the ponderous engine off from its feet, and strands it across the track! Well done, snow! That was a notable victory! Thou mayest well consent now to yield to scraper and snow-plough!

However, it was not *our* engine that got off the track, but another one beyond Morristown. Ours could not get off nor get along. It could only push and stop. The pushing was a failure, the stopping was very effectual. It kept us till nine o'clock before we reached the lecture-room. But the audience had waited with wonderful patience till we got there, and then, with a patience even more exemplary, till we got through — at half past ten.

In the morning, returning, we gloried over the last night's struggle; and shot with a comfortable velocity down the inclined plane, up which we had vainly toiled in the darkness and snow but so few hours before.

In a few weeks another silent force will come forth. And a noiseless battle will ensue, in which this now victorious army of flakes shall be itself vanquished. A rain-drop is stronger than a snow-flake. One by one the armed drops will dissolve the crystals and let forth the spirit imprisoned in them. Descending quickly into the earth, the drops shall search the roots, and give their breasts to their myriad mouths. The bud shall open its eye, the leaf shall lift up its head, the grass shall wave its spear, and the forests hang out their banners! How significant is this silent, gradual, but irresistible power of rain and snow, of moral truth in this world! "For as the rain cometh down, and the snow from heaven, and returneth not thither, but watereth the earth, and maketh it bring forth and bud, that it may give seed to the sower and bread to the eater; so shall my word be that goeth forth out of my mouth: it shall not return unto me void, but it shall accomplish that which I please, and it shall prosper in the thing whereto I sent it."

*

THE MOUNTAIN FARM TO THE SEA-SIDE FARM.

Lenox, August 24, 1855.

MY DEAR DOCTOR "C.": — Allow your friends to congratulate you upon the acquisition of a *sea-side farm*. For although it cannot be compared with a mountain farm, having too much sand and too little loam, yet any farm, even a *sea-side* farm, is better than none. Indeed, it hath advantages, now that I bethink me. The salt air is supposed to favor plums, or rather to be hostile to the curculio, which is the chief scourge of that excellent fruit. And then you have your market close at hand. You can draw out a breakfast or catch a dinner at a few moments' warning. Should an unexpected squad of visitors arrive, and the anxious housewife declare the coop empty, the butcher neglectful, the veal and lamb all gone, you have only to say, "Wait a moment, my dear, I know the very rock around which black-fish love to linger." In a half-hour you return, your basket heavy with yet flapping fish, eager to be cooked into usefulness. Then, too, you can keep a boat. You are not far, I presume, from Saybrook. No, I mean Stonington. But that Saybrook Platform was running in my head, and I got the wrong word. You knew, doubtless, that Stonington was famous for *yachting*. You knew that venerable divines thought it not inconsistent with their cloth to own a fast boat, and to win the first prize at a regatta. Why not? What is more innocent than sailing, unless it be rowing? No cruelty is enacted; no muscles are overstrained. And what sight upon earth is more exceedingly beautiful than a fleet of snowy yachts, blown like sea-gulls across the swelling water? Of course you will own a boat, even if you do not join the club. You will often choose to see how your bit of ground looks from a liquid standpoint. You will often cool your summer afternoons by the breezes off shore, and seek the ocean air long before it bears its coolness in upon the land. It is a very noble thing to see the sun go down upon a golden sea, whose tremulous swells and fretting crests flash the glory from wave to wave, and, breaking up the broad sheet of red light into myriads of sparkles and fiery circles, play with it, tossing it up and down, hither and thither, as if it were a liquid floating on the sea. Do you know how to manage a boat? to row, to scull, to set sail, to reef or take in sail? Pray be careful. Do not carry too much sail. I have long been of opinion that men and ships in our day carry too much top-hamper. While the wind is gentle you may spread everything; but these crank hulls and enormous sails are very tempting to capricious squalls, and some day, as you sit with your hand on the tiller, dreaming out a sermon, under which your good people will perhaps dream too, down will come a sudden swoop, and with one rattle and plunge you will be all overboard! Never go out without a life-preserver under your arms. It is awkward, to be sure, to sit trussed up with these inflated air-ruffles under one's arms; but it will be yet more awkward to flounder about in the water without them, especially if you cannot swim.

Shall you raise your own oysters? Do you intend to dig your own clams? Have you enough kelp growing about your rocks to yield the needed manure for your sandy soil? Do your exhausted pastures do better in pennyroyal or mullein? Do you intend to use white-fish for enriching your garden? If so, pray plough them in deep, or you will be in bad odor with all your friends. People will say you are not sound; that you have a taint.

Excuse these freedoms. They are fraternal. I am all too glad that you have a farm at all. A *sea-side farm* will bring you back toward both the patriarchs and the apostles, for the one tilled the soil and the other fished the sea, and you can do both. May the surf sing you to sleep with its undying anthems! May the storms that awaken your midnights with the thunder of waves and the rush of awful winds bring no shriek to your ear of shipwrecked men; and no visions to your uneasy sleep of drenched and drowning creatures, swept from the deck, and sinking to the bottom, aimlessly reaching out and clutching the waters. Rather may the storm proclaim to you evermore the majesty and might of Him who rideth upon the winds, who sitteth King upon the floods!

And as a ship is dandled on the bosom of the boundless sea like a child upon its mother's knee, and is sheeted with the silver light of morning or flooded with the gold of evening, glistening all the hours between in the unbounded light that God pours in eternal streams from the heavenly spheres, so may you never see such an airy thing, without a sweet and blessed utterance,—"Thus doth God convoy upon the sea of life those who trust in him! For no ship there is of human heart, caught in storm or troubled sea, that hath not its Christ, ready to be aroused to calm the sea and hush the wind!"

I forgot to ask, in the earnestness of my congratulations, whether the farm is yours? Whether it is paid for? I hope the deeds are recorded, without mortgage or lien of any kind. I hope no notes are drawing interest. No blister draws sharper than *Interest* does. Of all industries, none is comparable to that of *Interest*. It works day and night, in fair weather and in foul. It has no sound in its footsteps, but travels fast. It gnaws at a man's substance with invisible teeth. It binds industry with its film, as a fly is bound upon a spider's web. Debt rolls a man over and over, binding him hand and foot, and letting him hang upon the fatal mesh until the long-legged interest devours him. There is no crop that can afford to pay interest money on a farm. There is but one thing raised on a farm like it, and that is the Canada thistle, which swarms new plants every time you break its root, whose blossoms are prolific, and every flower father of a million seeds. Every leaf is an awl, every branch a spear, and every single plant is like a platoon of bayonets, and a field full of them is like an armed host. The whole plant is a torment and a vegetable curse. And yet a farmer had better make his bed of Canada thistles than attempt to lie at ease upon *interest.*

But you do not need these words. You are a shrewd and cautious man. Every dollar is paid. I only write to show you what amiable things I would have said had you needed them. May no greedy land-shark ever grab your land, or pluck it from beneath your children's feet! There may you rest for a few weeks each summer, away from the dust of wheels, the dust of books, and the dust of gold-seeking men. God says some things to the soul in the open field, along the sea-shore, or in the twilight forests, which he never speaks through books or men. Thank God for books! And yet thank God that the great realm of truth lies yet outside of books, too vast to be mastered by types or imprisoned in libraries. A book that leads us away from nature is knavish. Those are true books which, like glasses, serve to enlarge that which lies outside and beyond themselves.

May you walk upon your farm, when, silver-haired, you lean upon your staff, and see the round sun rise or set, day by day, waiting for your own release and glorified ascension! May your children, in after-life, have a rich and endless theme of remembrance in the word HOME. For home should be an oratorio of the memory, singing to all our after-life melodies and harmonies of old-remembered joy!

I do not mean a narrow-faced house in the city,

reaching wearily toward the zenith, with perpendicular stairs, cruel and perilous to much-enduring women; but a real, substantial country home, where they may smell the earth, walk upon carpets of pasture and meadow, that forever laugh at the patterns of the loom! May they hear great trees — let them be elm-trees — sing and pray all day and night above their heads! May they grow in love with crooked brooks winking at you from silver pebbles, with tufted willows and tasselled alders, with orchards and birds, with all insects, with grasses, flowers, rushes, and reeds! with flags and the stately cat-tail — Stop! There is a brilliant humming-bird singing with his wings at the mouths of our honeysuckle blossoms, just come for his morning draught. Beautiful fellow! you are the first at that banquet! None have emptied the nectar. The cups are full of untasted sweets. See! The flowers do not even quiver as he sounds their depths, so skilled is he to hang poised before them and carry his long bill to the very hidden seat of honey. No table is to be spread for thee, no dishes cleaned after thy meal, no servants run to serve thee, no chimney reeks for thine appetite. There is not a fly or moth the less for thy feeding; no seeds are plucked out of the feathery cells. God calleth thee by the voice of flowers, and thou art served with cups more rare than ever Cellini carved for the Medici. Up springs the little winged jewel, and, forsaking the honeysuckle, he hangs right before my window, eying me with his bright eye, as if pitying me for not being a humming-bird! And surely I should like to have a merry bout with you through the air, glancing through the trees, searching all odorous places, living upon flower-digested dew. And yet, sucking floral nectar and wheeling through sun-flashes must be but an empty life! Good for an hour, but not for a life; yet nobler natures there are that do less than that for life. But perhaps my pen attracts him. He has a fit of literature. Ah, sir, if it were Longfellow's, Bryant's, or Tennyson's pen, you might well suck rare honey from the quill. Mine, I fear, would be a little acid and somewhat bitter! He is gone. He did not fly, but flashed away!

Have you honeysuckles and humming-birds? Do you find singing-robins and bluebirds on the shore? Never mind, you have sea-gulls and kingfishers, and now and then, doubtless, an emigrant crow calls out to you from the pine-trees. Do you think gulls sing as finely as wrens, greenlets, or bobolinks?

What is the particular grievance on your farm? Is it nettles? Is it mosquitos? What is it? Something has stirred you up, or you would not have begun your epistle by attacking my dear little mountain farm! At first I was stirred up to resent the indignity. I fancied I could see the maples laughing; the elms and beeches curled their leaves and lips at the idea of the scrubby trees that exist, but do not grow, in the salt spray of the sea-side. The thick, plushy, succulent grass, in whose veins, had I a cow's eye, I could doubtless see milk and butter flowing, the red-top and herdsgrass, when they heard me read your opening lines, winked and ogled each other with laughing, blinking dew-drops, in very derision of the poor wiry salt-marsh hay, which doubtless is so salt that cows give butter and cheese already salted enough. Shall such a place be contemptuous of my emerald hill, which this valley holds up upon her bosom like a glistening jewel? And so I stirred myself to reply, and sat me down at the table, before the open window; but, as I looked forth, the air spake peace. The distant trees stood in peace. The green mountains abode at rest. I saw shadows cast blackly down upon them, and traverse their hollowed sides and ridged tops. But they peacefully bore the blot, and let them pass unrebuked away. The shadows of storms do not hurt the mountains; nor do the shadows of slander or untruth harm men. And so I looked across the sloping lawn, and saw the tranquil lake, nursing in its bosom all the fenced farms that lie upon its thither side, and all around the horizon stood the silent mountains; and above them all, mightily outstretched, the blue and gray dome of sky. All thoughts of conflict forsook me. Shall I be turmoiled in behalf of things which will never lose their own peace? They know their strength, and when storms rail they never answer back again. They know their worth of beauty, and neither boast nor defend it. They abide in stillness.

But tell me, what have you instead of mountains? All around us, on every side, stand innumerable piles, tree-clad, rock-built, carved and scarped along their slopes by ages of rain. Rain! whose soft architectural hands have power to cut stones and chisel to shapes of grandeur the very mountains as no artist could ever do! On their tops clouds love to walk or brood. The hills stand waiting for us in the morning, with their sides draped with mist-lace, wrought in mighty convolutions and patterns, such as royalty could never command from Mechlin or Valenciennes.

In a few hours they are folded and laid away in that great wardrobe above, from which such rare and endless dresses are drawn by the subtle hand of Nature. In these mountains are dells and gorges, caves and chasms, brooks and loud-crying torrents. There are forests that sing to themselves their grand old songs night and day, and none hears but God, into whose ear comes, doubtless, every sound of earth, — the murmur of leaves and the chanting of reeds, the whisper of grass-blades, and the very silence of flowers, as well as the voices of human sorrow and thunder of the city! And then the afternoon and evening phantasms of the hills! Who shall speak the nameless hues which the atmosphere spreads upon the evening hills in mountain regions? What fleet upon your ocean ever fills the eye as do the cloud-fleets the ethereal ocean in these mountain regions? There go very continents, not anchored like Europe or the Americas, but sailing quietly with all their mountains and valleys. Only think of the Alps, some fine morning, starting off upon a tour of the continent! The Apennines, the Andes, old Chimborazo, or the Himalayas, out upon a tour! Yet there they are, as sure as you have fancy in your eye, parading the heavens, and sunning their fiery peaks above old Greylock, or flashing the afternoon light with such dazzling whiteness that the eye can hardly look upon them!

But I forgot that you too have these airy mountains. The sweet ministration of a common atmosphere is yours too. You have my sun, my moon, my stars. The morning which gems our hills, kindles the flaming bosom of your ocean. One noon glows above us both. The angel that brings sleep to me hovers above you. The same heaven lies beyond this visible for us both; the same Saviour, and the same everlasting rest! May no joy by the way or entanglement hold us; and when we look together from its walls, we shall not be able to discern, for their insignificance, our proud little farms! Yea, the whole earth will have dwindled, and would have gone out, were it not for one glowing spot,—Calvary. For that mountain it shall stand forever, and, glowing through all space, shine as a mighty jewel that God hath set as a memorial of his everlasting love!

*

HAYING.

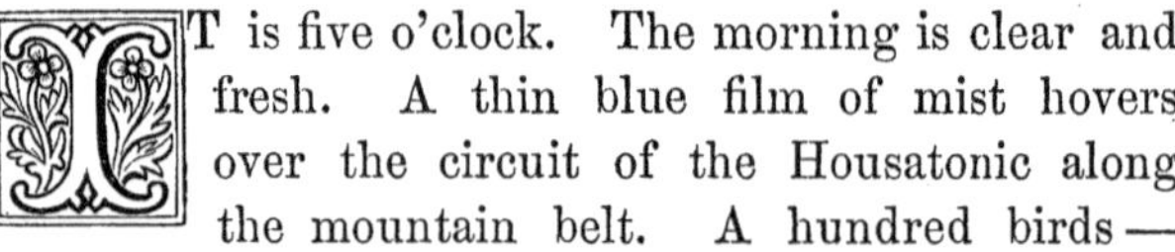

IT is five o'clock. The morning is clear and fresh. A thin blue film of mist hovers over the circuit of the Housatonic along the mountain belt. A hundred birds—yes, five hundred—are singing as birds never sing except in the morning. A few chimneys send up a slow, wreathing column of smoke, which grows every moment paler as the new-kindled fire below burns brighter. In our house the girls are astir, and the mystery of breakfast developing. The little dog is so glad after the lonesome night to see you, that he surfeits you with frolic. The men are in the barn feeding the horses, and getting everything ready for work.

The clouds hang low on the mountains on every

side. Their ragged edges comb the mountain-sides, and look as if they must sway the trees in their course. Yet they move with such soft and drowsy measure, that not a leaf stirs in their path. Will it rain to-day? The heavens overhead look like it. The clouds around the mountains hang low, as if there were rain coming. But the barometer says, No. Then a few rounds with the scythe before breakfast, just by way of getting the path open. There they go, a pretty pair of mowers! The blinking dew-drops on the grass-tops wink at them and pitch headlong under the stroke of the swinging scythe. How low and musical is the sound of a scythe in its passage through a thick pile of grass! It has a craunching, mellow, murmuring sound, right pleasant to hear. The grass, rolled over in a swath to the left, green and wet, lies like a loosely-corded cable, vast and half twined. Around the piece, step by step go the men, and the work is fairly laid out and begun. There sounds the horn! Breakfast is ready. A most useful and salutary custom is that of breakfast. One may work with the hands before breakfast, but not much with the head. The machine must be wound up. The blue must be taken out of your spirits and the gray out of your eyes. A cup of coffee, — real coffee, — home-browned, home-ground, home-made, that comes to you dark as a hazel-eye, but changes to a golden bronze as you temper it with cream that never cheated, but was real cream from its birth, thick, tenderly yellow, perfectly sweet, neither lumpy nor frothing on the Java: such a cup of coffee is a match for twenty blue devils, and will exorcise them all. Involuntarily one draws in his breath by the nostrils. The fragrant savor fills his senses with pleasure; for no coffee can be good in the mouth that does not first send a sweet offering of odor to the nostrils. All the children are farmer's boys for the occasion. Were Sevastopol built of bread and cakes, these are the very engineers who would take it. Bless their appetites! It does one good to see growing children eat with a real hearty appetite. Mountain air, a free foot in grassy fields and open groves, plain food and enough of it,—these things kill the lilies in the cheek and bring forth roses.

But we must make haste, and make hay while the sun shines. Already John Dargan is there whetting his scythe. John, tough as a knot, strong as steel, famous in all the region for ploughing, and equally skilful at mowing, turning his furrow and cutting his swath alike smoothly and evenly. If Ireland has any more such farmers to spare, they may come on in spite of all the Know-Nothings. The Man of the Farm strikes in first, as being the head man in this dominion, and John follows, and away they go right through the clover and herdsgrass, up the hill, toward the sun. The grass is full of dew, which quivers in the sunlight, and winks and flashes by turns all the colors of a rainbow. We follow after, as one that limps, having never attained the art of mowing; and being a late apprentice and mere learner, we prefer to let our betters go first. One swath will satisfy our zeal, and we shall then fall into the ranks of the spectators. Round and round the field they go, with steady swing, the grass plat growing less at every turn.

What a miniature forest is this tall grass full of

under-brush clover! How full of population! Vast communities dwell here of which we have but little knowledge, and for which we have but little sympathy. All manner of grasshoppers, field-crickets, bugs of every shape and color, worms, birds, young and old, and nameless life, swarm through these grassy forests, past all counting. One imagines the sudden surprise with which the crash of the scythe overthrows all their structures, obliterates their paths, destroys their haunts and societies, and buries thousands of them under each swath of grass. All the bright webs of spiders that sit up late at nights, the virgin webs that have as yet caught nothing but dew, and have caught a whole lapful of that, are swept in one stroke. A mower will, in half a day, disarrange the plans of myriads of his fellow-creatures, walking a conqueror through their desolated cities and dwellings, without once thinking, even, that he has wrought his task amid such multitudinous company. We, following on, turn over the grass, and watch the liberated captives, that take their disasters very patiently. Spiders forget to be voracious. Insects run over spiders without fear. All herd together in peace, made by a common misfortune. So we have read that bears, wolves, panthers, deer, rabbits, and foxes are sometimes pent up on some high ground, islanded by a sudden freshet, and forget their destructive habits, and live together peacefully until the receding waters let them forth again.

While we are musing upon the fate of bugs, a shout from the boys informs us that the mowers have disclosed a meadow-lark's nest. Sure enough, there goes the gibbering bird over into the next field, to complain and mourn over her most unexpected loss. Five speckled eggs are not so easily laid as to be given up without a thought! How many fond hopes are here crushed by one swing of Time's scythe, — or John's scythe it was, I believe! They are warm and smooth. How good they felt to the warm-breasted mother! Here she sat mute, reflecting upon the joyful times when she should inform her mate that the shells were broken, and both of them should bring a dilapidated worm to the ugly-looking mouths of their callow young! But when did a child ever look ugly to its mother! And larks doubtless think their featherless, discolored, yellow-mantled squabs more beautiful than full-grown humming-birds. And now the bereaved mother is flying upon the fence, and thence to the top of a near bush, to see the issue. We carefully put up sticks about the nest, and took oaths of humanity from all the boys, and caused horse-rakes and cart-wheels to respect the nest. But when the grass was cleared from the field, and the nest was left wide open to the sun, without shade or protection, the owners held a council over matters, and resolved to abandon the desecrated nest, set the eggs down to profit and loss, emigrate to another meadow, and begin life again! After two days' waiting, some of the kind friends, without our knowledge, removed the desolate nest and placed it upon our writing-table, and there it now lies before us, with a vine of green leaves and a few spikes of yellow sweet-clover twined about it. Poor eggs! No lark shall ye ever be! Ye shall not shake dew from the grass, nor pick worms from the earth, nor sing a mournful minor song, as I hear your kindred now doing from out of the field before my window.

Meanwhile all the boys have been at work spreading the grass. The hay-cocks of yesterday have been opened. The noon comes on. It is time to house it. It is brave work to see men pitching and loading hay. We lie down under the apple-trees and exhort them all to diligence. We are surprised at any pauses to wipe the perspiration from their brows. We are very cool. We think haying a beautiful sport. We admire to see it going on from our window! We resist all overtures of the scythe and the fork, for we think one engaged in the midst of it less favorably situated to make calm and accurate observations.

The day passes and the night. With another morning, and that Saturday morning, comes up the sun without a single cloud to wipe his face upon. The air is clear and crystal. No mist on the river. No fleece upon the mountains. Yet the barometer is sinking,—has been sinking all night. It has fallen more than a quarter of an inch, and continues slowly to fall. Our plans must be laid accordingly. We will cut the clover which is to be cured in the cock, and prepare to get in all of yesterday's mowing before two o'clock. Not till about ten o'clock is any change seen. Then the sunlight seems pale, though no cloud is before it. Some invisible vapor has struck through the atmosphere. By and by clouds begin to form,—loose, vast, cumbrous, that slowly roll and change their unwieldy shapes, and take on every shade of color that lies between the darkest leaden gray and the most brilliant silver gray. One load we roll in before dinner. While catching our hasty meal affairs grow critical. The sun is hidden. The noon is dark. All hands are summoned. Now if you wish to see pretty working, follow the cart, and see long forks leap into the cocks of hay, and to a backward lift they spring up, poise a moment in the air, shoot forward, and are caught upon the load by the nimble John, and in a twinkling are in their place. We hear thunder! Lightnings flash on the horizon. Jim and Frank and Henry Sumner are springing at the clover, rolling it into heaps and dressing it down so as to shed rain. There are no lazy-bones there!

On the other side of the road there is a small piece of this morning's cut grass lying spread. Even we ourselves wake up and go to work. All the girls and ladies come forth to the fray. Delicate hands are making lively work, raking up the dispersed grass, and flying with right nimble steps here and there, bent upon cheating the rain of its expected prey. And now the long winrows are formed. The last load of hay from the other fields has just rolled triumphantly into the barn! Down jumps John, with fork in hand, and rolls up the winrows into cocks. We follow and glean with the rake. The last one is fashioned. A drop pats down on my face. Another, and another. Look at those baseless mountains that tower in the west, black as ink at the bottom, glowing like snow at the top edges! What gigantic evolutions! They open, unfold, change form, flash lightnings through their spaces, close up their black gulfs, and move on with irresistible but silent march through the heated air. Far in the north the rain has begun to sheet down upon old Greylock! But the sun is shining through the shower, and changing it to a golden atmosphere, in which the mountain lifts up its head like a glorified martyr amid his persecutions! Only a look can we spare, and all of us run for the house, and in good time. Down comes the flood, and every drop is musical. We pity the neighbors who, not warned by barometer, are racing and chasing to secure their outlying crop.

*

MOWING-MACHINES AND STEAM-PLOUGHS.

Lenox, August, 1855.

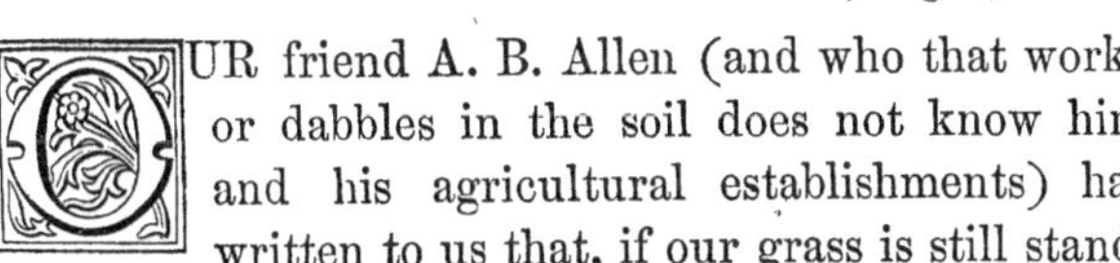

OUR friend A. B. Allen (and who that works or dabbles in the soil does not know him and his agricultural establishments) has written to us that, if our grass is still standing, he will, at his own expense, send up one of his new mowing-machines, and give us a day's work with it, for *he* thinks that it is the best machine yet out. Alas! our grass is all cut, except a small strip near the White Violet Grove, a gore in the swale on the west side of the hill, and some coarse stuff, for litter, down in the muck swamp. To be sure, this could be cut by a mowing-machine, especially one of which our friend says, "It is impossible, I think, now to clog the knives even in the wettest, greenest, shortest, thickest, finest grass!" But all the grass left standing would not be a mouthful for such an iron fellow, and yet why not send the machine up? Let it remain here! We shall have a large second crop on that part of the farm which has been deeply ploughed and dressed with muck. This slaty loam seems to love muck dearly, and holds out its grassy hands in gratitude for any particle given to it. And then, too, next summer we shall be ready for the mower. Do not hesitate, friend Allen, we will take good care of the machine, and if it performs half as well as you affirm, and as we believe that it will, we will give the world the account of its doings in the best English which we can command. When shall we look for it?

But if Allen's Mower had taken a notion about the time we did to come to Lenox, what a world of work would have been spared to human muscles! Here are thirty-five or forty acres of grass, over which, in half-circles, advancing four or five inches at a clip, the men have crept, shuffling along with their feet, crouched and sweating, hot, and tired in the small of the back. Two men will mow, say four acres a day, besides looking after that which was cut yesterday. Here are ten days of work. But throwing out the Sabbaths and throwing in the rainy days (which this year have striven to wipe out the memory of every day of last summer's drought), and there will be at least ten days more, or full three weeks of haying; i. e. mowing, watching the barometer (that is my part of the work), dodging showers, or nesting in the dry hay, with the showery west coming down upon us with black banners flying and thunder-trumpets sounding. However, these occasional matches between the storm and the farmer's whole family are not the least interesting and exciting of country sports. There is no game of ball like it, no rowing-match can be compared to it. As for a horse-race, it is a mere piece of vulgar cruelty in comparison.

The farmer, you see, would n't believe the barometer, and wanted yesterday's mowing to get a few hours more sun before housing. About three o'clock he did not like the looks of things in the west. Away went the boys after the brown horses, Major and Larry. Old Gray was put before the horse-rake, and Frank was told to put in his best kicks to hurry long-legged Gray over the field. About four o'clock we came forth to see what all this meant. What a bother was here! Maria and Ann and Nelly all with rakes, — the sister, wives, the daughter, and the daughters big and little, were flying about; the little boys and middling-sized boys, — in all, four; spry Jim and nimble John and the farmer, and last of all, and quite undisturbed by any fear of losing hay, we ourself, — in all sixteen human creatures, raking, rolling, piling up, pitching up, loading, and trimming down the precious fodder.

The rain made haste, and so did we! We saw it coming down, with the sun straining through it, far in the northwest. In a few moments it had covered in several hills more. It advanced rapidly from swell to swell and from peak to peak. The sunlight went out, gray haze ran skirmishing forward before the black heavy artillery. Now the mountains west of Lenox, Baldhead and all, stood up solemn as death, and as dark as night, right against the leaden grayness of the rain-cloud. In a moment their tops were caught and wrapped round with rain. The mountains are gone out. Now the sheeted rain makes at the church-hill, and the white belfry disappears; it comes skipping from point to point hitherward. Nothing can turn it from its path!

Work, boys, work! We felt a drop on our face, and another on our hand. A breath of wind gives a wild puff and dies away and is still. We can hear the roar of the rain as it comes through the wood yonder! The birds are all silent there. A single melancholy whistle is heard from the north beyond us. The last forkful has gone up on the load, and away goes the creaking, overloaded wagon, a man on each side holding up the towering, swaying mass with propping forks. It rises on the barn doorway, it hesitates, it touches, it grazes at the top, down sinks John to save his head a thump, but bawls out smotheringly from the hay at the horses, who jump and slip but spring again and buckle to with all their force for a last pull! Up comes the load, it rolls in, and the howling rain comes pouring down on the roof, but a little too late! In that race we think the farmer had slightly the advantage!

Let us see; how did we get to this spot? Ah, we started with a mowing-machine. Well, we wanted to say, that if, instead of these slow but peaceful scythes, we had had one of these mowers with iron sinews, that is never hurt or tired or sweaty, but rolls quietly along over twelve acres a day, and then tucks up its knives at night as if it had been out walking for a little sport in the grass, how much time would have been gained, how much struggle saved, how easily on the few fair days — fair, but hot — might we have cut and cured the whole crop without being chased out of the field by storms.

In that case we should have had our barley all harvested before this. Now it is crinkled, and will require twice the labor to secure it. Our wheat too — spring wheat (not the club-wheat, bought of Allen & Co., but the Mediterranean or Black-Sea wheat, —

Crimea wheat, for aught that we know) — would have been attended to before this. Now it is all down. Maybe it is sprouted. Perhaps it will mildew, or it may rust.

The midge may get into it, the fly will attack it, — not our harmless house-fly, a native, every drop of whose blood is American, — but that hateful foreign fly, which the British brought over with their mercenary Hessians. We could whip the British and the Hessians, but not the Hessian fly. *That* could never be brought to sign articles of peace. As we were saying, the midge, the fly, the weevil, the rust, the blight, the sprout, — in short, all the desperate maladies which attack newspapers about the time of wheat-harvest, — may be impending over our wheat (two acres and a half there are of it), because, for the want of a mowing-machine, the grass obliged us to neglect the wheat! But there is some consolation on a farm for everything. If it is bad hay weather, it is good potato weather. If it is too hot and dry for pastures, it is just right for corn. The same rain that vexes our first mowing is bringing on the second growth, or *rowen*.

We are accustomed to regard the improvements in machinery chiefly in their relations to manufacturing and locomotion. But nowhere else will a greater change be wrought by machinery than upon the farm. We are in the infancy of agriculture.

The knowledge of the elements with which we deal, and which compose rocks, soils, plants, and animal fibre, that organic chemistry puts into our hands, gives direction and accuracy to our processes, but does little to abridge manual labor. Mechanics step in at this point, and promise to set men free, and to make a servant of iron that will toil for him without fatigue, and with quadruple speed.

Great as is the saving of labor achieved by reapers, mowers, threshers, etc., they are all as nothing in comparison with that which must come before long, — THE STEAM-PLOUGH! What a revolution would take place, when a gang of five or six ploughs, cutting from fifteen to twenty-four inches deep, shall plow from thirteen to fifteen acres a day! A farm of twenty acres will then be equivalent to a hundred acres now. A hundred acres so cultivated will yield unexampled crops. It will be better for small farmers than it would be to make every man a present of four times as much land as he had before.

Then, too, large farming could be carried on without the drawbacks which now hinder it. A thousand acres ploughed, tilled, and reaped by machinery could be handled as easily by the proprietor as now he handles a hundred acres.

As yet we have only scratched the surface of the earth. We have never fairly harnessed mechanics, or made a farmer of science.

The man who invents a steam-plough, that will turn twelve or fifteen acres a day, two feet deep, will be an emancipator and civilizer.

Then labor shall have leisure for culture. Thus working and studying shall go hand in hand. Then the farmer shall no longer be a drudge; and work shall not exact much, and give but little. Then men will receive a collegiate education to fit them for the farm, as now they do for the pulpit and the forum, and in the intervals of labor, gratefully frequent, they may pursue their studies; especially will books be no longer the product of cities, but come fresh and glowing from Nature, from unlopped men, whose side-branches, having had room to grow, give the full and noble proportions of manhood from top to bottom. God speed the plough!

*

P. S. A critic, near at hand, thinks the storm in this letter very much like the one in the last. It is *not* the same storm, but another just like it. Nature has not been afraid of repeating her storms every day; and surely we should not be blamed for doing our storms once a week.

CITY BOYS IN THE COUNTRY.

Mountain Rest, Matteawan, September 1, 1857.

HIS is the first day of autumn. Summer is gone; gone how swiftly and unperceivedly! It has seemed to me like a green leaf floating upon a silent river. It came quietly toward me from above, then moved past in a shadowy and spectre-like way, and now has floated down and gone past the bend in the river, and I shall see the summer leaf no more. In like manner, the gold leaf of autumn has been glistening in the distance, and drawing daily nearer. It too, in turn, will glow and shine upon the spotted stream of time and go past. Then comes winter. It hath no leaves to give. It offers frost particles and flakes of snow instead.

To-day is a goblet-day. The whole heavens have been mingled with exquisite skill to a delicious flavor, and the crystal cup put to every lip. Breathing is like ethereal drinking. It is a luxury simply to exist. The whole air is full of inarticulate music. Birds have given way to the autumnal choir. Crickets, locusts, and katydids are chirping and harping away at the most astonishing rate.

When birds sing they never *fill* the air. They sing in multiplied voices, and yet there is always seeming room for more. But katydids and crickets surfeit the air. They are "mixture-stops" of not four or five sounds, but forty. Unlike birds' singing, there is no individualization. It is a vast body of sound. Sometimes one imagines them as jolly fiddlers at a revel; and we can see them lying back and fiddling with the most enjoying relish. At other times, they remind you of an orchestra in the anteroom chording their instruments. They seem to twang and thumb, to scrape and draw, without ever coming to concert-pitch or getting ready for the overture. Then, again, one fancies that they are fairies chattering in the grass, and imagines as best he can what cricket mirth must be; what grasshopper rivalries amount to; what locust passions and sentiments are. It would be curious to look at life from their point of view. Their notions of man would be a chapter in mental philosophy full as wise and profitable as the most of those which have amused sober sects, and fooled them into philosophy.

Probably there are dandy grasshoppers, which strut about in the grass, exhibiting their graceful legs; athletes, proud of the prodigious muscle of their thighs; amorous locusts, that execute all fantastic observances fitted to their state. Are there not castes and ranks, and distinctions of society, in the grass as well as above it? Shining crickets, jet, handsome, — these are doubtless despising the rusty ash-colored fellow, who knows no better than to wear the jacket which Nature made for him. But we sat down to write upon something besides these stridulous gentlemen of the grass orchestra; something quite as noisy in their way, but of a good deal more interest. We mean Boys!

A boy is a piece of existence quite separate from all things else, and deserves separate chapters in the natural history of man. The real lives of boys are yet to be written. The lives of pious and good boys, which enrich the catalogues of great publishing societies, resemble a real boy's life about as much as a chicken picked and larded, upon a spit, and ready for delicious eating, resembles a free fowl in the fields. With some few honorable exceptions, they are impossible boys, with incredible goodness. Their piety is monstrous. A man's experience stuffed into a little boy is simply monstrous. And we are soundly sceptical of this whole school of juvenile *paté de foie gras* piety. Apples that ripen long before their time are either diseased or worm-bitten.

So long as boys are babies, how much are they cherished! But by and by the cradle is needed for another. From the time that a babe becomes a boy, until he is a young man, he is in an anomalous condition, for which there is no special place assigned in Nature. They are always in the way. They are always doing something to call down rebuke. They are inquisitive as monkeys, and meddlesome just where you don't wish them to be. Boys have a period of mischief as much as they have measles or chicken-pox. They invade your drawers, mix up your tooth-powder with hair-oil; pull your laces and collars from their repositories; upset your ink upon invaluable manuscript; tear up precious letters, scatter your wafers, stick everything up with experimental sealing-wax; and spoil all your pens, in the effort at spoiling all your paper.

Poor boys! What *are* they good for? It is an unfathomable mystery that we come to our manhood (as the Israelites reach Canaan) through the wilderness of boyhood. They are always wanting something they must not have, going where they ought not to be, coming where they are not wanted, saying the most awkward things at the most critical times. They will tell lies, and, after infinite pains to teach them the obligations of truth, they give us the full benefit of frankness and literalness, by blurting out before company a whole budget of family secrets. Would you take a quiet nap? Slam-bang go a whole bevy of boys through the house! Has the nervous baby at length, after all manner of singings, trottings, soothings, and maternal bosom-opiates, just fallen asleep? Be sure an unmannerly boy will be on hand to bawl out for permission to do something or other, which he has been doing all day without dreaming of leave.

Who shall describe the daily battle of the hair and the bath, the ordeal of aprons for the table, the placing and moving up, and the endless task of good manners? If there is one saint that ought to stand higher than another on the calendar, it is a patient, sweet-tempered children's nurse! Talk of saintship, simply because a man lived in a cave, and was abstemious, or because he died bravely at the stake! What are fagots of fiery sticks for a few hot moments compared to those animated fagots which consume nurses and governesses for months and years, to say nothing of the occasional variety of parental coals!

Are we, then, not on the boys' side? To be sure we are. It is not their fault that they are boys, nor that older people are not patient.

The restless activity of boys is their necessity. To restrain it is to thwart Nature. We need to provide for it. Not to attempt to find amusement for them, but to give them opportunity to amuse themselves. It is astonishing to see how little it requires to satisfy a boy-nature.

First in the list we put *strings*. What grown-up people find in a thousand forms of business and society, a boy secures in a string! He ties up the door for the exquisite pleasure of untying it again. He harnesses chairs, ties up his own fingers, halters his neck, coaxes a lesser urchin to become his horse, and drives stage, — which, with boys, is the top of human attainment. Strings are wanted for snares, for bows and arrows, for whips, for cat's-cradles, for kites, for fishing, and a hundred things more than I can recollect. A knife is more exciting than a string, but does not last so long, and is not so various. After a short time it is lost, or broken, or has cut the fingers. But a string is the instrument of endless devices, and within the management and ingenuity of a boy. The first article that parents should lay in, on going into the country, is a *large ball of twine*. The boys must not know it. If they see a whole ball the charm is broken. It must come forth mysteriously, unexpectedly, and as if there were no more!

For indoors, next, we should place upon the list pencils and white paper. At least one hour in every day will be safely secured by that. A slate and pencil are very good. But as children always aspire to do what men do, they account the unused half of a letter and a bit of pencil to be worth twice as much as any slate.

Upon the whole, we think a safe stream of water near by affords the greatest amount of enjoyment among all natural objects. There is wading and washing; there is throwing of stones, and finding of pebbles; there is engineering, of the most laborious kind, by which stone and mud are made to dam up the water, or to change the channel. Besides these things, boys are sensitive to that nameless attraction of beauty which specially hovers about the sides of streams; and though they may not recognize the cause, they are persuaded of the fact that they are very happy when there are stones with gurgling water around them, shady trees, and succulent undergrowth, moss, and water-cress, insect, bird, and all the population of cool water-courses.

But boys are not always boys. All that is in us in leaf is in them in bud. The very yearnings, the imaginings, the musings, yea, the very questions, which occupy our later years as serious tasks, are found in the occasional hours of boyhood. We have scarcely heard one moral problem discussed in later life that is not questioned by children. The creation of the world, the origin of evil, divine foreknowledge, human liberty, the immortality of the soul, and various other elements of elaborate systems, belong to childhood. Men trace the *connections* of truths, and their ethical applications and relations, but the simple elements of the most recondite truths seem to have gained in them very little by the progress of years. Indeed, all truths whose root and life are in the Infinite are like the fixed stars, which become no larger under the most powerful telescope than to the natural eye. Their distance is too vast to make any appreciable variation in magnitude possible. They are mere points of light.

Boys have their soft and gentle words too. You would suppose by the morning racket that nothing could be more foreign to their nature than romance and vague sadness, such as ideality produces in adults. But boys have hours of great sinking and sadness, when kindness and fondness are peculiarly needful to them.

It is worthy of notice, how soon a little kindness, a little consideration for their boy-nature, wins their confidence and caresses. Every boy wants some one older than himself to whom he may go in moods of confidence and yearning. The neglect of this child's want by grown people, and the treating of children as little rattling, noisy imps, not yet subject to heart-throes because they are so frolicsome in general, is a fertile source of suffering. One of the most common forms of selfishness is that which refuses to recognize any experience as worthy of attention if it lies in a sphere below our own. Not only ought a man to humble himself *as* a little child, but also *to* little children.

A thousand things are blamed in them simply because, measured by our manhood standard, they are unfit, whereas upon the scale of childhood they are congruous and proper. We deny children's requests often upon the scale of our own likings and dislikings. We attempt to govern them by a man's regimen, and not by a child's.

And yet, badgered, snubbed, and scolded on the one hand; petted, flattered, and indulged on the other,—it is astonishing how many children work their way up to an honest manhood in spite of parents and friends. Human nature has an element of great toughness in it. When we see what men are made of, our wonder is, not that so many children are spoiled, but that so many are saved.

The country is appointed of God to be the children's nursery; the city seems to have been made by malign spirits to destroy children in. They are cramped for room, denied exercise, restrained of wholesome liberty of body, or, if it be allowed, it is at the risk of morals.

Children are half educated who are allowed to be familiar with the scenes and experiences of the open country. For this, if for no other reason, parents might make an effort every year to remove their children for some months from the city to the country. For the best effect, it is desirable that they should utterly leave the city behind them. It is absurd to go into the country to find all the luxuries of a city. It is to get rid of them that they go. Men are cumbered and hampered by too much convenience in the city. They grow artificial. They lose a relish for natural beauty and the simple occupations of rural life. Our children need a separate and special training in country education. We send them to the Polytechnique for eight months. But for four months we send them to God's school in the openness and simplicity of the country. A diploma in this school will be of service to body and mind while life lasts.

*

A TIME AT THE WHITE MOUNTAINS.

FTER a week or two among the White Mountains, I have concluded not to write about them. They are a university of mountains. One must enter regularly, pursue the course of study, and graduate, before he is worthy of a mountaineer's degree, — and before he undertakes to write in any worthy manner. As I am only a freshman, and in the first term at that, I do not propose to set forth and write out the whole of the White Mountains. In riding along these green lanes, we often break off — or twist off, rather — a branch of birch, and, bruising the skin, carry it for the sake of its delightful fragrance. In like manner, I will give you just a sprig of my experience.

The descent from the top of Mount Washington, toward the Gibbs House, had in it one half-hour of extreme pleasure and two hours of common pleasure. After leaving the summit hill, I shot ahead of the fifteen or twenty in the party, and rode along the ridge that separates the eastern and western valleys. Beginning at our very feet as little crevices or petty gorges, the valleys widened, and deepened, and stretched forth, until on either side they grew dim in the distance, and the eye disputed with itself whether it was lake or cloud that spotted the horizon with silver. The valleys articulated with this ridge as ribs with a backbone. As I rode along this jagged and broken path, except of my horse's feet there was not a single sound. There was no wind. There was nothing for it to sing through if there had been ever so much. There were no birds. There were no chirping insects. I saw no insects except spiders, that here, as everywhere, seemed well fed and carried plump bellies. There was perfect peace, perfect stillness, universal brightness, the fulness of vision, and a wondrous glory in the heaven and over all the earth. The earth was to me as it were unpeopled. I saw neither towns nor cities, neither houses nor villages, neither smoke nor motion nor sign of life. I stopped, and imagined that I was as they were who first explored this ridgy wilderness, and knew that as far as eye could reach not a white man lived. And yet these thoughts were soon chased away by the certainty that under that silvery haze were thousands of toiling men, romping children, mothers and maidens, and the world was going on below just as usual. How are the birds to be envied who make airy mountains by their wings! Could I rise six thousand feet above the ground, that were substantially to be on the mountain-top. Then, when the multitude wearied us, and the soul would bathe in silence, I would with a few beats lift up through the air, and seek the solitude of space, and hide in the clefts of clouds, or ride unexplored ranges of crystal-white cloud-mountains, that scorn footsteps, and on whose radiant surfaces an army of feet would wear no path, leave no mark, but fade out as do steps upon the water!

And so, for a half-hour, I rode alone, without the rustle of leaves, without hum or buzz, without that nameless mixture of pipes, small and great, which fill the woods or sing along the surface of the plains. There were no nuts to fall, no branches to snap, no squirrel to bark, no birds to fly out and flap away through the leaves. The matted moss was born and bred in silence. The stunted savins and cedars, crouched down close to the earth from savage winds, as partridges crouch when hawks are in the air. The forests in the chasms and valleys below were like bushes or overgrown moss. If there were any wind down there, if they shook their leaves to its piping, and danced when it bid them, it was all the same to me. For motion or rest were alike at this distance.

There is above every man's head a height into which he may rise, and whether care and trouble fret below, or tear on, they become alike silent and powerless. It is only our affections that mount up and dwell with us, where bickerings and burdens may never come.

Out of these chambers of the air I remembered the world afar off, as one remembers the fairy tales of his childhood. The cities we had trodden seem in the mind like pencil-traced pictures half rubbed out. The real New York seemed too impossible even for a dream. That Boston really lay sweltering by the sea-side excited a smile of incredulity. As I rode along, I tried the effect of speech. I called out aloud. The sound fell from my lips, and ceased forever. No mountains caught it and nourished it in echoes. I called again. But there was in a second no voice, and none that echoed. I called a third time with better success, for one of the gentlemen of the party had crept upon my loitering, and, supposing himself called, gave me back a very unexpected and most unwelcome answer. The bubble burst! My half-hour, like a sweet dream interrupted, fled away, and I could not dream it again!

Reaching the hotel in due season, tired and sweaty, a bath must be had. We went toward the Notch, and turning to the right at the first little stream that let itself down from the mountains, we sought the pools in which we knew such streams kept their sweetest thoughts, expressing them by trout. The only difficulty was in the selection. This pool was deep, rock-rimmed, transparent, gravel-bottomed. The next was level-edged and rock-bottomed, but received its water with such a gush, that it whirled around the basin in a liquid dance of bubbles. The next one received a divided stream, one part coming over a shelving rock and sheeting down in white, while the other portion fell into a hollow and murmuring crevice, and came gurgling forth from a half-dark channel. Half-way down, the rock was smooth and pleasant to the feet. In the deepest part were fine gravel and powdered mountain, commonly called sand. The waters left this pool even more beautifully than they entered it; for the rock had been rounded and grooved, so that it gave a channel like the finest moulded lip of a water-vase; and the moss, beginning below, had crept up into the very throat of the passage, and lined it completely, giving to the clear water a green hue as it rushed through, whirling itself into a plexus of cords, or a kind of pulsating braid of water. This was my pool. It waited for me. How deliciously it opened its flood to my coming. It rushed up to every pore, and sheeted my skin with an aqueous covering, prepared in the mountain water-looms. Ah! the coldness: every drop was molten hail. It was the very brother of ice. At a mere hint of winter it would change to ice again! If the crystal nook were such a surprise of delight to me, what must I have been to it, that had perhaps never been invaded, unless by the lip of a moose or by the lithe and spotted form of sylvan trout! The drops and bubbles ran up to me and broke about my neck, and ran laughing away, frolicking over the mossy margin, and I could hear them laughing all the way down below. Such a monster had never perhaps taken covert in the pure, pellucid bowl before!

But this was the centre part. Not less memorable was the fringe. The trees hung in the air on either side, and stretched their green leaves for a roof far above. The birch and alder, with here and there a silver-fir, in bush form, edged the rocks on either side. As you looked up the stream, there opened an ascending avenue of cascades, dripping rocks, bearded with moss, crevices filled with grass or dwarfed shrubs, until the whole was swallowed up in the leaves and trees far above. But if you turned down the stream, then through a lane of richest green stood the open sky, and lifted up against it thousands of feet Mount

Willard, rocky and rent, or with but here and there a remnant of evergreens, sharp and ragged. The sun was behind it, and poured against its farther side his whole tide of light, which lapped over, as a stream dashes over its bounds and spills its waters beyond. So it stood up over against this ocean of atmospheric gold, banked huge and rude, against a most resplendent heaven!

As I stood donning my last articles of raiment, and wringing my over-wet hair, I saw a trout move very deliberately out from under a rock by which I had lain, and walk quietly across to the other side. As he entered the crevice, a smaller one left it, and came as demurely across to *his* rock. It was evident that the old people had sent them out to see if the coast were clear, and whether any damage had been done. Probably it was thought that there had been a *slide* in the mountain, and that a huge icicle or lump of snow had plunged into their pool, and melted away there. If there are piscatory philosophers below water half as wise as those above, this would be a very fair theory of the disturbance to which their mountain homestead had been subjected. As I had eaten of their salt, of course I respected the laws of hospitality, and no deceptive fly of mine shall ever tempt trout in a brook which begets pools so lovely, and in pools that yield themselves with such delicious embrace to the pleasures of a mountain bath.

And so, as the sun was gone, it was time for me to go. Step by step I climbed the moss-carpeted rocks; slipped in due degree, leaped the wide-set stones, got caught on the dead branches of the cedar, climbed astride over the birch, and reached the road.

*

OUR FIRST EXPERIENCE WITH A SEWING-MACHINE.

AMONG the things which we did not, but now do believe in, is the SEWING-MACHINE. One thing after another had been invented, one machine after another had superseded manual labor, until human hands seemed about to go out of use, for any other mechanical purposes than those of lovers' pressures, orators' gestures, and for beaux' and belles' gloves. But we always consoled ourselves, that one or two things there were yet which no machinery could perform. We could imagine children put through a whipping-machine, and we had long been accustomed to see them taught by automatic machines. There was the time-honored business handed down to us without a break, from the Garden of Eden, of courting, — and kissing as one of its ordinances; — no machinery could ever perform that! Machine-poetry and machine-sermons we were familiar with. Babbage can make machines for ciphering, for computing logarithms, for casting up interest; but can he invent a machine for *saving* interest, — and capital too, for that matter? And oh! can there ever be a machine for answering letters? We would pay any price for a machine into which letters being put, and a crank turned, there should drop out at the other side answers as good as the letters, folded, directed, and stamped!

But machines have steadily gained ground, and the iron muscle has relieved the flesh hand; — machines for boring, sawing, cutting, planing; for making bread (I wish there was one for eating some of it), for pumping water, for making cattle draw their own drink. But, notwithstanding, we firmly believed that some things would never be done by any fingers except human, and eminent among these impossible things was SEWING! Nothing we were sure could ever perform that, except the latest and best invention of Paradise, — woman!

When the rumors began to prevail, then, respecting an invented sewing-machine, we lifted our eyebrows gently, and went on our way with a quiet consciousness that we could not be taken in by any such story. We regarded it as of a piece with new-found morality in old politicians, with the thousand annual rumors of some heaven-dawned virtue in Washington City, — a mere device to catch the credulous.

But day by day the clatter grew. Indeed, we surprised ourselves with a coat, sewed in important respects by machine. We saw linen pyramids of sheeting made for hotels and steamboats by sewing-machines.

The case was growing serious indeed; and at last it came to a head, when the head of the family informed us that a woman was to come in a few days, with her Wheeler and Wilson, and do up the family sewing. Of course we submitted without a word. And the three capable persons of this household began to prepare matter for the machine, to an extent which showed how perfectly they had been fooled by the story of its executive ability. Piles of large stuff lay in each corner; little stuff covered the table; and miscellaneous stuff lay everywhere. We ran against cotton heaps, were in danger of getting tangled in webs of linen and sheeting at every turn; and such ripping and tearing and cutting and basting as went on would lead one to imagine that an army was to be clothed.

The day dawned. The woman came, and the iron Wheeler and Wilson came with her; only the lady had to act as beau, and offer her aid to wait on Messrs. W. and W. After a little, there arose a hum from our chamber, not unlike the buzz of a wheat-mill, such as we have heard in summer, sitting under willow-trees on the edge of a stream, over against a red mill, white-dusted. Soon we heard excited exclamations. Everybody seemed stirred up. The girls left their work, the children forsook their playthings, and we followed the example.

There sat before the simple machine-stand a fair young woman, some sixteen years old, whose foot, like that of old-fashioned flax-spinners, was working the treadle with the nimblest motion. Then came the conviction, for the first time, that sewing was conquered and vanquished! Long sheets, entering the fatal pass, streamed through, and came out hemmed, in a ridiculously short time. An hour's work was done up before your eyes in one minute. A shirt was set in of such dimensions, that (we call Baron Munchausen to witness!) a man could not get round it by fair walking in less than — well, in some time! It streamed through the all-puncturing Wheeler and Wilson about as soon as a good-sized flag, being hoisted, would unroll and flow out to the wind. A bundle of linen took its turn, and came forth a collar, a handkerchief, a cap. There goes in a piece of cloth!

there comes out a shirt! We were bewildered. Not much was done for some hours in that house but gaze and wonder. We mistake; a good deal more was done, and done more effectually than had ever been done in ten times the time before! What heaps of towels; what piles of sheets; what bedfuls of small trumpery; what bureaus full of fine trash; what carpet-littering stacks of unmentionable matters that make up the cloth-inventory of household wealth!

The dismayed woman of the house saw her three days' prepared work melting away before noon, as a three days' April snow disappears in a few hours!

The voracious machine began to show its teeth and to demand more food; and now it was a fair race, whether two women could prepare as much as one machine could perform! It did our very souls good. At last we hoped that this was working fast enough. O, what early hours has our lamp been made to illumine! Ah, what breakfasts have we eaten, and seen cleared away, long before the sun touched even the cheek of day. What impetuous industry has glowed about the house, — forenoon, afternoon, night, midnight, never enough, never overmatched! We grew tired even to look at it! At last, said we, You 've got your match. Now, then, we will sit down and see this race with a satisfaction that shall include years of revenge for disturbed indolence!

For a long time the match was doubtful. Sometimes it was the machine that had the advantage, and sometimes it was not. The contest was passing into the middle of the afternoon. It was doubtful. Sometimes the fast-driven needle evidently gained; then again, in rounding up a sleeve-gathering, the needle flagged, and then the hand-worked scissors gained! But iron and steel are more enduring even than a housewife's courage. And though, for any single hour, the hand could prepare faster than the machine could execute, yet, taking the day through, Wheeler and Wilson had the advantage, and came out at dark decidedly ahead. That settled it. There was a revolution in this household. Our Miriam sounded her timbrel, and triumphed over the cruel Pharaoh of the needle, whose dynasty and despotism were ended!

Now sewing is the family amusement. Our Wheeler and Wilson is played on a great deal more than our Steinway piano, — and is the cause, too, of more real music than is ever got out of that instrument; for two canary birds, perched on either side of the book-case, understand the first click of the sewing-machine to be a challenge, and while the machine sings *staccato*, they warble *ad libitum*, — and between the *solfeggio* of the one and the *cantabile* of the other we go crazy.

*

HUNTING FLIES.

1855.

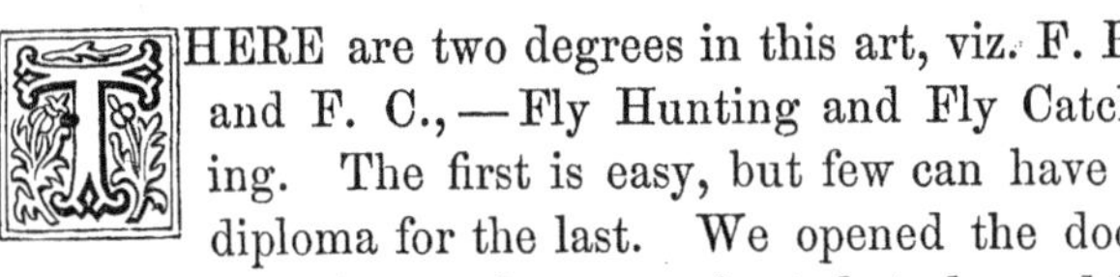

THERE are two degrees in this art, viz. F. H. and F. C., — Fly Hunting and Fly Catching. The first is easy, but few can have a diploma for the last. We opened the door to let the warmth out of our over-heated study, and in came a boisterous fly, almost as big as a bee, and ten times as important. One would think him a courier before all the emperors on earth, or the chief of politicians about to utter a speech, or a Monsieur Jullien, lecturing his hundred instruments, each in his own tongue.

It was an annoyance; for when one has a little bit of an inspiration of his own, and is about to make a flourish on paper, he does not care to have himself burlesqued. Did you ever undertake to drive one fly out of a large room, with a high ceiling? We took our broom and struck at the busy fellow, with only the effect of immensely quickening his activity. Whereas, before, he buzzed in stately circuits, he now set about such a series of nimble whirls, now near the floor, then, before we could detect him with our eye, up by the ceiling; now by the door, then by the window, and giving out a sound like a wheel in a factory, until our anger changed to mirth, and the attempt at hitting him became ludicrous. We smote here and there; we beat the books, the wall, the carpet, the stove, — everything but the fly. He seemed to be the only one that fully enjoyed himself. At length we sat down, hoping the busy impertinence would settle somewhere. So he did, — right before our face, on the desk, and crept about with such a nimble, pert, business-like air, that one could not help thinking that he said, "Were you not looking for us, sir, just now? Is there anything that you particularly want? Can't we serve you?" — and with that, undoubtedly unable to restrain the laughter that swelled his blue jacket, he flew up and whirred and whirled, bounced and buzzed; bumped the window, and bizzed against the wall, and went through all the waltzes, polkas, schottishes, that ever were conceived of, — a perfect aerial quadrille.

Well, this is amusing enough on a small scale; but it is rather sad to see it on a large scale. New York has been after its corrupt and corrupting aldermen for months past, swinging the broom of justice after them; smiting here and smiting there, but always hitting the place that the rogues had just left. And nobody is so happy, so fat, so nimble, so amiable and familiar with justice, as these amazing aldermen.

Methinks we see our example imitated, also, in the grandest style, by no less a broom-holder than the President of these United States. He shakes his broom, now at Disunionists, now at Free-Soilers, and then at all who hate both of them. Indeed, his task is worse than ours; for he has flies to drive out, and flies to drive in, and a part of the time it is very uncertain which is which. Lately several big flies have been buzzing in the custom-house, so that the President could get no peace even in Washington. And less ever since he has been flirting the broom than before.

*

BACK AGAIN.

E are always glad to get out of the city in summer, and always glad to get back again when the vacation is up. Ten months of city labor prepare one for the luxury of rest, or, what is better, light occupation and country scenes. A man in the country may, and often does, work incessantly, and up to the measure of his strength; and a city clergyman can do no more than that. Yet the labor of a city pastor is more exacting and more exhaustive of nervous vitality. Unless he shut himself up, and bar and bolt his seclusion, he knows nothing either of leisure or rest, in the sense of quietness and being let alone. The very roar of the street is an imperceptible excitement. To walk through the thoroughfares, to see the rush and whirl and anxious haste of so many men, imparts something of anxious haste or feverishness to your mind. Then there is an endless succession of things to be done, that require time for the doing, but leave you nothing to show at the end of the week. There are committees and consultations, there are private meetings and public meetings, there are new movements to be initiated, and old ones to be kept up. Everybody has everything to do, and clergymen are the ones expected to advise everybody about everything that does not come within limitation of business partnerships. The sick have a right to the minister. If they be strangers and poor, a yet better right. The poor have a right to expect that he, at least, will have concern for them. The afflicted look to him. Those who are in comfort, whose friends are good counsellors, do not know how many thousands there are in the city that have no one to go to. A widow wishes to put her boy to a good trade; who shall advise her? Who shall ascertain for her if the place thought of be safe and the man honorable? A young man is run down and discouraged; lacks a place and means of livelihood. Where, among strangers, can he find help, if ministers do not give it to him? Parents are troubled about their children, just passing through the crisis of life; they are not boys any longer, nor are they men. It is a help and a comfort, if they have not better advisers, to go to their minister.

One sort of men think of clergymen simply as the *preachers of sermons*. They think their life and labor is deep and subtle, — study through the week, and utterance on Sunday. Others think of clergymen simply in their relations to public enterprises. They ought to lead here, and lead there. They ought to appear in this meeting, and in that. If a man do not preach ably, he is good for nothing, some think. If he be not a reformer, a thorough progressive, then others think he is worse than useless. Now we surely wish every minister were a good and able preacher; and we wish it were the conscience-necessity of every minister to lead his people, and, as far as his influence allowed, the community, in all well-considered advance movements. But these are not all his functions. These are the *public* aspects. His private work, his ten thousand services to individuals, to the unfriended, the tempted, the poor, the afflicted, the perplexed; the giving of counsel to the weak, encouragement to the desponding; the taking care of men one by one and in detail, as well as generic and wholesome movements for communities and mankind, constitute an immense proportion of his labor. It is that part which takes the most out of him in time, strength, and nerves. It is that which he feels more than study or speaking. It is that of which his people have the least conception. They naturally judge by what they see, and they see that which is in the pulpit and on the platform.

It is six o'clock in the morning. The day is begun. The family are emerging. Breakfast will be ready in half an hour. You look for the *Tribune*. The bell rings. A man has called thus early, for fear you might be out. You despatch his business. Sitting down to breakfast, the bell rings, and the servant says the man will wait. But what pleasure can one have at a meal with a man up-stairs waiting for him, and the consciousness of it hastening the coffee and the toast on their way? You run up. Can you marry a couple at so and so? That is settled. Prayers are had with the family. The bell rings, once, twice, three times. When you rise, there are five persons waiting for you in the front parlor. A young man from the country wishes your name on his circular for a school. A young woman is failing in health by confinement to sewing; does not know what to do; behind in rent; cannot get away to the country; does not wish charity; only wishes some one to enable her to break away from a state of things that will in six months kill her. Another called to inquire after a friend of whom he has lost sight. While you are attending to these, the bell is active, and other persons take the places of those that go. A poor mother wants to buy her son's wife out of slavery. A kind woman calls in behalf of a boarder who is out of place, desponding, will throw himself away if he cannot get some means of livelihood. Another calls to know if I will not visit a poor family in great distress, in —— Street. A good and honest looking man comes next; is out of work; has "heard that 'your riverince' is a kind man," etc. Another man wants to get his family out from Ireland, can pay *half*, if some one will intercede with ship-owners to trust him the balance. A stranger has died, and a sexton desires a clergyman's services. Several persons desire religious conversation. It is after ten o'clock. A moment's lull. You catch your hat and run out. Perhaps you have forgotten some appointment. You betake yourself to your study, not a little flurried by the contrariety of things which you have been considering. You return to dine. There are five or six persons waiting for you. At tea you find others, also, with their divers necessities.

This is not overdrawn; and for months of the year it is far underdrawn. There is no taxation comparable to an incessant various conversation with people for whom you must think, devise, and for whose help you feel yourself often utterly incompetent.

Yet it is right that people should have some one to go to. It is right that Christian ministers should be the persons. It is religion in its form of benevolence thus to stand on the side of weakness, want, ignorance, repentant wickedness, — for their relief.

But when ten months of incessant attrition have exhausted one's nervous store, the bell becomes an affliction; we dread its sound. We long for calmness, for solitude, for rest. We seek the coolest, most secluded spots. There must be many attractions of scenery; but, before all other things, there must *not* be many people there.

Six weeks of rest change all that. The feverish impatience is gone. Your old love of work comes back. You return to your post with secret joy. You are eager for work. The old bell is musical. You begin again to listen, to urge or dissuade, to counsel or to direct, those who come. You find the fountains of speech flowing once more. The face of the great congregation is inspiring to you. And, after your vacation, you are worth a great deal more to them than if you had plodded on without cessation or relaxation.

*

A WESTERN TRIP.

October, 1855.

HEN we first visited the West, in 1834, there was but one single strip of railroad in the whole country west of the Hudson, and that was between Albany and Schenectady. We thought ourselves fortunate in reaching Cincinnati in ten days from New York. But now we leave New York at 6.30 (to use the new railroad idiom) on Monday, and expect to take supper in Chicago on Tuesday evening. The only difference between expectation and realization was, that we arrived on Wednesday forenoon, being out two nights instead of one. We missed the connection at Toledo, and so our delay arose.

The cars on the Erie road were crowded more than we ever before saw them, giving sign that people are recovering from their absurd prejudices against this most comfortable of all roads. But though every place be filled, the cars cannot, after all, be said to be *crowded*, so spacious are the wide seats.

We went through the usual experience of travellers. We talked till our throats ached, for we were fortunate in having Dr. Bellows, of New York, as a companion. We thumbed the guide-book, and reckoned how far we had come, and how far it yet was to Dunkirk. We got out at wood and water stations, and saluted the engine, and bought apples of the boys, and ran down banks for asters, golden-rod, and purple beech-leaves, and scampered back again fast as feet could carry us, when the whistle began, like a fretting old woman, to scold and scream that they would leave us if we did not come back instantly. But we were always too nimble for the engine, whose speed is not in its start where ours *is*. At eleven o'clock at night Dunkirk was reached. We had the huge, dreary, chilly depot as a waiting-place till the Buffalo cars came in. They were late. They were yet later when we started for Cleveland, and more than two hours behind time when we reached that city in the morning, after a night's sleep in the cars; which made you think that you were a kaleidoscope, and at every jolt and turn new and ridiculous combinations were taking place in the fragments of your internal being, and one looks back on the contents of such a night as upon a wild hallucination. But if the night was disturbed, what was the screaming tumult of the morning at the Cleveland depot? Bells ringing, gongs roaring, porters shouting, passengers being disgorged by hundreds, with wrinkled-up children, squeezed and uncombed and unwashed. The Cincinnati train, the Toledo train, and other trains had been patiently waiting for our tardy arrival; and the locomotives were roaring off their extra steam, and whistling for very nervousness, and prancing about, running in and out, just to keep themselves from blowing up with mere ill-humor and impatience. Meanwhile, the hand-trucks were changing baggage, and rattling, with huge piles of luggage, all over the depot.

Is there anything on earth so much to be pitied as a trunk? What awful violence it suffers in packing; what crowding and straining, to get in twice as much as it can possibly hold. Then comes the shutting, the getting on the lid, the jumping and jamming, the red-faced vexation because the latch will not quite catch, the final triumph, the twirl of the key, the strapping and cover-fastening. How trying to weak human nature is a strap and buckle! You pull till the blood threatens to burst from your head, and *almost* bring the hole up to the buckle-tongue. You give it a quick jerk to let it in, but it only springs back. You try again, and lose it again, and your patience with it. You jerk, and protest, and *will* have it come right. At length you propose a compromise, and cut another hole in the strap half-way; and deceive yourself with thinking that you have had your own way. This may end *your* troubles, but it is but the beginning of the trunk's. The hackman drops it; the porter slings it aboard. The baggage-master fires it into the heap as if he meant to make it strike fire. At night it is to be changed at Dunkirk, say. They are pitched out of the car like bombs. Two or three employees seem possessed with very spite at them. They catch them by the handle, give them a prodigious twirl on one end, and the trunk spins like a top to a corner of the baggage-space, and smashes up against its fellows. Again at Cleveland, they are sent out like shot from the cars, piled up on the trucks, little ones at the bottom, and big ones at the top, some are smashed, some are dented, some are ripped, but all go headlong and heterogeneously into the new limbo of baggage. It is very interesting, then, to examine some of these trunks, which a kind aunt has labelled, "Please lift it by the handles"; or, "Keep this side up." One might as well put a label on a Paixhan shot, giving directions for its careful journey. Well, our "*Crouch and Fitzgerald*" trunk seemed peculiarly lucky. It had the knack of escaping contusion and abuse, and when we reached Chicago, came forth from its canvas, shining like a new one. But we look on it as a miracle. Nothing would have persuaded us that such an escape was possible. A mathematical calculation of chances would make the course of a trunk from New York to Chicago to be like the chances of grain through the mill-stones. And a man might well expect to receive, at the end of his journey, only a bag of dust mixed up with fragments of leather and raiment.

But we are thankful for a safe reaching of this extraordinary city of Chicago. No man has seen the West who has not seen Chicago. Nature has done little for its harbor, and government has done less. The ground was not meant for a city. The place has no adaptations for a fine city. It is low, flat, muddy, or dusty. But such is the concentration of enormous business here, that before many years all natural difficulties will have been overcome. The grade will be raised artficially; the streets paved; the sidewalks, now of wood, converted to stone; the river tunnelled; the harbor cleaned out and enlarged, and the whole river, in both its branches, be wharfed in and lined with lumber-yards and warehouses. But as yet Chicago is anything but a city of desirable aspect to the eye or the feet. It would seem to be a merchant's *beau ideal* of paradise. It fairly smokes and roars with business. There is no room for the caravans of teams. The river is choked with craft, and the harbor is filled with vessels. The streets are filled up with boxes and bales, the stores are like hives in spring weather, with swarms going in and out with incessant activity; — buying and selling, buying and selling, buying and selling, — that is Chicago. The merchant cannot get goods from the East fast enough. His yesterday's arrivals are gone to-day, or picked over and made thin. The warehouses cannot hold the grain; the shipping cannot convey it away fast enough; and *demand,* on every side, drives up the business-men with incessant importunity. Huge hotels, that seem large enough to accommodate an army, were running over; and having occasion to stop a moment at the Briggs House, we found the hall leading to the dining-room packed with scores of men, though yet fifteen minutes to dinner, waiting for the opening of the door. But it was the Agricultural Fair that had, without doubt, made such a terrific crush in town, during the few days that we tarried there.

We visited the grounds of the Fair, and made a rapid inspection of stock, products, machinery, fabrics, and men, women, and children. The occasion was very creditable to the managers. While examining the ploughs, some farmers, supposing that we were the exhibitors, asked us to explain the operation of one. Fortunately, it was the double Michigan plow, and we knew its peculiarities. Accordingly, we fell into our blandest manner: "Gentlemen, this is an admirable plough! We will suppose that a furrow has been opened all around the field or *land.* When this plough sets in, the first share, which you see here, takes some four to six inches of the surface, and inverts it into the furrow. The second share raises some ten to twelve inches more of the subsoil, and throws it upon the surface soil, so that the soil is exactly reversed; the top soil is turned from fifteen to twenty inches, and the subsoil is brought to the top. This will not do on gravelly and shallow soils. But when you have a good subsoil, that only needs air and mellowing, these ploughs are admirable." Having got safely through that speech, the farmers were disposed to enlarge our sphere, and asked an explanation of several other inventions and machines that were quite beyond our reach, so that we found it convenient to slip off, and leave the place, while our reputation remained good.

Much stock changed hands on the ground, and at large prices. Our only purchases were of two potatoes of a South American kind, and a bushel of Mexican ditto. Likewise we procured two kinds of corn. With these our zeal closed.

*

THE LECTURE SYSTEM.

1855.

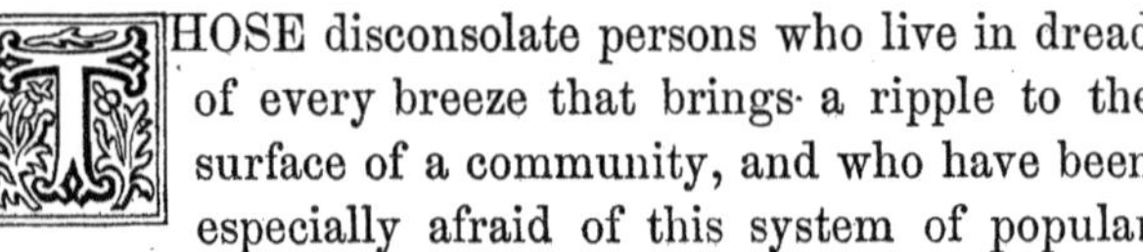

THOSE disconsolate persons who live in dread of every breeze that brings a ripple to the surface of a community, and who have been especially afraid of this system of popular lectures which has so suddenly grown up and into such strength, have fresh occasion for alarm. The demand for lectures was never so strong and earnest as now. Feeding does not satisfy it. The number of able lecturers every year increases. The arrangements for lectures have assumed something of the stability of institutions. The places where lectures have prevailed longest are the very ones where the interest is deepest. It must be given up, then, as a thing past recall, and lectures will henceforth be ranked as a part of our necessities. Is there no consolation for these sad-eyed and disconsolate persons? We think there is, and much.

Every lecturer has an opportunity of hearing an expression of opinion respecting those who have preceded him, and I have been struck with the general truth of the judgments formed, and the evidences afforded of good sense and critical sagacity among the common people. Men find their level in this walk of life as much as in the professions. The people are reasonably content with plain sense; they are better pleased with sound sense dressed with learning or ample experience. If to this is added wit and fancy, they repay all that with proper appreciation. And if the whole be inspired with a deep moral impulse, and breathe the breath of a noble heart, every one recognizes that too.

It will probably be the testimony of all who lecture, that every year audiences grow more difficult. In other words, every winter's course educates their critical judgment and their taste. They require abler performances. They can less easily be imposed upon by brilliant trick or learned dulness. And we were never so sure as now, that the most popular lecturers are those who deserve to be so. That success does not depend upon superficial glitter, but upon intrinsic merit. Of this we shall speak again in a moment.

One should remember that a lecture is but just begun when the lecturer has finished its delivery. The audience have laughed and clapped, glowed or wept, admired or yawned, as the case may be, and social sympathy has carried them along pretty much together. Now they disperse. They begin to talk on the way home. The father and mother draw the children out, to know how much they heard, and what impression was produced on them; they discuss it, and the family for several days is a debating-society. Young men in an office, clerks in a store, mechanics in the shop, boys in the academy, all overhaul the lecture, and for a week it becomes a theme of reflection, discussion, and active criticism. In this way one lecture controls another. If a lecture is but interesting in the delivery, and full of meat afterwards for a whole week's picking, it sits in judgment on another lecture, brilliant in delivery, but leaving no permanent impressions, no questions, no facts, no reasonings, for after-discussions. It does not take a community long to perceive that some lectures instruct them wearisomely, that some instruct and inspire, that some inspire but do not instruct, that some, like fire-works, are magnificent while going off and nothing afterwards, and others, like a pomological show, are fine in the exhibition, and very juicy and refreshing afterwards. What else is there in our towns and villages throughout the land that produces such a degree of pleasure and such universal mental excitement? Is it better to have young people at balls and dances, or at convivial gatherings and bar-rooms?

It is often said that popular lectures produce superficial habits, and that, instead of reading and reflection, young people become fascinated with easy and brilliant knowledge, to the detriment of sober and reflective information. This may be true in single cases; but in regard to the greatest number who attend lectures, the choice is not between knowledge judiciously gathered by their own industry and knowledge superficially got from a lecture. In respect to the greatest number, it is true, that, if they do not get it from the lecture, they will not have it at all. And the real question is, whether it is better for the young to grow up without general knowledge, or to obtain a relish for it from lecturers.

Not long since we read a captious paragraph in a paper, stating that Professor So-and-so, of such a college, had gone to such a village, and but a handful came to hear him; whereas the next week, Mr. Barnum lectured there, and the house could not contain the crowds, — and the application made was, that even New England audiences ran after chaff, and did not care for wheat.

But is this a fair statement? Did the writer take pains to ascertain what opinion was formed of Mr. Barnum's lecture; whether people *afterwards* were as much pleased, as before they were curious? Would they go again in such numbers? And, on the other side, did Professor So-and-so have any previous reputation in that village which should draw people to hear him? Perhaps they had heard him before, and therefore stayed away. We have heard college professors that were stupid, even to genius in that direction. There are professors in colleges with gifts at instructing classes, who have no gifts at instructing promiscuous audiences. It is one thing to lead a class along, day by day, opening in successive parts a large subject, and another to project a subject, group it into life form, and set it forth in an hour's time, so that common minds can grasp it, and be entertained withal. But if our disappointed professor was all that it is necessary for a lecturer to be, and the people did not come to hear him, he is in the condition of every young man before the public find him out, — *a probationer*. Let him go again, and a third time, and if then those who came at first do not return, and few others supply their place, instead of charging the town with stupidity, might he not better undergo a process of self-examination? Sometimes the people are smart, and the lecturer stupid. We are speaking, of course, in the general; for we know neither the person named by his injudicious friend in the paragraph alluded to nor the circumstances of the town. And, for aught that we know, next year Professor So-and-so, a little roused up, will prepare a living lecture, written for people that are not students, and will deliver it with such genial animation, that everybody will say that it was *the* lecture of the season, and then the intelligence and appreciativeness of the popular mind will go up above par.

TOWN-HALLS. — One of the fruits of the lecture system is seen in the multiplication of admirable town-halls. Every town ought to have a good hall of its own for popular assemblies and for town-meetings. But such reasons would wait long before people would consent to be taxed for an expensive building. But once let the lecture spirit arise, and people be for a few seasons crowded into a court-room, or into a church, which is soon shut against them, (because men of doubtful orthodoxy are invited to lecture, or because the audience laughed and clapped the speaker, or for a far better and more justifiable reason, — because men, calling themselves gentlemen, besmeared the carpets and pews with filthy tobacco-spit,) and the enterprise of a town-hall gains favor, and one or two years sees it built, and the whole town proud of their public spirit. These remarks are suggested by the new building just erected in Hudson, N. Y., where we are now writing. Three years ago we lectured in the court-house; last winter, in a church; but last night, in an ample and admirable town-hall, which is very creditable to this place.

Ought not such places as New Haven, Bridgeport, Hartford, Springfield, Poughkeepsie, to have public halls bearing some relation to the taste and public spirit of the citizens?

VENTILATION. — If they *do*, will they not procure one thing, — a *supply of air*. It is astonishing that God should have set such an example before us, and provided such wondrous abundance of air, and men take no hint from it of the prime necessity of this substance for health, brightness, and enjoyment. Almost without a single exception, new halls and old ones are *unventilated.* The committee will point you to an auger-hole in some corner of the ceiling, and tell you that arrangements have been made for ventilation! You might as well insert a goose-quill in a dam to supply all Lowell with water for its mills! These contemptible little holes, hardly big enough for a fat rat to run in without disarranging his sleek fur, are hardly enough for one breather, and they are set to do the work of a thousand people! Besides, no provision is made for the introduction of *fresh air* from below, to supply the place of that which is supposed to pass off. The air-trunk of furnaces ought to be double the usual size, and the hot-air trunks that lead from the furnace-chamber to the room should be four times as large as is usual, so that large volumes of mild air can come in, instead of fierce currents of intensely hot air, out of which the moisture has been dried, and the oxygen burnt, by contact with a red-hot furnace. A room that will seat a thousand persons should have not less than *four* ventiducts, each one of them larger than a man's whole body. They can be placed at the four corners of the building; or they may be arranged along the sides of the wall, the number being increased as the diameter of each is diminished. But the square inches of the mouths of the ventiducts should be at least *one third greater* than of the mouths *of the heat-trunks* which come from the furnace.

As soon as a speaker begins, he usually finds his

cheek flushed, his head full and throbbing. Bad air is at work with him. The blood that is going to his brain has not been purified in his lungs by contact with good air. It has a diminished stimulating power. It is the first stage of suffocation ; for all that is done, when a man is hung, is to prevent the passage of air down his windpipe ; and if you corrupt the air till it ceases to perform a vital function, it is the same thing in effect ; so that a public speaker, in a tainted atmosphere, is going through a prolonged process of atmospheric hanging.

The people, too, instantly show signs of distress. Women begin to fan themselves ; children grow sleepy ; and well-fed men grow red and somnolent. How people can consent to breathe each others' breath over and over and over again, we never could imagine. They would never return to a hotel where they were put into a bed between sheets that had been used by travellers before them, — no, they must have *fresh sheets.* They would go without food rather than eat off a plate used by several parties before them. Clean, fresh plates are indispensable. But, while so delicate of their outside skin and their mouth, they will take air into their lungs that has been breathed over twenty times, by all sorts of persons, and that fairly reeks with feculence ; and nothing disgusts them but a proposal to open a window, and let in clean and fresh air. That brings up coat-collars, and brings down scowls, and amiable lips pout, and kind tongues declare that they will not go to such a place again, if they do not have these matters regulated better for the health !

*

HOME REVISITED.

LEAVING Chicago a second time, we rode all night toward Indianapolis, Ind. It was strange to make in a single night, with ease, a journey which used to require four hard days' riding in the best season of the year! Leaving Michigan City at about eleven at night, we reached our former home at seven in the morning. There can be no place so memorable to our after years as that in which we began life, and received our first development. This is true, whatever a man's calling may be; but there is that in a pastor's office which gives peculiar interest to all his first efforts.

There stands yet that academy, in the second story of which we first preached on settling in Indianapolis. It would hold scarcely more than one hundred. The first sermon there is as vivid a picture to-day as it was at the time. The persons present, the transient expressions which the faces wore during the exercises, their dress, and the little incidents, — as where an old man put his cane, the knocking over a pile of hats, the crying of a child, — we see them all now in memory, more distinctly than we were conscious of seeing them at the time. In this room we preached the first *real* sermon that we ever uttered. We had delivered hundreds before, but till then, the sermon was the *end* and not the *means*. We had a vague idea that truth was to be preached, and that then it was to be left to do its work under God's blessing as best it might. The results were not satisfying. Why should not preaching do now what it did in the Apostles' days? Why should it be a random and unrequited effort? These thoughts grew, and the want of fruits was so painful, that we determined to make a careful examination of the Apostles' preaching, to see what it was that made it so *immediately* efficient. We found that they laid a foundation first of historical truth, common to them and their auditors; that this mass of familiar truth was then concentrated upon the hearers in the form of an intense personal application and appeal; that the language was not philosophical and scholastic, but the language of common life. We determined to try the same. We considered what moral truths were admitted by everybody, and gathered many of them together. We considered how they could be so combined as to press men toward a religious state. We recalled to mind the character and condition of many who we knew would be present, and then, after as earnest a prayer as we ever offered, and with trembling solicitude, we went to the academy and preached the new sermon. The Lord gave it power, and ten or twelve persons were aroused by it, and led ultimately to a religious life.

This was the most memorable day of our ministerial life. The idea was born. Preaching was a definite and practical thing. Our people needed certain moral changes. Preaching was only a method of enforcing truths, not for the sake of the truths themselves, but for the results to be sought in *men*. *Man* was the thing. Henceforth our business was to work upon *man;* to study him, to stimulate and educate him. A sermon was good that had power on the heart, and was good for nothing, no matter how good, that had no moral power on *man*. Others had learned this.

It was the secret of success in every man who ever was eminent for usefulness in preaching. But no man can inherit experience. It must be born in each man for himself. After the light dawned, I could then see how plainly Jonathan Edwards's sermons were so made. Those gigantic *applications* of his were only the stretching out of the arms of the sermon upon the hearts and lives of his audience. I could see it now, and wondered that I had not seen it before. But having caught the idea, I went eagerly through Edwards to see how he took aim. I found his sermons to be either a statement and establishment of a plain principle, or an exceedingly abundant collection of Scriptural teachings around some great central truth. This was not, however, the sermon; it was only a battery thrown up. The guns were in place. The cannonading was yet to come on. Then from these bulwarks and batteries came a fire upon the life, the hearts, the character, the conduct, of living men, just as they lived in Edwards's days, such I think as no uninspired man ever surpassed, if any ever equalled it. It was a kind of moral inquisition, and sinners were put upon argumentative racks, and beneath screws, and, with an awful revolution of the great truth in hand, evenly and steadily screwed down and crushed. I never could read that sermon, "*Sinners in the hands of an angry God*," at one sitting. I think a person of moral sensibility alone at midnight, reading that awful discourse, would wellnigh go crazy. He would hear the judgment-trump, and see the advancing heaven, and the day of doom would begin to mantle him with its shroud.

But we have wandered, — not exactly wandered

either, — for the Book of the *Acts of the Apostles* and *Edwards's Sermons* were the two masters at whose feet we sat while learning that preaching is only another name for taking hold of men and moulding them. This was sixteen years ago. What a crowded memory rose up through all that period! Children are men, men are turned to spirits. Almost every house I met sprung out to me with a memory. In that one, I remember an only daughter's funeral, her mother a widow. The first children baptized in the Academy room were twins; one is grown nearly to manhood on earth, the other quite, but in heaven. The mother that was broken-hearted has gone thither after her children. The eldest daughter has mounted thitherward, rejoicing too.

There was the church building, almost every nail of which we saw driven. We did not see simply the church made with hands, but the church of souls. In the semi-subterranean lecture-room what glorious scenes were enacted! We went thither and sat down in the old place, and called back the former times; we saw the faces again; we labored again, and prayed again, and wept again. For the trance was complete, and we lived in the ten years ago. It did not seem that we had been away. It seemed the most natural thing in the world to begin just where we left off, — to take up the thread and stitch just where we laid them down.

In the church on Sabbath morning how strangely were the real and the unreal blended! Each face that we saw flashed upon us the whole history of the man. This one was converted in such a year.

We remembered the first time he spoke to us, where we were, just what he said, our own silent thought, the whole progress and issue of the case. Mothers were there with their little children, whom we had carried as little girls. But many were not there. Some made shipwreck; some by faith have inherited the promises.

On Monday we walked the streets, searching out the old places. The ten-acre pasture near our little dwelling is now a nest of houses checkered with streets. The places where we searched for quails will never see wild game abound again. Poage's Run is now cut and shaped, and walled in and bridged, until its old acquaintances do not know it, even if it knows itself. There was not a tree that had not its story to tell. Every street had a claim upon memory. The former houses were written over within and without, like record-books. The kind citizens, rejoicing in the growth and prosperity of their city, naturally wished that I should see the *new* things. I turned away. It was the old things that I cared for. There was no tongue in the new. But the old spoke, and told me, if not "all that ever I did," yet a good deal of it. As I left the place, in my very soul I felt what the Psalmist meant when he said, "Peace be within thy walls, and prosperity within thy palaces. For my brethren and companions' sakes, I will now say, Peace be within thee."

By the favor of influential friends, I was allowed the privileges of the road when I took the cars for Lawrenceburg and Cincinnati. I therefore determined to go upon the locomotive, the better to see the ground over which, or rather through which, in earlier years I had waded wearily on horseback. No man knows anything of mud until he has lived in the West. Three days to Cincinnati, in my day, was good travelling. Now about four hours is required!

Mounted on the engine, I rode in triumph over the swamps, across the corduroy roads, along the black, deep river-bottoms that used to have such terrors. I gloried over them. I could not help fancying that there was a subdued look to the roads and rails, as if they felt that they were conquered and humbled.

Thus ended the pleasant part of our Western trip.

*

HOW TO WAKE IN THE MORNING.

ETTING up early is venerable. Since there has been a literature or a history, the habit of early rising has been recommended for health, for pleasure, and for business. The ancients are held up to us for examples. But they lived so far to the east, and so near the sun, that it was much easier for them than for us. People in Europe always get up several hours before we do; people in Asia several hours before the Europeans do; and we suppose as men go toward the sun it gets easier and easier, until somewhere in the Orient probably they step out of bed involuntarily, or, like a flower blossoming, they find their bed-clothes gently opening and turning back, by the mere attraction of light.

But as far toward sundown as we are, the matter becomes more difficult. Expedients of every kind are resorted to. Some men have heads with the organ of Time so largely developed, that they have only to select the hour, fix attention upon it, and then, as it were, wind up their minds, and sure enough off they go at the appointed time. We have tried this with success ourselves. But it induces a habit of waking up every half-hour through the night, to see whether it is time to wake up finally.

Alarm-clocks are very good, provided they do not stop, and *do* go off. But if there is one day in the year on which the machine fails, it will be that very day that, of all others, it was necessary for you to start early.

Servants are much relied upon for waking you up in hotels and at friends' houses. But of course they oversleep on that very morning when you must get the early train, or lose all the connections, and half a dozen appointments. And of course, too, everybody says, "How surprising that the servant did not wake! Was never known to miss before. Always had been reliable!"

We have found one plan of waking to be very effective. Let one preach a rousing sermon over night, become thoroughly excited, and he will wake early enough the next morning. We never miss Monday morning, whatever may be the fate of other days.

The indefatigable E. M., — whose observations of weather have made him renowned, and whose reports have given to newspapers quite a set of weather-phrases, — has been in the habit for years of making hourly observations of the thermometer, day and night. Of course, the waking at night was an important part of the business. He was the lucky owner of a dog that sympathized with his master, and divided the labor with him. For the intelligent little fellow, every time the clock struck at night, would spring up and scratch at his master's door, till E. M. came forth. Such nocturnal labors at length wore out his constitution, and science mourns the departed martyr of thermometric zeal and broken rest.

Good healthy children, that are put to bed at night when birds and chickens retire, are admirable wakeners in the morning. When they have slept their sleep full, there is no help for you. Wake they will, coo and frolic they will. All your hushing and humming are vain. Your efforts to put them to sleep only serve to wake you up! A bouncing boy, a year old, creeping out of his crib slyly, and pouncing upon his father's face, with chirp and chuckle, is better than any alarm-clock. A clock will soon run out its cacophonous rattle, but a child never runs down, or ends his fun.

But we have discovered a new method of waking early. Perched up upon our green hill-slope beyond Peekskill, we have found it difficult to sleep after about four o'clock of summer mornings. For a countless multitude of birds, in all the trees and shrubbery, aim their notes at us with such sweet archery, that we are pierced through and through with the silver arrows of music. It is in vain that you wrap the pillows about your ears! It is vain for you to reflect that you need sleep, and will not get up. Every one knows that an effort of will sufficient to resist the annoying or attractive sound is itself the end of sleep. While we are resisting, we are wakening. Thus, this very morning, all the trees about our little old house were belfries, and rang out more chimes than were ever heard at Cologne or Antwerp. And, after the first recognition, we turned resolutely to the wall, determined to sleep on. But "That 's a robin," said our ears; and "That 's a bobolink," — "There goes a wren"; and sparrows, larks, phœbes, catbirds, and many of their cousins in the orchard and woods, all joined to laugh us out of the idea of sleeping. Now, if any one wishes to know how to get up early, we will tell him. Go out of the city early in the day. Seek some tranquil place in the country where guns are never heard, where fruit-trees and shade-trees abound, and where the shaking of the leaf, or the distant crow of chanticleer, is the loudest sound ever heard, except of birds. And then, after walking all day among the fields and hills and forests, and supping upon milk that never dreamed of a city-milkman, go to bed by nine o'clock. If you do not wake before five the next morning, report your case to us, and we will make a fresh prescription.

*

LETTER FROM THE COUNTRY.

Office Editors of The Independent: —

EAR SIRS: — Do you own a cow? Every good man ought to. For a cow is the saint of the barn-yard. Not one of those final saints, who are born afar off from goodness, and fight their way to it, but one of those mild, meek, harmless, natural saints. If homeliness is necessary to goodness (and there is a strong presumption for the theory), a cow has this prime qualification. For nothing can well be more devoid of all beauty than a genuine milker. There is not one line of beauty. There is not one limb that seems to have regard for another. The muscles are thin, the shoulders and neck flat and poor, the hind quarters wide across and gaunt, and the whole form is meagre, lathy, and poverty-stricken. But when we reflect that all this comes from a cow's benevolence, and that she eats, ruminates, digests, and, in short, lives, for the sake of others, our sense of her benevolence at length clothes her with a kind of moral beauty. She could be fat if she would only be selfish. But she economizes beauty, that she may be profuse in milk. Blessed saint! And yet, in all the symbolism of saints, we do not remember a single instance in which the cow is advanced to signify anything in holy figure. Bulls and oxen, sheep and lambs, and holy rams, abound in pictorial legends. Lions and bears, dragons and eagles, serpents, bees, doves in endless repetition, stags, horses, crowing cocks, falcons, ravens, wild geese, fish, dogs, and wild boars, and we know not how many other creatures that swim, or fly, or walk, or creep, have been made glorious in stone and wood and paint, for some sake or other of the great multitude of saints whom the books record. But this noblest symbol of all, the very ideal and pattern of a saint, who is as poor as if living a life of maceration, who gives her whole strength to lacteal benevolence, who is patient, gentle, guileless, contented, — and yet, with two exceptions, no saint can be found (by us, at least) with a cow. These two saints are St. Ello and St. Perpetua. The second has wild cows by her side, and the first has cows with oxen about her. Let dairymen pay respect to the shadowy memory of St. Ello and St. Perpetua.

If we were to speak of the musical voice of a cow, people would laugh. But the sound will depend upon circumstances. Let a man be lost in the woods, and suffer the terrible excitement which comes with the first flash of conviction that he is *lost;* let him dash wildly forth, and after an hour's running and hoarse hallooing, find that he has only swept a circle and come back to the very spot from which he started; let him, toward the going down of the sun, weary, famished, and yet wandering, hear the low of cows not far off! No trumpet was ever so sweet on the march, and no lute ever charmed a lover with more delight than this uplifted sound of a cow to a wood-sick man. And when, running to the sound, he comes out near some farm-house, if tears gush, and he would fain even throw his arms around the neck of homely old brindle, let no one laugh or deride. Go and try the experiment, and see if you would not do it yourself! Besides, the *face* of a cow *is* handsome. It is the only thing about her that is beautiful, except by association!

But we need not go to all the trouble of being lost to reach the conclusion that a cow has a musical voice. Sitting on a summer evening on the sward, under the high, pendent elms, only enough conscious of being in the body to receive through it the most ineffable sense of the beauty of sights and sounds, and then, while birds are carrying the alto, and bees are making tenor, let the long and repeated low of cows coming home, and longing for their calves, rise as a bass, and tell me whether a cow has not a musical voice!

If one is of a devout turn, and would like some Scriptural associations, we can almost give him some. For, although oxen it was that were about the manger, according to all pictures, yet cows are the mothers of oxen. We read, too, in Scripture of "the pure milk of the Word"; and the qualifying adjective would seem to imply that teachers in those days imitated the milkmen of ours, and gave a diluted article. From this great company of patient creatures, let us mention a few more eminent, such as St. Alderney, St. Ayrshire, St. Durham, and St. Homebreed. These are the most illustrious of milk-saints. But goodness is not confined to any of these denominations. There are capacious udders, patient dispositions, mild-eyed mothers, home-loving and pasture-browsing saints, without name and fame, in every neighborhood.

And now, do you ask, wondering reader, what all this preludes? Just this: that we are a three-cow gentleman-farmer! Again, we know what is the real taste of milk. We have once more, before we die, seen cream! Twenty-six pans of milk were skimmed this very morning; and now, if you were riding past, you should see twenty-six inverted pans on the fence, in the sun, shining like silver, and sweetening themselves all day, in the air and sunshine, for the night's milk! Even the pigs fare better here than citizens do in New York. For although we take off the cream, we never think of giving them anything weaker than skim-milk! — four pigs, that once were longer than broad, but which are rapidly growing to the shape of a marble.

And now, having given this introduction, it may be expected that we shall go on to make some sound practical remarks about feeding, milking, making cheese and butter. And so we could if we chose to. And so we will, perhaps, by and by. But now we shall close by holding up the cow to all persons, as a model of disinterested benevolence not only, but as an instance of its reward. For though the homeliest creature on the farm, such is the effect upon the imagination of real goodness, that at length, by association, men come to think a cow handsome. And thus it will be with all of us plain, common, and homely people. Let us do well until our neighbors see our characters rather than our faces; and then, though born without beauty, we shall die handsome.

The looking-glass may say what it pleases. The heart of friends is the mirror of good men. And in that glass we shall be beautiful enough, if we are good enough!

*

WEEDS IN PICTURES.

WEED is said to be "a plant out of place." An excellent definition; for what is there, when appropriately placed, that deserves this name for vexatious worthlessness? But a weed is often in its very place when well painted. We have learned to look upon many vegetable reprobates with an eye of favor. Some weeds are exquisitely beautiful in structure, in flower, or in leaf-forms, when closely examined. The habits of others make them subjects of great interest. We recollect once, while standing with one of the first landscape artists of America, before one of Baddington's views of the Thames, whose banks were clothed (pictorially) with magnificent aquatic plants, being surprised to hear him say, that in America we had few large, succulent plants fit for an artist among our native weeds. Since that time we have never gone into any meadow or field without noticing the plants as subjects of portraiture. And I feel sure that there can be no excuse for barrenness in the foregrounds of landscapes from want of material. It is the want of industry, or the want of *real love* for weed-like plants, that occasions such meagre or conventional pictures. It is seldom that we see *plants* rendered as Landseer or Rosa Bonheur render animals, with an enthusiasm of love that never tires, that never can enough repeat them. If our right hand had been endowed with cunning, we believe that the humbler growths of the field should occupy much of its skill. But one must

love well to paint well. If a man does not respect a plant, if it exerts upon him no positive and pleasurable influence, he is unfit to represent it. A nurse that does not love children can never take good care of them; and an artist that does not love what are called weeds cannot do them justice. Some ridicule has been thrown upon our young artists for painting grasses so much. That they paint them at all is their praise; and that they confine themselves to so few, and repeat their work so often, as if there were but half a dozen species in the world fit for admiration, is their real fault! Instead of but few striking and effective plants, in any direction, growing abundantly, there are so many that one might well be embarrassed by riches.

There is the dock family. None can be less pretentious or more meritorious. What if it does grow in dank and shaded places? What a breadth of leaf the burdock exhibits, what vigor of health, what an oak-like spread of branches, when its blossom-stem is fully extended! There, too, is the relishful horse-radish, of a broad and long palm. The elecampane is another plant of generous leaf. Laying aside all prejudices, who can deny great merit, as a robust and vigorous plant, to the skunk-cabbage? What if its odor is an indisputable fact? Art, in this respect, has the advantage of Nature. In a picture its peculiar and delicate green would be beautiful, without the least odor.

Among upright plants the milkweed is notable. Not for its grace, but for its full habit and generous bearing. The thistles, the brier family, the sedges, the cat-tail, the water-plantain family, the bind-weed, the woodbine, and the blackberry, both upright and creeping, than which, in early leaf, in blossom, or in fruit at every stage, nothing can be more graceful and beautiful, — these all deserve careful *study.*

The mullein need hardly be mentioned, as it figures in pictures already. But what would be more exquisite than the spray of asparagus, if well rendered? There, too, is the golden-rod, the aster, the iron-weed (*Vernonia*), the smart-weed, the teasel, and a hundred more, — admirable chiefly for ornamental designs and decorative patterns, but likewise fit elements for the foregrounds of landscapes. It is worthy of notice, that the plants most valuable for culture on our continent are those which are most beautiful for ornamental design; namely, wheat, rye, and barley, the Indian corn, the cotton and tobacco plants, the grape-vine and its fruit. The potato, poor homely fellow! has no merit except in its blossom; but almost all the plants which form the staple crops are universally beloved of artists.

It is amusing to read the descriptions of weeds in agricultural books. Editors are bound to look upon weeds only in relation to farming. If a thing be prolific, tenacious of life, and voracious of food, no matter how graceful its form or comely its blossom, it is hated, and all the ugly names of the vocabulary are heaped on it. But that should not prevent the admiration of those who have no crops to tend. A pestilent weed may yet be exquisitely ornamental.

We are quite sure that it is the artist's fault if he is deficient in succulent foliage, in herbaceous riches, in all graceful stems and twining vines. Instead of a destitution of such elements, our woods, our low, wet meadows, our hedges and hill-sides, are full of them. It requires only diligence in finding and industry in representing them to make every landscape artist's portfolio rich in vegetable treasures.

*

THE RIGHT KIND OF FARMING.

THERE are few places for a visit more delightful than a large and well-kept farm.

The farm-house spacious, unpretending, neat, convenient; the barns large, and clean; the out-houses for pigs, poultry, tools, etc., well arranged; the bees humming endless music in thin, long row behind the house; the garden, the fields, the forest; these, together with the coming and going of herds, the steady progress of various kinds of work, the unwasteful abundance of provisions which in cities are doled out in close measure; eggs fresh every day, sweet milk oppressed with cream, all manner of fruits in their season, and, above all, vegetables fresh from the garden, whose true flavor is unknown in cities, — no wonder that a farm excites the imagination, and raises up a picture of delight and enjoyment. Speaking of vegetables, it may be cruel to say to people in the city, that they have no idea of the flavor of *peas* or of *corn;* not unless they remember how they used to taste when they lived in the country.

They must be eaten alive, or they are poor luxuries. They should be plucked only long enough to be shelled or shredded for cooking.

Then, in the sultry days of July and August, as the great tureen comes steaming with the one, and the huge platter smoking with pyramids of the other, who cares for meats, or for all costly confections? Peas alone are a feast; and sweet corn, in its various methods,—on the cob, cut off and mixed with cream, or raised into the ineffable glory of *succotash*,—is a banquet which would have made all the gods forget ambrosia and nectar, and stroke their beards with celestial satisfaction.

But this is a mere episode. To *visit* a farm as good company, to have horses at your disposal, to sit in the shade and hear the hens cackle for eggs laid, and cau-cau-caukle for contentment; to watch the workmen at their task,—all this is quite charming. But to carry on a farm is another thing—quite!

A farm is a vast manufactory. Instead of buildings and machinery, you are to carry on manufacturing operations through the agency of the soil. No laboratory turns out a greater variety of products; none requires for its highest success more knowledge, skill, and business tact. If a chemist were obliged to evolve his various products in such a way, as at the same time to build his houses, create his furnaces and implements, his task would be like the farmer's, who, while raising crops, is also bringing up the condition of his ground, and fitting it for its best functions.

It is not difficult for a man to raise good crops, if he has *money enough*. A rich man can walk out of the city upon a poor farm, and in one year put ten thousand dollars' worth of expense upon it. He can *make* a soil, if he has money enough. But wheat that sells for a dollar a bushel will cost at least three; and corn for seventy-five cents, will have cost two dollars. It is not hard to get good crops, if *profit* is of no account. A rich man plays with a farm, as children do with babies, dressing it up to suit his fancy, and quite indifferent to expense or profit. It is his fancy, and not his pocket, that he farms for. Such men are not useless. They employ many hands. They try a great many experiments which working farmers cannot afford to try. They show what *can* be done. And American farmers, although they will not imitate, will do better than that; — they will take hints in this thing and that, and, by gradual improvement, they will raise their own style of farming many degrees. Every township ought to have one gentleman farmer who aims to show what soil can be made to do. In *his* case it may not be remunerative. But, take the country through, the indirect effect will be very remunerative. His very mistakes will be useful. A mistake is often more instructive than a success. But it is not everybody who can afford so dear a schoolmaster.

But, even with a pocket full of money, and with a farm as a mere play-ground, a rich man may carry on very foolishly. A careless, scheming foreman may waste vast sums of money, without producing one useful result, either to his employer or to the community. Indeed, we scarcely know of any other sponge that will suck, in so short a time, so vast a quantity of money, as a farm recklessly carried on! But, unlike a sponge, no squeezing will give back the precious contents. Buildings in bad taste and wrongly placed; trees planted by the thousand, and dying almost as fast as planted; the grounds drained at great expense, so as to require draining again in two or three years; costly cattle and sheep bought, and then neglected; experiments begun with great outlay, tired of, and given up before half completed; — these, and such like things, are follies which have scarcely any compensating side.

Although we use the word farming as including every variety of operation based upon the soil, yet the word covers occupations more dissimilar than are the occupations of the lawyer and the clergyman, or the schoolmaster and the blacksmith. What similarity is there in farming for fruit or farming for herbs? What can be more unlike than a grazing farm, for stock or the dairy, and a grain farm, for sale or fattening stock? How unlike is the conduct of a great plantation, raising one or two staples, and the farm of a score of acres, of mixed crops, raised by the owner's own hand for his own use.

Leaving to the mood of other days some excellent remarks on these various kinds of farming, we avow our own preference, among all kinds and varieties of agricultural procedure, to meditative and imaginative farming. Sitting in our barn-door, which, looking south, is raised one story above the yard beneath, what do we see? Not the Hudson rolled out so wide as to take the name of Haverstraw Bay, nor the mountains beyond, nor yet the green and rounded tops of the near opposite hills, nor the fringes of forest which divide the several sections, nor the slopes, and basins, and tree-ruffled dwelling-houses. What do we see? You would say that the object of our regard was a compost-heap. And by that polite term let it be called. But you and I do not see the same thing when looking at that soil and straw and turf and litter. You see a round heap of fermenting materials. I see flowers and vegetables and fruits. Out of that heap blossom, to my eye, mignonette and phlox, and geraniums, roses, petunias, verbenas, asters, and dahlias! I see regimental rows of currants, strawberries, and raspberries. Great yellow-bellied pumpkins orb up to my sight from among the withering stalks of ripened corn. Compost, indeed! That is a grove of trees, a young orchard, long lines of elms, clumps of balmy evergreens. That is not undigested straw, but peas and flowering beans; that is not lumpish manure, but wheat and grapes! Why, this barnyard is a garden, if only looked at aright, purpled with innumerable flowers; it is a vineyard, all of whose broad leaf-hands cannot cover up the purple clusters; it is an orchard, — see the trees bending with fruit, or humming with insects and bees, that are regaling themselves in its blossoms! Ah! here is rare delight! Here sit I, a farmer indeed, all of whose fields, planted in imagination, tilled by fancy, are reaped in visions.

My crops never fail. Weather never thwarts me. Everything succeeds. Men are always skilful, seed is always good, the hay is never caught by showers, the wheat escapes rust and fly that afflict newspapers so dreadfully about these days; and, in short, as long as I have a comfortable support aside from these grounds, I mean to raise imaginations and meditations on this farm. It is a capital soil for such crops!

*

ARE BIRDS WORTH THEIR KEEPING?

WE receive many pleasant notes from rural friends upon country subjects. Two before us are on birds and weeds. The first we publish, with remarks, below; the other, from an artist in trouble, we shall give, with suitable comfort, by and by.

"Your special contributor, 'perched upon his green hill-slope beyond Peekskill,' writes about birds; but there are some things about birds which he left unsaid. It is very well to speak in their praise, but we should not be altogether blind to their faults. I enjoy their sport in the grove, as they leap from branch to branch, or hover around, cleaving the air ever and anon with swift wing. I am delighted with their beautiful and varied plumage. I am charmed with the sweetness and variety of their ceaseless songs. But, with all this, I am compelled to say, they are inveterate and incorrigible thieves and robbers, imbued with mischief as the human heart with depravity. I give my experience.

"I am owner of a half-acre upon a 'hill-slope,' not on the banks of the Hudson, it is true, but bounding the valley of the Chemung. I planted upon it a grove and an orchard. I invited the birds to lodge and sport in their branches and find shelter beneath their foliage, and they accepted the invitation. Sweet was their song, and gay was their sport. Among my fruit-trees was a cherry producing rare, sweet, and early fruit. I watched its growing trunk and expanding branches from year to year, and in due course of the times and seasons hailed its opening blossoms. Day by day I marked the growth of the fruit, and at last saw the daily deepening blush overspreading its cheek and betokening speedy ripeness. I promised my wife and children and myself a rich feast of the first fruit of the season. But, alas for human hopes! The birds had promised themselves the same thing, and in one day they plucked every cherry approaching toward ripeness from my tree. This they did every day, till not one remained.

"But my tree was then small, and I thought as it should enlarge and produce more fruit, the birds would, after satisfying themselves, leave a little for me; and so I waited, but in vain. The present season I determined, if possible, to get a taste of my cherries, and when they began to ripen I placed a scarecrow in the tree. But the birds soon became acquainted with the scarecrow, and stole the fruit unterrified. I watched hours with stones, which I hurled at them, but they soon learned the uncertainty of my aim, and stood fire unmoved. I threatened a gun, but my wife and daughters said it was a pity to shoot such pretty birds, plucking the cherries so cunningly, and that they would rather go without the fruit than see them killed. So the birds again completed their robbing, and to this day I have never tasted a fully ripe cherry from my favorite tree. I am a friend to the birds, whether they waken me early in the morning or not, if they will only abstain from my choice cherries. But with my present experience, I have no other alternative but to denounce them as thieves and pests — in cherry time. **

"Corning, N. Y."

There is no unmixed good in this world except dying, which cures all ill and inherits all blessing. But while living, what is there without an admixture of evil? Even that wife, who properly restrained you from harming the birds, and evidently is a good woman, has probably some slight infelicities of disposition. The very children, that carry the doubled excellences of their parents, have they not some strokes of mischief? Indeed, sir, do you not find that you are obliged to take even yourself with some grains of allowance? Why, then, should you demand that birds should be more perfect than anything else in this world?

Let us state the case. Although birds undertake to furnish you with the most admirable amusement, and with music such as no orchestra could be hired to give, they do not charge you a penny for their services. You never have to wake them. You have no care of their toilet. You are asked to provide nothing for their breakfast, nothing for dinner, nothing for supper. They draw on you for no linen for their beds, and no space for tenement room. They come to you early in spring; they stay with you till the red leaves grow brown, and even then they leave a rear-guard to watch the winter, and every bright day till after January is sentinelled with some faithful, simple bird on duty.

And what is the service they render? A thousand sparrows there are, without remarkable song, but whose very name recalls to you the memorable words of Christ. There is not another truth more needed and doubted by sorrowing and hard-used men, than that of God's personal care over human interests.

There is scarcely a land on the globe now where the Bible does not say to men, "Are not two sparrows sold for a farthing? And one of them shall not fall to the ground without your Father." And there is scarcely a rood of ground on the earth where this little bird does not flit before our eyes every day, tiny, homely, with only a chirp for a song; but a text-bearer, a mission-bird, a remembrance to every discouraged soul of Christ's words of sweet assurance. I would feed a thousand sparrows with all the cherries that their little crops could carry, for the sake of that very truth which God has associated with their name, and which they recite to me every day. For what cherry or currant or berry that they pluck from my trees can be worth to me what that fruit is which they bring to me from the Tree of Life?

But there is another sparrow, — the tribe is large, — the song-sparrow, whose note is the sweetest, we sometimes think, of all the summer's birds. It is a perpetual songster. It comes early and stays late. It sings all day. We have heard its soft, clear, and exquisitely sweet little snatch of melody, from out of the tree overhead, at two o'clock on a sultry day, with the thermometer at 90° and no wind stirring! Is not that fidelity? Dear little soul, I would give it all the cherries on the place for itself and fellows, and bushels more, if it would deign to confer upon me still the favor of such sweet utterances! For, in good sooth, men are the beneficiaries and birds are the benefactors! It is arrogance and egotism for us to regard insects, birds, and innocuous beasts, as honored in our mere tolerance! They too are God's creatures. They too are a part of the filling up of the grand picture of his earthly cathedral. They have an errand of their own, a place of honor; and no one is to despise or patronizingly to *condescend* to notice that which God made, and makes, and rejoices over in every land and field upon the globe!

Next to these, we hear every day, just now, the wren. A pert, *petite*, smart, brave little animated spark is he! His song is a twisted thread of sweetness. His amazing assiduity in doing nothing is quite edifying. He is brave in battle, — as human bustling do-nothings seldom are, — and will whip twice his weight of martins and swallows.

But none of these mentioned birds are particularly fond of fruit. Seeds and insects form their diet in chief. The same is true of that artist, the bobolink, that sings at the North in a black and white livery; but going South changes his coat and his note, and, like many another northern-bred black-coat, drops into good living, and grows fat in the rice-swamps, and forgets to use his voice, except to call for more food, or raise an alarm-cry when there is some danger of losing what he has got. The chief depredators of the garden are the robin, the blue-jay, the oriole, and the pea-bird, or wax-wing.

A man that would shoot a robin, except in fall, when, in flocks, they are gathered together to caravan the air in their long pilgrimage to Southern glades and forests, and then really and conscientiously for food, has in him the blood of a cannibal, and would, if born in Otaheite, have eaten ministers, and digested them too.

Indeed, if it were not too much trouble to re-write what we have said of the song-sparrow, we would say that the robin is our sweetest summer singer. This universal favorite has a variety of songs. All are sweet, but one rises far above all the rest. At evening, the sun gone down, the cows returned from pasture, the landscape radiant in its salient points, but growing dim and solemn underneath, then, as you sit musing in your door, you shall hear from a tree on the lawn, a little distant, a continuous calling song, full of sweet importunity mingled with sadness. It is the call for its absent mate. Sometimes it rolls and gurgles for but a moment, when a shadow flits through the air, and a sudden flash of leaves, the song stops, two birds glide out upon the sky, and fly to their home. But at other times the bird's grief is your gain. No coming mate shortens his song. Some remorseless boy has brought him down, to sing, and build, and brood no more; some cat or hawk or gazing snake has dined upon the fair thing. And so, though the twilight falls, and the evening grows darker, the song calls on, pausing only to change the manner, throwing in here and there coaxing notes and staccato exclamations of impatience, but going back soon to the gushing, pining, yearning home-call. Take all my strawberries if you want them, O singer! Come to-morrow for my cherries! You pay me in one single song for all that you can eat in a summer, and leave me still in your debt. For there is no such thing as *paying* for that which touches your heart, raises your imagination, wings your fancy, and carries you up, by inspired thoughts, above the level of selfish life. The heart only can pay the heart for good service. As to cherries, I'll take my chance when my betters are served. Eat what you wish, sweet sir, and if there are any left, I will think them all the sweeter, as a part of your banquet.

As to the orioles, there are but few of them. I wish there were more. The jay too, though a brave eater, and a large one, sticks to the woods, for the most part, and comes but seldom to the garden. Its note is as terrible as the music of the Scotch bagpipe. We should think the spirits of a dozen old pipers had entered into every particular blue-jay, and their notes quarrelled and jangled in its throat which should be most cutting and cacophonous! Yet the blue-jay won its way to our regard, and in this wise. When living in Indiana they sang a great deal about our little one-story house, and screamed and shrieked with such terrible vigor that our nerves gave way. We had had chills and fever,—were weak, and a little *edgy*. We took our gun and began an indiscriminate warfare. The jay is tenacious of life, and dies game. After a day or two of shooting, we began to admire the soldier-like quality of these splendid and high-plumed fellows. And when, with our last shot, we brought down a splendid specimen, half shot to pieces, but full of pluck, his eye bright, his courage up, fighting for his life, that ebbed away, and dealing blows right and left at our hand with his stiff bill, and dying without flinching, pluck to the very last gasp, we were conquered, and vowed that we would never shoot such a brave bird again! We never have. We never will.

But, now, as to the wax-wings, or the little crested, yellow pea-birds, that never come to cheer you, that eat none of the marauding insects, that only sing a sharp "*pee ze*," while they are gobbling down your fruit, or ripping out the peas from the tender pod,—

why, we must say, that if any birds are to be shot, these are the ones. We do not recommend it. For it may scare the song-birds, and wound the feelings of robins and their fellows. All the cherries on earth could not be so sweet in our mouth as are the notes of robins in our ears. These drops of sound are the true fruits, and the wide air is that garden universal which rears and shakes them down for all whose senses are refined enough to know how to feed by the eye and the ear, more than by the mouth!

*

COUNTRY STILLNESS AND WOODCHUCKS.

NOTHING marks the change from the city to the country so much as the absence of grinding noises. The country is never silent. But its sounds are separate, distinct, and, as it were, articulate. The grinding of wheels in paved streets, the clash and din of a half-million men, mingling, form a grand body of sound, which, however harsh and dissonant to those near by, becomes at a little distance softened, round, and almost musical. Thus, from Brooklyn heights, New York sounds its diapason, vast and almost endless. The direction of the wind greatly influences the sound. When the air is moist, and the wind west, the city sends a roar across like the incessant break of surf upon the ocean shore. But with an eastern wind, the murmur is scarcely greater, and almost as soft, as winds moving gently in forests.

But it is not simply *sound* that acts upon us. There is a jar, an incessant tremor, that affects one more or less according to the state of his nerves. And, in leaving the city by rail-cars, the roar and jar of the train answer a good purpose in keeping up the sense of the city, until you reach your destination. Once removed from all these sound-making agencies, and one is conscious of an almost new atmosphere. Single sounds come through the air as arrows fly, but do not fill it. The crowing of a cock, the cawing of a crow, the roll of a chance wagon, and the patter of horses' feet, — these, one by one, rise into the air to stir it, and sink back again, leaving it without a ripple. For a time, this both excites and soothes. During the wakening hours the very stillness plays upon your imagination with importunity. You *feel* how still it is. You murmur to yourself, "O how quiet! how tranquil!" On a side-hill, with a wide look-out, upon a rock, or under its shade, you lie for the hour stupid in the bath of stillness. The wings of birds that fly past you are audible. A leaf falling on a leaf reports itself. The squeak of field-mice, in their petty synods, the frolic and bark of squirrels, become very prominent sounds.

I cannot say that such scenes are favorable to *thought*. It is fancy that moves quickest then. It is a nourishing of the sentiments and feelings. The past and the future play together, and memory and expectation pitch sweet fancies to each other.

We said that country silence was also soothing. Let the few first nights' sleep bear witness! In the first place, men's habits right themselves. We dine at noon, not at sundown. We take tea in the broad light of the sun. And by nine o'clock the evening has become very late, and we nod and yawn, and drop off to bed. You look out first to see if all is right. The moon has it all her own way up there. There is not a breath of wind. The leaves hold as still as if they did not know how to swing and quiver. The cricket is singing. A whippowill stirs up fond remembrances. Some super-serviceable dog lets off a bark, as if he had pulled the trigger by accident, then shuts his muzzle, and leaves the great round heavens almost empty of a sound. Ah! these long country nights, full of unwakening sleep!

To find yourself in the morning just where you lay down! To sleep without a wink, a roll, or the slightest change, eight hours, — that is to get back far toward boyhood again.

Speaking of boyhood, did you ever hunt woodchucks? We remember well what venatorial perturbation our young bosom used to suffer on seeing a woodchuck popping up his head above the grass, and with what headlong zeal we plunged after him, invariably to just miss catching him as his tail disappeared down his hole. This region seems to be a favorite haunt for these marmots. Some dozen, we judge, are tenants on our farm. The boys have made several sagacious forays upon them with arms and dog, but Sir Marmot has always been just a little too deep for them. Not so the dog. Jocko had been down upon a visit to a neighboring dog, talking of rabbits, cats, and other things which have power over dogs' imaginations. On his way home, a young woodchuck, whose ma did not know that he was out, inadvertently exposed himself. The temptation was too strong for Jocko. With one or two tremendous bounds, a nip, and a very busy shaking, the work was done. For all the good his parents had of him, the woodchuck might as well not have been born. John skinned him neatly. He was roasted. The family sat around. The lady of the house peremptorily refused to touch the "varmint." The eldest son agreed to support the father, and the two younkers were fierce to eat woodchuck! The head of the family disposed of one mouthful, and looked around. Being watched, he boldly took a second, and was imitated. But about the third taste made it plain that woodchuck satisfies the appetite very speedily.

These singular, chubby, nimble fellows have a very good time of it, on the whole. They wake up from a winter's sleep; enjoy the spring, summer, and autumn. They have no migration to attend to. They lay up no stock of winter food. When the time comes, they roll up into a heap in the chamber of their burrow, poke their nose into their belly, and tuck their tail around, to make a good finish, and then they outsleep storms, snow, and winter. But we have saved one member of this family even this trouble. We have looked in the Prices Current of *The Independent* in vain to find the ruling prices of *woodchuck-skins*. Can any one inform us? From the amazing enterprise shown by the boys, hitherto, they might turn an honest penny yet, in selling packs of woodchuck-skins!

Meanwhile, my young marmots, you are welcome to all the clover you can eat, to all the holes you dig. You may sit serene after your morning feed, and sun yourselves without fear of the boys, for really, jesting apart, they are not half as smart as you are. Don't flinch if they shoot, especially if they take aim. But beware of the dog. He does not say much. He is apt to perform first, and promise afterwards.

*

A CANNON-BALL IN THE HAT.

HEN I was a lad of thirteen years, my father removed from a country town to Boston. Nothing of all its sights produced upon me such an impression as the ships. The outlying bay, the ocean beyond, its mystery, the ships coming in and going out, the masts and rigging, standing up against the sky, — these things produced an indelible impression on my imagination. All the world rose up to my fancy. Real and fabulous things commingled, — voyagers and buccaneers, merchantmen and pirates, fleets of men-of-war, came before my inward sight, and all distant lands and famous islands. Long Wharf has taught me a great deal of geography and sea-history.

But the Navy-Yard, in the adjoining town of Charlestown, separated only by Charles River from Boston, was my especial wonder and glory. I became familiar with all its marvels. I crept down to the bottom of its huge and dismantled ships, I climbed up to the decks of those which were building in the covered ship-houses, I watched the construction of its famous stone Dry Dock, I ranged along the silent mouths of its massive cannon.

One day I visited some ill-constructed vaults where shot had been stored. The six and twelve pound shot were extremely tempting. I had no particular use for them. I am to this day puzzled to know why I coveted them. There was no chance in the house to roll them, and as little in the street. For base-ball or shinty they were altogether too substantial. But I was seized with an irresistible desire to possess one. As I had been well brought up, of course the first objection arose on the score of stealing. But I disposed of that, with a patriotic facility that ought long before this to have sent me to Congress, by the plea that it was no sin to steal from the government. Next, how should I convey the shot from the yard without detection? I tried it in my handkerchief. That was altogether too plain. I tried my jacket-pocket, but the sag and shape of that alarmed my fears. I tried my breeches-pocket, but the abrupt protuberance was worse than all. I had a good mind to be honest, since there was no feasible way of carrying it off. At length a thought struck me. Wrap a handkerchief about it, and put it in your hat.

Now all the world knows that a boy's hat serves as a universal pocket. There he carries handkerchief, papers, twine, letters for the post-office, tops; in short, whatever traps the pocket cannot hold, or whatever contraband thing would show through, goes to the hat. Is a hen's-nest found out, the hat takes the eggs. Is fruit to be gathered, the hat takes it. Is the boy heaping up stones to fire at cats, birds, dogs, and strangers, the hat collects and carries them to the heap. Does a boy want a butterfly, the hat is his net to cast over it. Would he smack a fly or a bee, his hat is better than a bat. It is his fan when hot and his protection when cold. And as age gives it suppleness, it mounts into the air as a poor foot-ball. By that very signal, too, you may know when school is let out: hats go up. And Sunday morning may be detected, if one has lost his reckoning, by the style and sobriety of boys' hats. It is the only day of rest for hats as well as for boys.

The iron ball was accordingly swaddled with the handkerchief and mounted on my head and the hat shut over it. I emerged from the vault a little less courageous than was pleasant, and began my march toward the gate. Every step seemed a mile. Every man I met looked unusually hard at me. The marines evidently were suspecting my hat. Some sailors, leering and rolling toward the ships, seemed to look me through. The perspiration stood all over my face as an officer came toward me. Now for it! I was to be arrested, put in prison, cat-o'-nine-tailed, or shot for aught I knew. I wished the ball in the bottom of the sea; but no, it was on the top of my head!

By this time, too, it had grown very heavy; I must have made a mistake in selecting! I meant a six-pounder, but I was sure it must have been a twelve-pounder, and before I got out of the yard it weighed twenty-four pounds! I began to fear that the stiffness with which I carried my neck would excite suspicion, and so I tried to limber up a little, which had nearly ruined me, for the shot took a roll around my crown in a manner that liked to have brought me and my hat to the ground. Indeed, I felt like a loaded cannon, and every man and every thing was like a spark trying to touch me off. The gate was a great way farther off than I ever had found it before; I seemed likely never to get there.

And when, at length, heart-sore and head-sore, with my scalp well rolled, I got to the gate, all my terror came to a culmination as the sentinel stopped his marching, drew himself up, and, looking at me, smiled. I expected him to say, " O, you little thievish d—l, do you think I do not see through you?" — but, bless his heart, he only said, "Pass!" He did not say it twice. I walked a few steps farther, and then, having great faith in the bravery of my feet, I pulled my hat off before me, and carrying it in that position, I whipped around the first corner, and made for the bridge with a speed which Flora Temple would envy.

When I reached home, I had nothing to do with my shot. I did not dare show it in the house, nor tell where I got it; and after one or two solitary rolls, I gave it away on the same day to a Prince-Streeter.

But, after all, that six-pounder rolled a good deal of sense into my skull. I think it was the last thing that I ever stole (excepting a little matter of a heart, now and then), and it gave me a notion of the folly of coveting more than you can enjoy, which has made my whole life happier. It was rather a severe mode of catechizing, but ethics rubbed in with a six-pound shot are better than none at all.

But I see men doing the same thing, — going into underground, dirty vaults, and gathering up wealth which will roll round their heads like my cannon-ball, and be not a whit softer because it is gold instead of iron, though there is not a man in Wall Street who will believe that.

I have seen a man put himself to every humiliation to win a proud woman who has been born above him, and when he had won her, he walked all the rest of his life with a cannon-ball in his hat.

I have seen young men enrich themselves by pleasures in the same wise way, sparing no pains, and scrupling at no sacrifice of principle, for the sake, at last, of carrying a burden which no man can bear.

All the world are busy in striving for things that give little pleasure and bring much care; and in my walks among men, I often think, There is a man stealing a cannon-ball; or, There 's a man with a ball on his head; I know it by the way he walks. The money which a clerk purloins for his pocket at last gets into his hat like a cannon-ball. Pride, bad temper, selfishness, evil passions, will roll upon a man as if he had a ball on his head! And ten thousand men in New York will die this year, and as each one falls, his hat will come off, and out will roll an iron ball, which for years he has worn out his strength in carrying!

MY POCKETS.

POCKET, if not a faculty of the human mind, or an organ of the human body, must be regarded as an indispensable adjunct to both. The Pocket is the badge of civilization, and what it contains, the very element of discrimination between man and man. My pockets have been the occasion of great trouble to me, ever since I was married. It ought to be understood that I have a wife whose very life-pleasure consists in taking good care of her husband. I dare not say that she is perfect. Perhaps that might cause her death, for the scarcity of such persons living makes me sure people die as soon as they become perfect.

But she is as nearly perfect as it was thought that such a poor sinner as I am could endure. Not only does she review my clothes, bring all buttons and button-holes every week to the general muster, return my stockings to the drawer without a hole, save the necessary one for foot-entrance, and give me immaculate linen, but she examines my pockets, and calls me to a strict account both for what she finds there, and yet oftener for what she does not find!

All those obliging little notes, those pleasant letters of sentiment which it is so agreeable to receive and so awkward to explain, if by any negligence I leave them in my pocket, bring me into the most affectionate catechism. So, too, if I run up a little cosey bill for books or engravings, — a mere private matter of my own, in no way chargeable to family expenses, — unless I am on hand before the first of July and January, (those two J's are like executioners' spears to many a moneyless wretch!) the thoughtless shopkeeper sends them to me by post. Of course they come during my absence. They are accidentally opened! But, after all, — what a blessing they occasion. But for them, I should lose that laying on of the hand upon mine, that sad, earnest look, and those excellent counsels, which I might call golden were it not that they spring from the very absence of gold!

Then, again, I am commissioned to deposit a letter

in the office, and put it for carriage into my pocket, and wickedly continue carrying it there a whole week, without excuse or extenuation! And I do wonder that I am let off as easily as I am. And if I take a letter *from* the office, instead of bringing it directly home to its superscription, it goes circuiting about in routes not laid down in any mail contract. Of course such things bring a man into disgrace in any well-regulated family.

But all these things are mere mishaps, compared with the regular, chronic, incurable fault of my pocket in *money matters*. It seems as if I were foreordained to lose money. Yet I am free from all vices; I do not gamble, drink, smoke, race, or bet. The worst that I know of myself is an addiction to book-stores, print-shops, and picture-dealers' haunts. No, I *lose* it. It must be the fault of my pocket. At first, I pleaded the shallowness of my vest pockets. My wife then transferred my wallet to my pantaloons, but with no change in my misfortunes. I had my pockets examined, but no hole was found. New ones were made, deeper ones, of better cloth, with the best of buttoning adjustments. Alas! the same thing continued! I tried my neighbor's tailor. My neighbor *never* lost money. A ten-dollar bill went through the week unbroken, as surely as a ship goes through a summer voyage. Nobody had ever been known to pick his pockets. Many people had tried to introduce a kind of burglarious instrument, called Benevolence, known to be very adroitly used in easing the pocket. But all failed here. These were the pockets for me! I got a pair of pantaloons of the same cloth which he wore, with the same pockets. Now was I proud and presumptuous. And soon was I abased to the very dust before my wife, having lost all my money, and being able to give no sort of satisfactory account of it.

This long series of misfortunes has very much broken my pride and quenched my hopefulness. I no longer dream that I shall earn the name of the full-pocketed gentleman; the man of a long pocket; the man of an impregnable pocket! And I am sure that hopelessness is making me more and more careless. Almost anybody can get access to my pocket. Children subtract from me. The poor subtract from my pockets. All unfortunates seem to know where my pocket is. Every man that has curious things, old books, venerable old maps, etchings, engravings, or pictures, has heard about my pockets. Every bookseller in town drives through them as easily as through a city gate. Is there any remedy?

Is there no such thing as a pocket-fastener? Are inventions all used up, or can there yet be invented something that will stop up leaky pockets? We can caulk the seams of ships, mend leaky roofs, keep in and keep out moisture by india-rubber garments; but can there be no remedy for leaking pockets? I am prepared to give one half of all that is saved to the man who will make my pockets trustworthy, and he will find *that* to be ample enough for a contented man to live upon respectably!

P. S. The thing is invented! The discovery is made! It was just whispered in my ear, as I wrote the last line. "Take your wife *with* you whenever you go out." Here, good woman, I will pay as I promised. You shall have the half of all you save!

JOYS AND SORROWS OF EGGS.

BORN in the country, our amusements were few and simple; but what they lacked in themselves we supplied from a buoyant and overflowing spirit of enjoyment. A string and a stick went further with us, and afforded more hearty enjoyment, than forty dollars' worth of trinkets to our own children. Indeed, it would seem as if the enjoying part of our nature depended very much upon the necessity of providing its own pleasures. There are not many of our earlier experiences which we should particularly care to renew. We are content to renew our wading and grubbing after sweet-flag root only in memory. The nuttings were excellent in their way, the gathering of berries, the building of snow-houses, and the various games of summer and winter, on land, ice, or snow. We keep them as a pleasant background of recollection, without any special wish to advance them again into the foreground.

But one thing we shall never get over. We shall never lose enthusiasm for hen's-nests. The sudden cackling outcry of a faithful old hen, proclaiming the wonder of her eggs, we shall never hear without the old flush and wish to seek and bring in the vaunted trophy. The old barn was very large. It abounded in nooks, sheds, compartments, and what-nots, admirably suited to a hen's love of egg-secretiveness. And no lover ever sought the post-office for an expected letter with half the alacrity with which we used to search for eggs. Every barrel, every manger and bin, every pile of straw or stack of cornstalks, every mow and grain-room, was inspected. And there was always the delightful hope that a new nest would suddenly open up to us. For every one properly born and well brought up knows that hen's-nests are fortuitous, and are always happening in the most surprising manner, and in the most unexpected places. And though you bring all your great human brain to bear upon the matter, a silly old hen will tuck away a dozen eggs, right under your eyes, and will walk forth daily after each instalment with a most domestic air and tone of taunting, saying, as plain as inarticulate sounds can proclaim it, "I've laid an egg! I've laid an egg! I've laid another!—You can't find it! You won't find it! I know you won't!" And sure enough we can't find it, and don't find it, until, after a due time, the gratified old fuss leads forth all her eggs with infinite cluckings responsive to endless peepings! Behold! there was the nest in a clump of grass not a yard from a familiar path!

The knowledge that a nest might dawn upon us at any time kept our youthful zeal more alert than ever Columbus was to discover this little nest of a continent. Sometimes we detected the sly treasure in the box of the chaise; sometimes an old hat held more in it when cast into a corner than in its palmy days. The ash-bin was an excellent spot. The fireplace under an old abandoned Dutch-oven was a favorite haunt. We have crept, flat as a serpent, under the whole barn, fearless of all the imaginary monsters which, to a boy's imagination, populate dark holes, and have come forth flaxed from head to foot with spider's-webs, well rewarded if only a few eggs were found.

Ah, how it comes back to us now! The round, rosy face of a younger brother; the quiet, dreaming search of a sister, who always was looking, and never finding what she did look for, and always finding what she did not. And then, when the spring was wide-awake, rearing her brood of flowers, and the air smelt of new growing things, and showers were warm, and clouds were white and fleecy, and wandered about the pale blue heaven, like straggling flocks of pasturing sheep; and new-mated birds kept honeymoon in every bush and tree, and sang amatory poems that Burns might have envied; and new furrows in every field attracted flocks of worm-loving blackbirds, and everything was gay and glad and musical, the very flies having music in their wings; and bees, like wicked poets, singing of the flowers which they had robbed; — (well, let 's see, this long sentence has bewildered us, and we forget exactly what we started for. O, now we remember.) Well, in these fervent, soft, brooding days, even hens felt the celestial fire, and piled up their poetical duties in full and overflowing nests, till boys' hearts fairly throbbed with delight, and the pans in the closet swelled up in rounded heaps, until egg could no longer lie upon egg!

Now it sometimes happened that, when busy about the "chores," — foddering the horse, throwing down hay to the cows (yet requiring a supplemental lock at night to eke out the day's pasturage), we discovered a nest brimming full of hidden eggs. The hat was the bonded warehouse of course. But sometimes it was a cap not of suitable capacity. Then the pocket came into play, and chiefly the skirt pockets. Of course, we intended to transfer them immediately after getting into the house, for eggs are as dangerous in the pocket, though for different reasons, as powder would be in a forgeman's pocket. And so, having finished the evening's work, and put the pin into the stable-door, we sauntered toward the house, behind which, and right over Chestnut Hill, the broad moon stood showering all the east with silver twilight! All earthly cares and treasures were forgot in the dreamy pleasure, and at length entering the house, — supper already delayed for us, — we drew up the chair, and peacefully sunk into it, with a suppressed and indescribable crunch and liquid crackle underneath us, which brought us up again in the liveliest manner, and with outcries which seemed made up of all the hen's cackles of all the eggs which were now holding carnival in our pockets! *Facilis descensus Averno, sed revocare gradum*, &c., which means, It is easy to put eggs into your pocket, but how to get them out again, that 's the question. And it was the question! Such a hand-dripping business, — such a scene when the slightly angry mother and the disgusted maid turned the pockets inside out!

We were very penitent! It should never happen again! And it did not — for a month or two. Then a sudden nest, very full, tempted us, and we fortified our courage, as, of course, the same accident could not happen twice. The memory of the old disaster would certainly prevent any such second ridiculous experience!

But it chanced there was company in the house. Cousins and gladly-received neighbors. And amidst the gratulations and the laugh and the hand-shakings, they began to sit down, and we also sat quietly down, but rose up a great deal quicker! Our disgrace was total. Such a tale as we unfolded!

Three times within our melancholy remembrance did we perform this shameful act, until a hen's-nest affected us with peculiar horror.

Are we the only man that sits down on eggs? Is not the whole world hunting nests, and laying up their treasures in pockets behind them, and sitting down on all their spoils, when it is too late? Are there not other things beside eggs, which are very fair on the outside, and very clean if tenderly handled, which, when broken, are most foul to the raiment and the touch? Are there no men whose experience of long-sought love is but eggs in the pocket of one who sits down? Are there no men filling their pockets with thin-shelled, golden eggs, which fortune lays, and which they mean to carry home, and employ for all domestic uses, but which in the end are crushed and only soil their pockets?

We said we performed the feat three times. Why should we conceal the fact that we have understated the number? Let us make a clean pocket of the matter, and confess that it happened oftener, and even after we were grown up and married! The wife's admirable conduct on the occasion established her reputation. And if any one, before venturing upon the untried navigation of matrimony, would test the patience and gentleness of any angelic person, we would advise him to sit down on a dozen eggs in her presence, and witness then the developments of her disposition in the disaster. There are a hundred women who would follow Florence Nightingale into a plague hospital, where there is one who would put her hand into his pocket after such a drear experience as we have recorded!

THE DUTY OF OWNING BOOKS.

E form judgments of men from little things about their houses of which the owner perhaps never thinks. In earlier years, when travelling in the West, where taverns were scarce and in some places unknown, and every settler's house was a house of "Entertainment," it was a matter of some importance and some experience to select wisely where you would put up. And we always looked for flowers. If there were no trees for shade, no patch of flowers in the yard, we were suspicious of the place. But, no matter how rude the cabin or rough the surroundings, if we saw that the window held a little trough for flowers, and that some vines twined about strings let down from the eaves, we were confident that there was some taste and carefulness in the log-cabin. In a new country, where people have to tug for a living, no one will take the trouble to rear flowers unless the love of them is pretty strong; and this taste blossoming out of plain and uncultivated people is itself like a clump of harebells growing out of the seams of a rock. We were seldom misled. A patch of flowers came to signify kind people, clean beds, and good bread.

But in other states of society other signs are more significant. Flowers about a rich man's house may signify only that he has a good gardener, or that he has refined neighbors, and does what he sees them do. But men are not accustomed to buy *books* unless they want them. If on visiting the dwelling of a man of slender means we find that he contents himself with cheap carpets, and very plain furniture, in order that he may purchase books, he rises at once in our esteem. Books are not made for furniture, but there is nothing else that so beautifully furnishes a house. The plainest row of books that cloth or paper ever covered is more significant of refinement than the most elaborately carved *étagére* or sideboard.

Give us a house furnished with books rather than furniture! Both, if you can, but books at any rate! To spend several days in a friend's house, and hunger for something to read, while you are treading on costly carpets, and sitting upon luxurious chairs, and sleeping upon down, is as if one were bribing your body for the sake of cheating your mind.

Is it not pitiable to see a man growing rich, augmenting the comforts of home, and lavishing money on ostentatious upholstery, upon the table, upon everything but what the soul needs? We know of many and many a rich man's house where it would not be safe to ask for the commonest English classics. A few gairish annuals on the table, a few pictorial monstrosities, together with the stock religious books of his "persuasion," and that is all! No poets, no essayists, no historians, no travels or biographies, no select fictions, or curious legendary lore. But the wall-paper cost three dollars a roll, and the carpets four dollars a yard!

Books are the windows through which the soul looks out. A house without books is like a room without windows. No man has a right to bring up his children without surrounding them with books, if he has the means to buy them. It is a wrong to his family.

He cheats them! Children learn to read by being in the presence of books. The love of knowledge comes with reading and grows upon it. And the love of knowledge, in a young mind, is almost a warrant against the inferior excitement of passions and vices.

Let us pity these poor rich men who live barrenly in great, bookless houses! Let us congratulate the poor that, in our day, books are so cheap that a man may every year add a hundred volumes to his library for the price of what his tobacco and his beer would cost him. Among the earliest ambitions to be excited in clerks, workmen, journeymen, and, indeed, among all that are struggling up in life from nothing to something, is that of owning, and constantly adding to, a library of good books. A little library growing larger every year is an honorable part of a young man's history. It is a man's duty to have books. A library is not a luxury, but one of the necessaries of life.

MY PROPERTY.

KNOW few men as rich as I am. I scarcely know where I amassed all my treasures. I have but a few things at home, and they are very precious, animate and inanimate. But, dear me, if you suppose that *that* is all I own, you never were more mistaken in your life!

I have every ship that comes into New York harbor, but without any of the gross trouble which those deluded men have who think they own them. I never concern myself about the crews or officers, about freight or voyage, about expenses or losses. All this would be wearisome. I have certain men who look after these things, while I am left to the pure enjoyment of their beauty, their coming and going, the singing of the anchor-hoisting crew.

I go about the wharves, watch the packages going in or coming out of ships. The outlandish inscriptions, the ceroons of indigo piled up, the stacks of tea-chests, the bales and boxes, the wine and spices, all pass under my inspection. I say inwardly to the men: "Let these things be taken care of without troubling me," and I am obeyed. I have also many ship-yards, where they are building all kinds of craft. Other men pay the money; I take the pleasure, and they the anxious care!

The Yacht Club have been very obliging to me. At great expense they have equippod unequalled boats, that suit me to a nicety. I ask nothing better. They are graceful as swans, beautiful as butterflies. If I had them all to care for, my pleasure would cost me rather dear. But, with extreme delicacy, the gentlemen of the Club relieve me of all that gross and material part of it, and leave me the boats, the pleasure, the poetry of the thing; and once or twice in a season I go down the bay, on a breezy morning, and see these fine fellows sail their craft, and I do believe that if they were doing it for their own selves, instead of for my enjoyment, they would not exert themselves more.

Then, how much have I to thank the enterprising shopkeepers, who dress out their windows with such beautiful things, changing them every few days lest I should tire. It is a question of duty and delicacy with me whether I ought not to go in often as thus: "Good morning, Mr. Stewart, Good morning, Mr. Lord, or Mr. Taylor. I am greatly obliged to you for those fine goods in the window. I have enjoyed them amazingly, as I did the other patterns of last week. Pray, sirs, do not put yourselves to all this trouble on my account. Yet, if your kindness insists upon it, I shall be but too happy to come and look every day at such rare productions of the loom." In the same way I am put under very great obligations to Messrs. Appleton & Co. It is affecting to see such kindness as they have shown, in going to great expense to procure fine stereoscopic views for the entertainment of their friends. It must be a great expense to them. But then they are displayed, free as grass in meadow or dandelions by the roadside, and any one can look for nothing, and without any other risk than that of purchasing! On the same side of Broadway is a firm so benevolent that some Dickens ought to embalm them as a "Cheeryble Brothers," — of course, I mean Messrs. Williams and Stevens, who pay out great sums every year, in order to fill their windows with pleasant sights for passers-by. Some surly old rich men there are in New York who hoard and hide their pictorial treasures. Not so these benevolent gentlemen. They let their light shine; and with rare delicacy, lest the eye should tire of repetition, they change their pictures every week. Then here is Mr. Seitz, who has ransacked all Europe for brilliant impressions of the rarest classical engravings, and has brought together a collection which cannot probably be equalled or approached by any similar concern in the world. Only to think of such pains-taking kindness! And then if one loves books, how many are there besides Messrs. Appleton or Mr. Scribner who will rejoice in seeing you before their shelves, warming in kindred feeling to these children dressed in calf. I am sometimes overwhelmed with the sense of my riches in crockery and china, in sewing-machines, in jewelry, in furniture, in fine wall-paper, in new inventions.

And then how many men build handsome houses for me to look at, and fill their yards with flowers for me to nod to, and place the most beautiful faces of the family in the window to cheer me as I pass! Surely this is a kind-hearted world! And then how many fine country-seats are built, and grounds laid out, for my enjoyment. The fee simple may be in some other man, but I own them. For he owns a thing who understands it best, and gets the most enjoyment from it!

This world was made for poor men, and therefore the greatest part of it was left out of doors, where everybody could enjoy it. And though men have been building and fencing for six thousand years, they have succeeded in getting very little of the universal treasure sequestered and out of sight. Suppose you cannot plough that fertile field, or own the crops, or reap the harvests, is there no pleasure to you in a fine field, a growing crop, a good harvest? In fact, I sometimes fancy that I enjoy ploughing and mowing more when other people are engaged in them than if I were working myself. Sweat away, my hearties, I say; I am in the shade of this tree watching you, and enjoying the scene amazingly. I love to go into the pasture and look over those sleek Devonshires. The owner is very kind. He has paid thousands of dollars for them; he has spent I know not how much for the barns and premises; he keeps several careful men to tend them, and all for my enjoyment and yours! We walk through the fields, handle their silky vests, discuss their points, and enjoy the whole herd, full as much as the so-called owner!

Sometimes I go out to look after my farms, for I own all the best ones hereabouts. And the orchards, the gardens, the greenhouses, the stately forests and exquisite meadows that I possess, divested too of all vexation of taxes, care, or work, are enough to make one's heart swell with gratitude.

Besides all this, there is a royal artist that rises earlier than I do every day, and works gloriously every hour, painting pictures in the heavens, and over all the earth, giving inimitable colors, unexampled *chiaro-oscuro*, filling the day and the world with scenes that the canvas never equalled. And this stately gallery, with a dome like heaven, stands open without fee or impudent janitor, to every poor man that has eyes. And the best of all is, that, glorious as is this manifestation, it is but a hint and outlying suggestion of a world transcendently better, not made with hands, eternal in the heavens!

MEN NEED WHAT THEY DO NOT WANT.

IF one will take the trouble to watch his own mind, or — which he will find to be a great deal more natural — to watch the conduct of his neighbors, he will observe how readily men listening to discourse believe more firmly what they believed before, and allow themselves to be influenced in the very qualities which are already strongest and most active.

Men love to read "on their own side," to hear the things which they already believe enforced with new arguments; to hear their ministers or political speakers praise the things in which already they are fully established. But they are seldom willing to hear another side, to have enforced the truths which they do not believe, and the qualities which they do not possess. In this way men grow narrow: they intensify their opinions, rather than enlarge their knowledge, and become selfish and bigoted.

If I were to urge the benefits of an easy and good-natured contentment in life, the anxious and the careful would shake their heads, and fear that these qualities would lead to carelessness and mischief. Whereas, all the heedless and jovial, who live for one day at a time, and never provide for to-morrow, would jump at the doctrine and rejoice in its wisdom. But those who refuse it are most in need of it, and those who accept it do not need it at all.

If I urge the claims of sobriety and foresight, those who are already too anxious about the future, and too sober for the present, will listen eagerly and nod approval, and talk all the way home of the wisdom of my speech. But it was not for their sakes that this truth was propounded, but for the careless, giggling, heedless creatures who take none of it to themselves. If I praise generosity, they who are already carelessly generous receive a fresh impulse in that direction. If I exhort to frugality and economy, all the shrewd and close-managing men in the congregation repeat the words, and nudge their neighbors, and look around exulting. But if I sharply expose the meanness of being penurious and stingy, all the parsimonious men are deaf, while the spendthrifts fairly laugh out with approbation.

When I inveigh against pride, the proud are the last that take it; but if I expound the benefits of a firm self-reliance and self-respect, all those already too strong in self-esteem straighten up, and say, Amen!

Men strengthen each other in their faults. Those who are alike associate together, repeat the things which all believe, defend and stimulate their common faults of disposition, and each one receives from the others a reflection of his own egotism. If the slow and prudent would associate with the sanguine and zealous, the peculiar faults of each would be mutually corrective. If the timid and the courageous would walk together, one would rise toward firmness and the other sink a little back from rashness. Men of a practical mind, who regard the imagination with contempt, are just the men that ought to associate with imaginative people, and clothe their barrenness with some beauty, and gain that finer insight which the imagination gives to the understanding.

People naturally select those companions who please rather than those who profit them most, and gratify their conceit at the expense of improvement.

There is manifest a wisdom in the divine order of society; men are thrown together without regard to their affinities and preferences. The old and young, the gay and sober, the thriftless and frugal, the selfish and generous, the poor and the rich, the high and the low, all dispositions, all pursuits, all sides of belief of all sorts, secular things and religious, authority and lawlessness, knowledge and ignorance, riches and poverty, cheerfulness and gloom, hopefulness and despondency, the nimble and the sluggish, the quick-seeing and the dull-eyed, — all are thrown together into the vast compound of human society, and made by their *interests* to defer one to another, to wait upon each other, to give up their own preferences, to respect in others traits which they do not themselves possess. And so the Divine Wisdom has made human life to be a school and educatory discipline. And we are not to regard it as our misfortune that we must mix with men and feel all their humors, and carry some part of their follies as burdens. No schoolmaster could teach men as much wisdom as those things do which men count it a misfortune to meet or to endure! And all the dreams and aspirations which men entertain, of retiring from society, of getting out from life into some secluded nook, are not only unwise, but contrary to the ordinance of Divine Providence. For men need men. And while it is *pleasanter* to meet men whose likeness to ourselves shall flatter our vanity or pride, it is *better* to be obliged to associate with those who will teach us new things, or even with those whose very faults will induce patience, forbearance, and philanthropy.

CONSULTING AN ECHO.

VERY self-willed and passionate man there was, in our boyhood days, who had long and loud disputes, sometimes with his wife and sometimes with his neighbors. Of course he was always in the right, and they, whoever they might be, were always in the wrong. It chanced that there was in his neighborhood a place remarkable for its echo. One echo was always to be had, and in certain positions, two and three. The vehement old gentleman used, when the dispute did not please him, to walk off in the direction of the echo-hills, talking to himself, and at every step more and more positively laying down his propositions, until, by the time he reached the ground, he would shout out, "I know I am right!" and immediately it was sent back to him, — "Know am right!" — "Am right!" — "Right!" "I say she lies!" he would cry out, encouraged with the first effort; and the echo replied, "Say she lies," — "She lies," — "Lies!" Catching up the hint, he would answer, — "Well, I do say so." And he was gratified with hearing, "Do say so," — "Say so."

This walk became a great consolation to the pragmatical old man. And he seemed, at length, to think that there was wafted to him some intelligent confirmation of his notions. Thus he was wont to hear himself, and listen to his own words reflected from the sides of the hill.

There are a great many persons of strong nature, inflexible will, self-opinionated, and intense in feeling, who never see anything in life, except themselves reflected from those whom they meet. It is not their wish to be advised, or to be modified in their notions. They give forth their own intense convictions, and pour forth their feelings out upon things and persons to such a degree, that everything is but a reflection of themselves.

Such persons will bear down upon men, in asking their opinions, with such a statement of their own, that timid and complying natures say yes to them, of course; and those who wish to please, or do not wish to offend, say yes, too. And those who say nothing are considered, of course, as giving tacit assent. And sensible men, of contrary opinions, would no more think of resisting them, than they would of catching a wild horse that ran with headlong fury through the streets. But how satisfied is he, after such a career! Rubbing his hands, he says, with lordly satisfaction, "I have asked a great many sensible people about this matter, and I have yet to find one who does not think as I do." The fact is, that he has been out hallooing and listening to his own echo!

If a man is prosperous and influential, there are multitudes who only desire to know what he would like to have advised. It is not always easy to get another's real mind. They stand off, they hesitate and question as if to get at the truth, whereas they are only getting at *you.* So soon as your bent and wish are discovered, they will, with great apparent candor, advise you just as you longed to have them! and you have got yourself twice over, — your own mind and its echo!

It is amusing to listen to a dozen gentlemen at a political consultation, or at a board of directors for some institution, or of a railroad company, upon a question which divides and excites all the number. Each of at least half a dozen men will assure you that he has not yet met a single man who does not think as he does. At least two or three irreconcilable opinions will be declared to be the current opinion of the community! Each man goes to those naturally accessible to himself, and hears himself reflected from them, and reports to his confederates one opinion, and that his own, echoed five or six times! Men usually find what they wish to find. What they look for, that they see.

Let a pretty woman, of agreeable manners, and musical way of talking, who is greatly exercised with some profound question of a Fair or Festival, and who leads the "Opposition," go among the admiring gentlemen who are her friends, and see if she does not come back in triumph to report that every one agreed with her!

Let some amiable pastor go out to see what his people think about his remaining with them, and we will venture to say that he will be almost unanimously fooled into the impression that every man in the parish wishes him to stay as much as he himself does! Consultation, with obstinate men, is only another way of propagating their own opinions.

The same thing takes place in public assemblies. Men who speak to temperance meetings are expected to say what the meeting already believes; the Democratic or Republican speaker is the echo of the audience, with variations; that preacher is sound, with his own people, who eloquently varies and embellishes their own beliefs.

Every considerate man should be aware of this subtle echo of selfishness or conceit. And a wise man should eagerly entertain those counsellings which are the least like his own. It is what others think that we need to ponder. Conceit is narrow. No man can be very broad who will build with nothing but that which he quarries from himself. There are men enough who think, when they hear themselves echoed, that a god spoke.

THE VIRTUE AND FANATICISM OF NEATNESS.

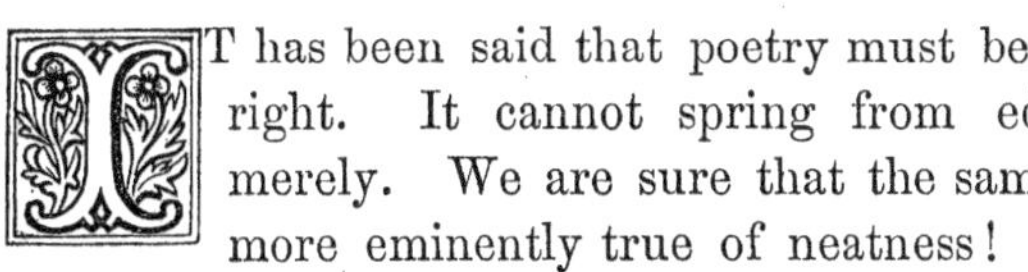

IT has been said that poetry must be a birthright. It cannot spring from education merely. We are sure that the same is yet more eminently true of neatness! A man must have an original genius for it, or he will not excel. We have good reasons for saying so. We admire pictures, without being able to paint them, and we admire neatness in the same way. We have a sort of reverence for a comprehensively neat and orderly person, as of a being of superior endowments. We could never gain an insight into that rare and wonderful mental mechanism by which everything is made to arrange itself without commotion, and things come to pass neatly. It is a matter of genius undoubtedly. Education may develop it, direct it, but never creates it. All the education in the world could not enable us to fold a shirt so that it would come forth with the creases in the right place. We can roll up a bundle, we can tumble up a garment, we can crowd into very narrow compass any amount of linen. But when it comes forth again, who can describe its condition? But another hand is put forth. Every thread knows its master. Each plait and every fold submit themselves. Creases vanish in despair. And a heterogeneous heap comes quietly into order and contact, so that a trunk is packed with as much harmony as are the muscles and tissues of the human body.

Then there is the mystery of bureau-drawers. We never put anything into them that it does not seem to shove everything else. We never take anything out, without discomposing all that remains. There is a fatality of disorder in our touch. But another soothes the drawer, brings peace to linen, and composure to ruffled handkerchiefs and heterogeneous stockings. If we hang up anything in the closet, it is sure to fall down again. If we want a coat, it is sure to be under two or three other garments, which always get out of the way in any but the right way. Our boots and shoes take every liberty with us, and despise regularity in arrangement. Indeed, our visit to any place is a sure indication that the place needs some attention. But if these easy things are difficult, what shall be said of books, of papers, of letters, of engravings, of pictures, and of all the multitude of nameless things that make up a collector's cabinet? Who can describe a gentleman's house when his family is away? Books accumulate on the floor; papers load down the table; pitchers, tumblers, plates, blink from among statuettes and vases on the mantelpiece; framed engravings and pictures are stacked against the wall six or seven deep; portfolios spread abroad their huge sides flat upon the floor; shawls and dressing-gowns are tucked upon the sofa; hats, caps, gloves, and shoes are promiscuous and diffusive; heaps of everything abound everywhere. There is a place for everything, and everything is in its place, and that place is — the floor. The ashes are forgotten and protrude far beyond decency and the fender; canes and fishing-rods confer together in the corner, and cups and balls roll and jingle in every drawer. All the tumblers in the house have been used for flowers, and all the pitchers have been brought up with water. And yet the man loves order, and no one has a keener sense of gratitude when the restoring hand at last arrives, and all things, as if conscious of a new influence, begin their march to their own domain.

But order and neatness are different things. A man may be forgiven for disorder, but not for dirtiness, and especially if it be personal. There are many persons scrupulously neat who are not orderly, and sometimes we find a man who is orderly but not neat; but generally neatness and order are twin sisters. And how beautiful!

We can pity and forgive the want of these qualities in man, but not in woman. All virtues and graces go for nothing in a slattern. A woman must be superhuman, indeed angelic, who could please without neatness. Probably the conviction of this truth accounts for the universal grace of neatness among women. There are occasional rumors of a contrary state of things. But we always tread them under foot indignantly as wanton slanders. Women *are* neat. If not, they are not women.

Nay. Women are in danger of excess in carefulness. They run into radical notions of order, and even flame forth into fanaticisms of neatness. Then neatness becomes most afflictive. It has long been a question with me, which was most dreadful, a disorderly house, or a dwelling given up to the insanity of neatness. In the sacred precinct of that dwelling where the despotic woman wields the sceptre of fierce neatness, one treads as if he carried his life in his hands. Order is the centre, and neatness the supreme law, of the house. Nothing is pardonable, nothing tolerated which does not nimbly and abjectly bow down to them. Sin and dirt are synonymous. Vain are Lesson and Catechism without precision and absolute neatness. All the instruments of this final quality become reverend. A child that would speak slightingly of broom, brush, or towel, is on the road to profanity! All moral qualities are inflections or subordinates of the supreme virtue of cleanly order. Men are divided into two classes, the neat and the filthy. The grades of respectability and the order of endowment are all measured by the relative capacity for neatness! Everything comes under this Moral Law. The horse must be neat, the cow must be neat, the dog must be neat, the pigs must be neat!

From cellar to attic there is the most fierce and vigilant hunt for the germ of dirt. There must not only be no spot, or soil, or litter, but not even the suspicion of any! What avail all virtues, all graces of speech, all helpful kindness, if, when the matron lays her head on the pillow, there is a probable shaving on the nursery floor, an undusted chair, or a bit of lint right out on the parlor carpet?

Common, ignorant folks have but a slight idea of neatness as a science. It is with many people of a neglected education a mere superficial quality. Have they ever classified the different kinds of dirt? traced them to their sources? and studied their habits? Do they even know that there is a Natural History of Dirt? There is mould, rust, mildew, dust, smoke-grime; dirt of wood, of woollen, of cotton, of fruit and vegetable, of paper, of leaves, of insects, of birds and beasts, of men and children, solid, liquid, gaseous, aerial, terraqueous, visible and invisible. There is the dirt of the crack, of the crack vertical and the crack horizontal, of the moulding and cornice, of the wall and ceiling, of the curtain and carpet, of cupboard and closet, of table and bed, of seasons. Each in kind, winter dirt, spring, summer, and autumn dirts, and each to be searched, seized, condemned, and annihilated.

The housewife becomes a knight-errant. Ghosts and giants are nothing to her. Castles and encounters of freebooters she turns over to nursery credulity. She has her broom and brush in hand, her armature of cloth and wash, for that deceitful, stealthy, ubiquitous foe of all domestic peace, universal dirt. All nature is her enemy. All winds are adverse which bring dust. All phenomena are regarded as good or bad, from their dirt-producing tendencies. The economy of life is arranged with supreme reference to virtues of order and neatness. Comfort is nothing, ease is nothing, happiness is nothing, good dispositions are nothing. Neatness is the one grace. That determines when you must get up, what you must wear, where you may sit down, what you may touch, what rooms are usable, what days of the week are home days, or endurable days. Life has not one moment's respite from unwinking vigilance! Not one moment is there that the great Arch-enemy of connubial felicity does not threaten a speck or a spot upon something. You live under a perpetual and sounding, "Take care." It is "Take care, don't touch that silver, you will tarnish it." "Take care of that sofa, it is newly covered." "Take care! don't sit on that clean chintz; you ought to know better than to sit down on such a chair!" "Take care! let that hat alone, you will soil it." "Take care! pray don't go near that side-board, you 'll scratch it." "Take care! a stick! a knife too!! Whittling in the parlor!!! Go out — out with you; go out of the yard, go into the road; go behind the barn, where the wind won't blow your shavings back." "Take care! don't eat apples in the sitting-room, — you always drop some seeds." "Take care, child, come away from that door. You are not going into that room; it is just put in order!" And thus, family discipline, domestic life, and the whole end of living seems to be, to avoid dirt, and secure neatness. Is there anything so tormenting as ecstatic neatness? O, for a morsel of dirt, as a luxury! How good dust looks! A ploughed field with endless dirt, — all hail! The great sentence itself, which consigns man finally to dust again, becomes a consolation!

NIAGARA FALLS, BUT NOT DESCRIBED.

NY attempt to convey to those who have not seen them "a realizing idea" of Niagara Falls, must be a miserable failure, even when the description is calm, detailed, and scientific; and much more when it is exclamatory and poetic. But, after one has himself been at the Falls, and subject to their influence, all reasonably well-written descriptions become interesting. One cannot but wish to know how other minds have been affected, and what were the secret reasons of different experiences. With some most literal persons the whole concern may be expressed in arithmetical figures; — the American falls are so high and so wide; the Canada falls are so much wider and so much lower; the water is so deep, and so many tons are estimated to pass over in an hour; the rapids descend at such an angle, and so many feet. There is to them neither more nor less than just what is before them, — a vast, roaring plunge of water. To another, we may suppose there is added a fine perception of form, color, and motion. He will have an artist's eye for each feature, — as if he were turning in his mind unconsciously the anatomy of the thing, and revolving how it could be rendered on canvas.

But to others, while this may not be wanting, there is a very different class of mental sensations. After the first bewildering excitement begins to assume a more settled form, and the confused and multiplex conceptions grow up each upon its own stem, one is conscious, at least I was conscious, that I did not so much see simply the Falls, as, seeing them, feel *thousands of associations* which they touched and vivified. And it seems that, besides their wondrous quality of beauty and force and grandeur, they have a yet more wonderful power of *suggestion*. Thus, while I was steadily gazing at these perpendicular waves, and thought that I was really *seeing* them, the mind had glanced back, and was experiencing a strange sense of the length of years, and unending, unintermitted work. For ages before an eye saw them, long before even an Indian wandered toward their mysterious thunder, — while Columbus was steering westward, while battles were destroying Rome, while Romans were sacking Jerusalem, while Israel wandered in captive lands, while David was penning in his psalm, "The voice of the Lord is upon the waters: the God of glory thundereth: the Lord is upon many waters. The voice of the Lord is powerful; the voice of the Lord is full of majesty. The Lord sitteth upon the flood, the Lord sitteth King forever," — these mighty Falls were making their solemn chorus. And not for one moment has there been check or pause. It seems to one, at first, as if they wrought for *him:* as if, when he departed, they must fade out somewhat as they do in his remembrance. And it comes with great power home to us, that they have thundered for ages, neither caring whether men heard or were deaf or absent, in winter and summer, amid storms or sunshines, dark or light; under the stars and under the sun. Our own emotions seem to be a part of the scene. That there should have been such long space in which no one shuddered or laughed, no one was solemn or glad, no one looked or lingered or yearned, while yet all this upheaved glory was active still, makes one feel what the unworthy disciple said, "Why was this waste?" It is like a drama enacted in a solitary theatre; a sermon discoursed unto emptiness. Then one wonders what the sensations must have been of the millions of diverse minds that have thronged these banks, in all degrees of capacity and sensibility, in all moods of sobriety and sorrow, in all experiences of gayety and joy, — young and old, wise men and fools, giggling girls for once hushed and overawed, before this stern and uncoquetting beauty that would as remorselessly swallow down babe and beauty as it would bear or log. Could the simple and natural experiences of all the souls which have been wrought upon before this Majesty of Waters be vividly recorded, it would be yet more wonderful than Niagara itself.

One is not long in discovering that he is seeking to express that which he sees by comparisons with familiar objects. I cannot till this moment, when looking upon the bubbling-out of jets of white from the face of the descending water, forbear to think that it is a process of blossoming. This takes place peculiarly upon the Canada side. The water at the centre angle comes to the plunge with unbroken surface, — a massive movement, a solemn dignity, as if conscious of the secret power which slept within. It bends without a wrinkle; it plunges; but, at less than a third of its descent, some projecting crag from beneath catches it, or the air hisses up through it, and white ebullitions evolve, growing more and more frequent, until, before the mass is hid in the mists which gather about its feet, it is sheeted all over with flowers. This is not a suggestion merely of color, but of motion. The evolution of these diamond bouquets is suggestive of the rapid opening of leaves, of the quick, final opening of flower-buds. Neither can one, by any process of reasoning, get rid of a sense of *life* in this cataract. It is felt in the Rapids above, in the long-descending Fall, in the infuriate and agonized uproar beneath the Horse-Shoe, and, perhaps even more than anywhere, in the race beneath and beyond the suspension-bridge, two miles below. You do not at all admit that you are so wrought upon in your inmost soul by a mere mass of inert water drawn down the cliff by gravitation. It must be a living voice that speaks to you. You attribute volition to it. No one thinks or speaks of it as a passive thing, irresistibly acted on; but as a fierce will, as an irresistible power, full of all caprices, of inordinate passions, surpassing in rage and fury and terrible strife all that we have conceived of in human conflicts, or the race of contending beasts, or the coil and twist of mightiest serpents. This sense of life grows more earnest and real the nearer you come to the water. At a little distance the sense of beauty takes precedence of all others; but stand at the foot of either sheet, or close upon the edge of Table Rock, or, more remarkably yet, descend beneath Table Rock, and, turning to the left a hundred yards, go down and out to the very edge of the stream, that, having made its leap, is hissing past in wild affright and immeasurable speed, and you will have a brave heart indeed or a very stupid one, if you do not feel as if you were looking in upon a chasm of perdition, and were in momentary danger of being clutched by weird spirits and hurried headlong to destruction. No one can look out over this particular scene, from the edge of it, without an impression of subterranean and infernal doings. At one moment, the innumerable jets, that never for two seconds wear the same form, — that are not water nor foam, but both, — that open and stretch out long hands, leaping up as if clutching at some invisible prey, and then rush together, and whirl round and round in a maze of fury, — suggest to you a liquid prairie full of raging and bedevilled water-wolves. If the eye changes a little, looks farther up towards the opening and shutting mist, it fancies that there are monsters beneath in horrible sport. The water swells up as if they were about to emerge, or bubbles and boils after them as they sink down again. You look for the serrated and knotted black back, you almost can see the huge sprawling legs and tentaculæ of the fabulous Norwegian Krakens, acre-large, sporting with all their young litter. There is one point where, above all others, you have a sense of power in a threefold form; going beneath Table Rock, as far as you can, without going behind the sheet, you see the force with which the water descends. It is not a steady pouring, but in successive bolts; it has the appearance of clenched fists, pelting downward toward the rocks. Behind this is the gloomy and mysterious mouth of the cave, swept across by violently blown mists. The wild eddying of these vapors was to me very impressive. I looked to see some storm-god issue forth, and these were his whirling couriers speeding out before him. Just below, an eddy swept round a point of rock, forming a whirlpool, some fifty or sixty feet in diameter. Into this had been sucked several trunks of trees, logs, planks, besides lesser trash. It was affecting to look at their attempts to escape. For surely they were alive, and conscious of their danger, and wildly heading out toward the raging waters, which mounted them, beat them down, whirled them back, and sent them round again in the endless circle. And so I watched them for a half-hour, and longed to do something to help them, — for it was plain that they could not help themselves. Doubtless they are whirling there yet, as I write; and yet, as you read. Nor could one of my profession refrain from thinking that thus stray men, swept by their passions, are caught and whirled nightly round and round, by currents that are easily entered, but that defy all escape, until their work is done, and they cast the mangled victim in fragments all along the shore!

One that had not seen could hardly be persuaded that over all these views there is spread the most dazzling and exquisite beauty. The very stream that rushes like a raging demon at you, and splits upon the rock on which you sit, is beaded all over with sparkling bubbles, that, every one, might teach a diamond how to shine. Those globes that belly up from the deep are sheaves of pearls; those wildest circles that shoot out like suddenly uncoiled serpents, give you every curve of beauty, and are white with efflorescent gems. The mind changes with perpetual and involuntary transitions from terror to admiration; from terrible power to exquisite loveliness. It is a scene of raging power covered all over with a robe of perfect beauty. The mists assume every form; rising as a stately pillar, or swept by the winds and diffused like clouds. Meantime the whole air is solemn with the undertone of the falls. The most obvious sound is a sharp and crashy roar. But down below, there is a suppressed thunder, as of an organ playing beneath the uplifted song of a thousand voices.

The sense of irresistible power is common to every part of this scene, when approached closely. The tumult and headlong rush of the Rapids, whirling, tumbling over each other, one wave devouring another, — the stately plunge of the solemn green water, the boiling and madness of the tormented chasm below, with very different effects in other respects, have all alike a sense of irresistible power that makes your own strength insignificant. You are the most helpless of all creatures. A gnat, a spider, a leaf, have as much power to resist as you. A struggle would be a folly. Even an outcry would be as if you were dumb. Such utter nothingness, before a presence upon which the hand of man can never be lifted, is a kind of annihilation. Courage, resistance, strength, contention, are words without any meaning to a man who steps three feet farther out beyond where I stand.

But different portions of this system of falls, — for it is not one fall, but an elaborate cataract system, — have very different expressions of feeling. Seen from a distance, as from Terrapin Bridge and the tower on Goat Island, the Rapids are not victim waves, hurried to execution, but they come down toward you with all tokens of joy, flinging up their arms, and rushing with an ecstasy of exhilaration, a very carnival of waters. Sometimes one thinks, when looking far up to the upper line of the Rapids, where they back against the sky, of a troop of bannered knights, filling the air with white pennons and streamers, and charging down toward you, and every few moments some larger swell, like a suddenly spurred steed, bolts upright and above all its fellows. At other times, when in positions that bring the sun aright, it seems as if, from below, water-sprites were ostentatious of their jewels, and flinging them by millions to glitter a moment in the sun, and then flash back to the wave again.

All hasty visitors, and almost all who think themselves thoroughly acquainted with the Falls, miss the only view of the Rapids which, once seen, one wishes to carry away in his memory, and that is on the Canada side, about two miles from the Clifton House, on the Chippewa road, at a place called Street's Mill. As compared with this, all other views of the Rapids are fragmentary. This one, at that particular point, gives them in such perspective, that they seem to stretch away ten miles, although not in fact half a mile wide. If one, on returning, looks from the hill, back upon the scene which he has just been viewing, he can scarcely be persuaded that the few strips of foam which he sees could have seemed so immensely outstretched. It is the most gloriously deceptive view around the Falls.

NEAT DRESSING IS NOT CLEAN HOUSEKEEPING.

AVING often met Mrs. Prim in society, I thought her the neatest woman in the world; and probably should have always thought so if I had not, very strangely, had access to her house. For, once, when I had praised the good woman, a mischievous girl whispered just loud enough to be heard, (exactly as if she was trying to keep it a secret, — cunning rogue!) "He ought to see her at home, if he wants to know what neatness is." This ran in my head, and stirred up a host of busy fancies and wondering thoughts. "Well, I do wish I could slip in some time, unexpectedly, and see if this fair show is a pretty piece of domestic imposture!"

Who knows what is before him? My wishes were gratified. For, that very night, I dreamed; and Mrs. Prim was the heroine of my dream. By that amazing power given unto dreams, I found myself the husband of Mrs. Prim, — the very Mr. Prim himself. Methought my lady had gone out to spend an evening; and after sleepily reading a paper for a while, I retired to rest. Entering the room, there lay a stocking sprawled out at full length on the floor, its mate coiled up into a dump by its side, just as it was turned off the foot. In the middle of the room stood a stack of underclothes, just as they had been stepped out of. Several pairs of shoes and several widowed ones, who long had mourned the loss of a companion, and had, for grief doubtless, much run down at the heel, were sprinkled around the room promiscuously. The washbasin, its contents creamed over with soap, stood in a chair; the towel lying half in it, the soap on the floor with a coat of dust be-feathering it. The washstand was covered with ends of candles, open and evacuated snuffers, scraps of fancy soap, a caseknife, a roll of brimstone, two tooth-brushes colored with powder, the one red, the other black; a shoebrush, a snarl of black braid for shoestrings, half a dozen empty perfume-bottles, and a Bible. The bureau was as much beyond the wash-stand in condition as in original size. Every drawer but one was open in different degrees, like Peel's sliding-scale of tariff. If Homer asked help of the gods when beginning his epic, how much more should I? He had only a city to describe, with a few armies, and the geography of earth and heaven; but I have a lady's bureau and all its drawers! The cloth, designed to cover and protect it from all scratches, had certainly been used for a towel at each corner, for there were the finger-prints. A pair of curls, several unmanufactured wads of vagrant hair, an upset box of tooth-powder, two dispersed squadrons of pins, — the one sort mere light infantry, the other full-grown dragoon pins, — hair-brushes, one, two, three; two long combs, one fine comb, so old as to have lost many of its teeth, and to have turned quite *gray;* pomatum, oils, uncorked *cologne*, *mille-fleur*, *lavender*, *patchouli*, *verveine*, and a host besides; wristlets, hair-bands, ruffles, laces, lockets, rings, thimbles, elongated hair-pins, side-combs, back-combs, refuse curl-papers, a pair of curling-tongs laid down too hot, and making the cloth to blush brown under them; a bundle of tracts, several notes and *billets-doux*, seals, wax, unrolled and unrolling spools of thread, several skeins of silk snarled and unsnarlable, a crushed cap or two, sundry ribbons, an odd volume of Hannah More's works, the constitution of a maternal society, gloves a score, black, white, yellow, blue, and brown, — and all this just on the top, for the drawers are yet to come! A tempest had evidently been dealing with these lower depths, for they were stirred up from the bottom. When, in dressing in hot haste, a collar had been sought, the sweet Mrs. Prim, beginning at one side, forced down to the other end each article which was not the one sought for; and then, returning, pawed them all down to the *other* side. Going to the next drawer, the ceremony was repeated. Some of the drawers were emptied into others; and then the contents put back by the handful and kneaded down to their proper compactness. Once, the candle — which was in a "melting mood" — was overturned into a heap of fine linens, but the mischief was effaced by shoving the ill-fated things, in disgrace, far back into the drawer and deep under many companions. Many things were torn open to see if something else was not in them. Stockings were unrolled and left; or a cotton and silk one rolled up together, a black one and a white. Thus much for the bureau; but it is only a hint, and not a full description. My coats and overcoat, overhauled daily to see if a stray dress or underdress had not hid itself among them, were thus well-trained to ground and lofty tumbling; and were becoming quite fledged with lint and feathers.

Out of such a chaos Mrs. Prim would come forth the sweetest-looking creature and the best-dressed woman in town, *when she was going into company!*

How came she forth when only entering her own family? With hair spreading in different directions, with a bestained and dirty dress, half hooked and half pinned with pins black and white, and with one of the backs of her dress an inch higher than the other; the skirt ripped out of the gatherings in spots; an apron tied on askew, ill-mated shoes, and no neck-handkerchief at all,—for, if the air is chilly when stepping out of doors, the apron is drawn around the neck. O, what a waking was mine, when morning broke up the dream, and divorced me from Mrs. Prim! Really, I do not suppose such a person ever lived or was thought of, except in a dream. If it *ever were* true, out of dreams, I do not think that husbands would respect their wives; honeymoons would wane, men would not love their homes, things would go at sixes and sevens, young married couples would grow indifferent to each other, wives would complain that husbands did not care for them, husbands would mutter something about being "taken in," both would learn to say, "I remember the time, Mr. Prim, when you would not have treated me so." "And I, Mrs. Prim, remember the time when you did not *look* so." "Well, my dear, whose fault is it, when I have nobody here at home half the time to care how I look?" "Well, love, who wants to wade knee deep in dirt, and call that home?" "Well, sir, you are a proper man to talk about dirt, you are *so* neat yourself; pray, sir, do give me a lecture; *do* show me how to keep things neat; could n't you write a little book about it? it would be very nice, Mr. Prim!—neat Mr. Prim!!—charming Mr. Prim!!!"

But as such things never happen, there is no use in writing any more about them.

OUR FIRST FISHING.

HERE is in the first experiences of life, the first hearty experiences of childhood, such a clear, full, and uncontrolled flow of pleasure, that we look back to them afterwards and wish, in later and riper life, that it were possible to have such simple and utter abandonment to our feelings. We go back to the scenes of childhood, and stand on the places that witnessed our early sports and joys, with an incredulous wonder. It seems more like a dream than a reality that we were once boys, capable of doing and being all that we remember.

We suppose scarcely a single person knows the locality called "The Old Saw-Mill." It is on the river *Bantam*. Of course every one will know where that is.

Well, that was a day above all days when we were permitted to go a-fishing all by ourselves! Off we darted for the spade, and a ten-year-old boy might have been seen at work on the north side of the wood-house, where the kitchen sink-spout made the soil very rich, digging worms with the most glowing industry. Then, with a straight line right across lots, we aimed at the *Old Saw-Mill*. And not one step did we walk, and every step did we run, till the stony bank was reached. There lay the pools of water nearly two feet deep. And there, hidden under projecting stones, lurked the longed-for fish. An alder-pole was good enough in those days, a piece of twine was the line. Our hook was soon baited with a worm that wriggled in a manner most deliciously tempting to any well-bred fish. With the most awful suspense we dropped the tempting morsel into the pool. Scarcely had it sunk to the flashing pebbles at the bottom, when a fish, that had evidently been made on purpose to delight a boy's heart, darted out, and seized the hook with such a pull as sent the blood through every vein in my body. The energy with which that fish came forth was such as to settle all question of cruelty. For such a violent jerk did we give, that the little fellow described a circle over our head, and was thwacked against the rocks with such force as to be dashed to atoms! But we had caught a fish! The thing was settled! A fish *could* be caught, and *we* could catch it. But a second and third endeavor resulted in the same way. The fish were *shiners*. They were as large as a man's finger, almost. And, when we went home at length, at least half that we caught had been dashed to pieces. How many times since then have we seen the same thing done in life-experiences. Men are so eager that they destroy their own ends! A parent is so roused up by a child's fault that he puts at him with such impetuosity that the boy is driven away from him, and refuses to be influenced.

A friend, by gentle treatment, might have been led out of an error, but intemperate eagerness only sacrifices him and his interests. If a man will have golden fish, let him go to the side of the stream of life calmly, put in his hook discreetly, and lift out his prey with an easy and even pull. But if he threshes back with full swing, ten to one he will dash his luck to pieces!

You cannot succeed in life by spasmodic jerks.

You cannot win confidence, nor earn friendship, nor gain influence, nor attain skill, nor reach position by violent snatches. One sort of men lose by too much caution, another kind by too much eagerness. One waits too long, another does not wait long enough.

First get your fish to bite. Then see that you so land them that they shall be worth something.

READING.

HERE are few who stop to consider the miracle of reading. That a few black marks upon paper should have such an informing and transporting power is scarcely less than miraculous. Four letters are put together, H, O, M, E. The moment the eye looks upon them the soul rises up, a picture comes forth; a house with its yard, its barn, its well, its fields and forests. Even its most minute features come to us with exquisite nicety. We see its inmates, an old man, a venerable woman, children, domestic scenes. Years that have long slept rise up and step forth again in newness of life. And all things are so refashioned that we no longer think where we are, or what we are, but seem to ourselves carried back scores of years, and walking up and down again the ways of childhood. And all this simply because there are four linear spots of ink on a sheet of white paper!

But if one considers more minutely what is taking

place in reading all the time, the marvel will still grow. The eye has learned to see without pausing to examine. The ready reader never thinks of *letters*. It is only the *word* that he sees. And even the word seems to lose individuality, and is but a member of something else, — a sentence. But even the sentence seems not to be seen, but to be seen through. We see the thought rather than the symbol by which it is set forth. And the act of reading, although it is a physical act, is yet so much more mental, that we lose all consciousness of the mechanical part of it, and follow a train of pure thought, or the flow of sentiment, or a description, as if the thing itself were transpiring! It is most curious to watch a person in reading an exciting narrative, or some stirring appeal, and to see how these dead letters lord it over every inward faculty. At this black spot of printer's ink we weep, at another we laugh, at still another we are angry. This line touches one feeling, that line another, and line after line they reach in, and, like the fingers of a musician, touch the chords and bring forth all the soul's activity.

But the same passage, read by different men, will affect them all differently. It is not probable that the same state of mind, in all its details, has ever been twice produced, exactly alike, by any text of Scripture or any passage in Shakespeare. Something is always varied.

It is worthy of notice, that, although when we are heartily engaged in reading we cease to see the lines and letters, and behold only their meaning, yet, when we are absent-minded, we read without seeing either the meaning or the words by which it is conveyed. We have, when much preoccupied, read whole pages aloud, to the edification of others, without being conscious either that we saw a letter or received a single idea. The eye saw, and the mouth vocalized, while our thoughts were busy with some memory, or in arranging some plan, or in some other variant activity.

The habit of reading proof and correcting it for press leads to some singular developments. A man *feels* mistakes rather than *sees* them. In glancing rapidly over the sentences, almost before the will can act, and while the thought is tending to hold its way right along, we feel a sort of mechanical grip, a putting on the brakes, as if something was wrong, and we go back to search and see what it is. And, behold, there is a word with *ie* put for *ei*, or an *m* is wanting, or but one *l* is put where two should be! That we did not see, but only felt the mistake, appears from the fact that when we search we have not the least idea of what the matter is, and we go back looking and groping to see what it was that stopped us with such a mind-jolt!

Every one's reflection will suggest other facts in regard to the marvellousness of the simple mechanical and mental act of reading. But *what* to read, and *how* to read, are more important than the marvels of the simple act itself; and these topics must not be begun at the heels of an article. And so, if our readers will wait, we will too.

SUMMER READING.

UMMER READING is a distinctly marked species in the great genus Reading. Everybody understands the term, but nobody can tell exactly what it means. There is a temperate zone in the mind, between luxurious indolence and exacting work, and it is to this region, just between laziness and labor, that summer reading belongs. A book, that — lying upon your back, while the wind shakes the leaves in your drowsy ears, and insects fill the air with a sweet tenor, and bees under your window hum and drone, and birds return thanks for the seed and worms eaten — floats you up out of sleep, which yet throws its spray over you, as the sea does on men who lazily float in a summer breezy day on raft or low-edged boat, — a book that now and then drops you, and then takes you up again, that spins a silver thread of thought from your mind fine as gossamer, and then breaks it as the wind does the spider's web, — this is a summer book. You never know where you left off, and do not care where you begin. It is all beginning, and all middle, and end everywhere.

Doubtless study has its dignities and claims; stiff-backed, hard-seated *study*, — that makes no luxury of books, but quarries them, and digs or blasts material for solid uses. A man turns his mind round and round like an auger in some oaken plank, and bores through the toughest subjects.

But venerable and praiseworthy as may be this long-bearded industry and midnight-lamp wisdom, it must not hold a lighter thing in utter contempt. There is a reading for fugitive moments; there is a luxury of reading when you are coiled up under a beech or elm tree around whose swollen roots a clear stream frolics that never goes to sleep, but plays in a perpetual childhood. I love clover-hay reading. Spread out on an ample mow, with the north and south barn-door wide open, with hens scratching down on the floor, and expressing themselves in short sentences to each other, now and then lifting up one of those roundelays or hen-songs that are no doubt as good to them as a psalm-tune or a love-song; with swallows flying in and out, and clouds floating over the sun, raising or lowering the light on our book. Can anything be sweeter than such reading of poet, or story-weaving magician, or magister? Yes. It is even sweeter to have tho lotters grow dim, and run about the page, and disappear, while the hands relax, and the book, gently swaying, comes down on your breast, and visions from within open their clear faces on you, and the hours go by so softly that you will not believe that the sun is low in the west, and that those voices are of folks out after you to come in to supper!

But there is a world of less indolent pleasure and of summer reading for cool mornings, for evening hours, and for the Sabbath, that never glows and rejoices with such fervor as in the country, in summer days. We yield up the old ponderous books to the shelf again; the histories, the controversies, the abstruse philosophies, the head-filling books of solid learning, and betake ourselves to books which teach us of plants, of insects, of birds, of fish, of all things that live and grow, or fly or creep. The summer seems a prolonged invitation to read God's Book of Nature.

WORTH OF MONEY.

E hear a good deal about the worth of property. A house is worth ten thousand dollars; that lot is worth fifty thousand dollars; a farm is worth eight thousand, a horse three hundred, a carriage five hundred, and so on endlessly. This is all very well in its way. But ought not the question, sometimes, to be put the other way, How much is a man's *money worth?* There is a wider range in the value of money than most persons think. And, upon a little inquiry, I suspect that it will be found that all men who possess money, or who long to possess it, have a way of measuring it, not by dollars, but by its value in some sort of pleasure or article.

One man earns a thousand dollars, and says to himself, There, that puts me one step out of debt. Money to him is a means of personal liberty. A man in debt is not a freeman. "The borrower is servant to the lender."

Another man sees in a thousand dollars a snug little homestead, a home for his children, a shelter to his old age, a place to live in, and a good place to die in. But his neighbor only sees one more link in the golden chain of wealth. It was thirty-nine thousand last month, he is worth forty this. And his joy is in the growing numerals. He imagines how it will sound, full, round, and hearty, when men say, "He is worth a hundred thousand dollars." Nay, when it comes to that, he thinks five a better sound than one, and five hundred thousand dollars is a sound most musical to his ear, — though he loves even better yet to call it half a million! That word *million* cuts a great swath in men's imaginations. All this estimate of money is sheer ambition. The man is vain. He thinks much of himself on account of money, not of character. A man who is openly proud of money is secretly contemptuous of those who have none.

Another man wishes to see the world. Every dollar means travel. A thousand dollars means Europe. Two thousand dollars means Egypt, Palestine, and Greece.

Boys dealing in smaller sums reckon in the same way. A penny means a stick of candy; sixpence is but another term for ball; a shilling means a kite; and fifty cents, a jack-knife.

The young "Crack" sees in his money a skeleton wagon and a fast nag, a rousing trot, a jolly drink, and a smashing party.

But many and many a weary soul sees in every shilling bread, rent, fuel, clothes. There be thousands who hold on to virtue by hands of dollars: a few more save them; a few less, and they are lost. Their gayer sisters see feathered hats and royal silks in their money, or rather, in their fathers' and their husbands'.

The poor scholar passes daily by the stall where books tempt his poverty. Poor clothes he is content to wear; plain and even meagre diet he is willing to subsist upon; and, as for all the gay dissipations and extravagant wastes of fashionable life, he looks upon them without even understanding what they mean, as a child looks upon the Milky-Way, in the heavens, a glowing band of far-away and unexplored wonders. But, O those books! He looks longingly at morning; he peers at them with a gentle covetousness at night. He imagines new devices for earning a few dollars. He ponders whether there is not some new economy which can save a few shillings. And when good luck at last brings a score of dollars to him, with what fever of haste does he get rid of them, fairly running to the stall, and fearing, at every step, lest some fortunate man should have seized the prize. Wasteful man! that night saw too much oil burnt out in poring over the joyful treasure. Books are what *his* money is worth! But others see different visions. Money means flowers to them. New roses, the latest dahlia, the new camelia, or others of the great houri band of flowers that fill the florist's paradise, — the garden.

Some men see engravings in money; some, pictures; some, rare copies of old books; some, curious missals. Others, when you say money, think of fruit-trees, of shrubbery, of arboretums, pinetums, and fruticetums. And we have reason to believe that there are some poor wretches who, not content with any one insanity, see pretty much all these things by turns.

But there are nobler sights than these to be seen through the golden lens of wealth: a father and mother placed in comfort in their old age; a young man helped through college, or established in business; a friend extricated from ruin; a poor widow saved from beggary, and made a suppliant before God for mercies on your head, every day that she lives; the sick and unfortunate succored, the orphan educated, the school founded, the village lined with shade-trees, a free library established, and a thousand such like things. A man is not to be known by *how much money* he has, but by what that money is worth to *him*. If it is worth only selfishness, meanness, stinginess, vanity, and haughty state, a man is not rich if he own a million dollars. If it mean generosity, public spirit, social comfort, and refinement, then he is rich on a few hundred. You must put your hand into a man's heart to find out how much he is worth, not into his pocket.

PET NOTIONS.

HE old grammars, and for aught we know the new ones too, divide verbs into regular, irregular, and defective. This is the very division which we should apply to men; only, instead of *defective*, we should say *streaked*, so that all men are divided into regular, irregular, and streaked. Of course, the first two include the moral elements, and the last is the term for all the whims, freaks, and eccentricities of men. When men are more remarkable for the things in which they differ from their fellow-men than for those in which they agree with them, they are eccentric.

Every village and every neighborhood has its queer men, its drolls, and its oddities. But, besides these streaked men, who do all things in a whimsical and uncommon manner, it is amusing to see single peculiarities in men of the regular class. As cattle and horses, though of a uniform color, often have some single spot, a white spot in the face, or a white hoof, so men, almost all men, have some queer spot. Often it is known only to their most intimate friends. Sometimes it works inwardly, and does not develop to observation until some trouble or great change in life lays it open. There are in old castles secret panel-doors, leading by hidden ways to concealed rooms, which the owner of the property keeps from the knowledge of all men, except some trusted servant, or his oldest son. But revolutions, and the pillaging of his castle by unmannerly soldiery, sometimes bring them to light. And so is it with many a curious taste, prejudice, affection, caprice, or whim, sometimes worthy, and sometimes foolish. Indeed, we have known hard and rugged men, of a severe face and stern bearing, hiding away, as if ashamed of it, some delicate and tender feeling, soft and sweet as a woman's. And when sickness or some sudden rending for a moment revealed the secret, they shrank from the disclosure almost as if it were a disgrace.

In this class of *streaks*, we have noticed none more common than that which leads men to be more vain of some quality quite aside from their profession, than of all the deserved and well-earned credit of their legitimate business.

Sir Walter Scott was accustomed to say, that, of all his *compositions*, he was most proud of his compositions for making trees grow. The same is yet seen.

Webster, if his secret heart were known, was more vain of his sheep and cattle than of his speeches. While the whole world is talking of some poet, whose ethereal works would lead you to think that he seldom touched the earth, except as birds do, with delicate wing, you shall be surprised to find, at his table, that he is more sensitive about his wine than about his verses. His poetry is his business. He expects to do well in that. But wine is out of his line, and he makes a pet of his cellar.

A merchant is envied by all his fellows for his clear-headedness, and his sagacious business operations. But we dare say he will feel more complimented if you praise his horses than if you admire his commercial sagacity. A fine, hearty, manly friend, admirably qualified for solid business, thinks that he has a peculiar gift for music. He sits down every night at his much-complaining violoncello, and scrapes and sings till our ears are as hoarse as his throat. And a delicate compliment to his musical talent brings upon you a flood of sunshine from his honest face, and establishes your reputation for discernment forever. Sometimes a merchant, making money easily, and just as easily keeping it, looks upon all his goods, property, and funds with discontent; for he longs to be an orator! He meditates speeches. At sundry little meetings he gives forth pet speeches. Ah, he tells you in a confidential hour, "I would give all that I am worth if I could only think on my feet, and move an audience to my words, as I will."

The old lawyer builds a country house, and lays out ten acres. That house of his own planning and those acres are more to him than all his skill with courts and his reputation for legal learning. Thus it goes. If a man is an orator, he does not look for that, but longs to *paint* with artists; while a successful painter is hankering after the laurels which are supposed to shade the brows of ready speakers.

We have known men quite addicted to sewing and knitting. They hemmed towels with an earnestness betokening a proper regard for this useful accomplishment of sewing. Some men write long essays, never to be published, but often reviewed with fond pride. Discoveries are made in sacred literature, — new theories of prophecy, new renderings, and perverse learning enough to set up a presbytery. Some men are always inventing, some tinkering, some building unshapely furniture, which the wife soon stores in the garret.

The deacon has a weakness for preaching; and, as he cannot quite succeed, he puts a white cravat on, sleeks down his hair, and *looks* as if he would burst out into a sermon, if you only touched him. The blacksmith writes poetry. The butcher, having had bad luck in his trade, thinks he has gifts for medicine, and practises alternately in each department.

And so the world goes. We are prone to undervalue the things which we can do easily, and therefore well, and to pride ourselves upon trifles, although we do them poorly, because men are surprised that we can do them at all.

These peculiarities are not simply amusing. They are a testimony, often, of a yearning after things more fine than belongs to a trade, more beautiful than every-day business furnishes, and purer and truer than many of the experiences of every-day life. Sometimes they may be but vanities; but it is charitable rather to imagine that they are irregular exhibitions of a longing in every one to be something more and better than he is.

REASONS FOR NOT WRITING AN ARTICLE.

R. BONNER: MY DEAR SIR, — I write to say that circumstances make it impossible for me to send you an article this week, and to ask you to excuse me. The fact is, that I am so busy with both eyes and ears that I have no time to write. You must know that I am not in the city at this present writing, but some forty miles up in Westchester County. Perched up on a side-hill, whose slope toward the south is just enough for the utmost grace in lines, is a pre-revolutionary farm-house. The timber is of old oak, — of oak that has heard the British cannon from the ships of war in the Hudson River without quaking. It is a one-story house, so low-jointed that I can reach the ceiling with my hand. The snug rooms are all of a suitable smallness, and, for summer, very cheerful. On the front, and running the whole length, are a piazza, a stoop, a portico, a veranda, a corridor, and a balcony, all in one. It is upon this said arrangement that I sit, and from this I must render a reason for not writing the article mentioned.

In the first place, the birds make so much noise that I can hear nothing else, except the wind in the trees, the occasional lowing of cows, the barking of my nearest neighbor's dogs (two of which he is fattening for the cattle-show), the crowing of a few oratorical roosters in the distance, and now and then the laughter of the men at work in the fields. This occupies my ears to a degree that unfits them for anything else.

And, as for my eyes, it is even worse. The hills in this neighborhood are arranged in such a manner that one's eyes are perpetually diverted from sober reading to look at their graceful, green slopes, their endlessly varied lines, their waving grain. Then the distant Highlands draw off my attention, to their endless diversities. Carved to every curve, their sides are scarped and grooved, ploughed and furrowed, until the whole view is a piece of gigantic engineering, — not by art and device of man's hand, but by the patience of slow-working Nature. Clouds have done what no edge of iron or steel in the hands of a million workmen could have done. For these floating engineers, with the soft touch of liquid drops sent down upon the mountain-side, have hollowed out valleys, and cut the hills into every form of simple or fantastic beauty. No lever can move such rocks as a frozen bubble displaces. No tool can chisel upon such a scale as do edgeless showers. And centuries sit brooding plans of change, and behold, here are their works!

Now, just beneath these garnished hills is the Hudson River. Every time I look at it I forget to look back upon my paper. It is not possible to write. Just now I had a thought. But ten sloops and schooners were just then flocking round the point in the river. I have always had an idea that North

River sloops were coarse and ugly craft, fit only for carrying bricks and lumber. But no mistake was ever greater. They are express works of art. They were built and are navigated for their fine effect. Every villa on the Hudson is incomplete without these fleets of sloops, that hover in the distance like so many butterflies sporting in the summer around the edge of roadside pools. Perhaps the crews, if there are any crews in such airy and graceful looking things, seen at this distance, think that they are carrying an inland trade. It may be that those near at hand can discover rude and unshapely things about these craft. But to my eye, perched on my front stoop, all these white fairies of the river are merely floating past the green hills for picturesque effect. No man need try to persuade me that they carry hay, salt, stone, lime, bricks. The very appearance of them, from these hills, contradicts the supposition.

There, now, just as I am getting ready to write again, up comes my neighbor to know about that stone-wall which bounds the maple-lined lane, by which, you know, we come up to this hundred-year-old farm-house. What do I know about stone-walls? Fix it as it *ought* to be fixed. That is plain enough. There are only two or three things required for a *good* stone-wall. It must be made so that chipmonks can run in and out easily; it must have woodbine enough, in spots; it must have a deal of mosses growing on it; and it must be broad enough on the top for one to walk on. I know of nothing else which a good wall requires.

Here comes a carpenter to ask about the kitchen which he is building in the rear of this venerable little dwelling aforesaid. But why am I to be disturbed by such things? Build the kitchen if you please, sir, in such a way that the cook shall always be good-natured, that the bread shall always be light, sweet, and *raised* just to the point of saccharine fermentation, but not a bit beyond it; for sour bread makes my temper sour. And also, Mr. Carpenter, please build the kitchen so that, if the cook be poor, somebody will always come and marry her off; and so that, if good, nobody can get her. With such directions, an ordinarily smart carpenter ought not to trouble me with questions.

Now everybody is possessed! Here is the mason, asking about the chimney! Well, sir, about the chimney; this is it. Build it so that it will never smoke; so that it will draw just enough, and not a bit too much; so that once in a while we can hear the storm-wind rumble in the flues; so that in winter great logs can be burned in its fireplace, and all manner of dreamy pictures fall upon its fleecy ashes; and, finally, build it so that cockroaches can't, and crickets can, run in and out of its crevices! Stop a minute! I want a brick oven, — none of your iron-cheeked stove-ovens will do for the country! Do you suppose that a genuine, old-fashioned *Indian baked pudding* could be made in one of your fuliginous modern iron stoves? Can anything but a real old brick oven bring forth *brown bread*, or baked beans, golden-russet, colored with a piece of pork cut criss-cross on the top, of a beautiful bronze color? There, now, you know all I can tell you. Go build your kitchen!

Now, my dear Mr. Bonner, can any man be expected to write articles under such circumstances? I must be excused. Tell your readers, if you please, that my "eyes and ears" are occupied upon other things, and cannot be used for literary purposes this week.

HEALTH AND EDUCATION.

A GREAT amount of information has been spread through the community in regard to the laws and conditions of health, and there has been a corresponding increase of knowledge. Nor has the movement been undertaken a moment too soon. Wholesome diet, the avoidance of feverish stimulants, pure fresh air, and out-of-door exercises are the simple expedients to which we trust. But, in so far as special efforts are required, they should be brought to bear upon the development of sound nervous force. The brain and nervous system are from an early age, in this country, brought under a very great excitement. Our people are constitutionally excitable: the climate is exciting, the customs and habits of society tend to bring forward our children very early; all the pursuits of life, with us, are conducted with intensity, and almost unrelieved continuity. Our public affairs partake of this inflammable tendency, and are begun and conducted with frequent and intense excitements of the whole community. In short, the whole character and condition of our people is such, that the brain and nervous system are kept under a very high pressure from an early age in life.

Against the evil tendency of this undue partial development there have been very few counteracting agencies. Our people have not been given to amusements. They are not encouraged to have holidays. Even those amusements which have maintained themselves have been, for the most part, of a kind that intensified the evil. When a man has all day long fevered his brain in the counting-room or office, he goes to a theatre or opera at night, substituting another cause of excitement, but directed upon the overtasked brain. Others, seriously inclined, attend religious meetings, young men's associations, debating clubs, and other like gatherings, which, in their own way, tax the brain.

Now, what is needed in the community is vigorous out-of-door recreation, developing the muscles and aiding digestion, accessible to all, and removed from special temptations to immoralities.

There is no one way of meeting this want. But the public should give encouragement to every wholesome recreation that takes people out of doors, and gives them real bone-building exercise. Yachting is good for gentlemen of property. A yacht is nothing but the *fast horse* of the sea. Lantern trots, and the Maria sails, but both of them are designed to run upon the fastest time-bill. But how many men can own the one or the other? It is said — how truly we do not know — that one of the most enterprising of all gentlemen of the press, in New York, has given ten thousand dollars for Lantern and his mate. If any one will provide us with the money, and another Lantern, we will do the same, and we will agree to find a hundred young men that would consent to do it too!

When a man puts his saddle on the back of ten thousand dollars for an evening ride, he may be said fairly to have got Mammon under him! We know that "money makes the mare go." But ten thousand dollars with bits in its mouth, and Jehu behind to drive, must carry a man at a fearful pace!

But it is not needful to ride lightning in order to enjoy a drive. Ten thousand men in New York and Brooklyn are able to drive out every afternoon with their families, with excellent, and not very expensive horses. Every merchant, lawyer, and business man, who can afford it, would do well to take this most wholesome exercise.

But only a hundredth or thousandth part of the community are thus provided for. It is well, therefore, that so many muscular games are coming into vogue. Base-ball and cricket are comparatively inexpensive, and open to all, and one can hardly conceive of better exercise. Boat-clubs for rowing are springing up in all our towns that have accessible waters. This gives an admirable development to the muscles. But all these are yet but a little for the thousands who need exercise.

There ought to be gymnastic grounds and good bowling-alleys, in connection with reading-rooms, in every ward of the city, under judicious management, where, for a small fee, every young man might find various wholesome exercises, and withal good society, without the temptations which surround all the alleys and rooms of the city, kept for bowling and billiards. It seems surprising, while so many young men's associations are organized, whose main trouble it is to find *something to do*, that some Christian association should not undertake this important reformation, and give to the young men of our cities the means of physical vigor and health, separated from temptations to vice. It would be a very gospel.

But while provision is made for the development of the physical frame, there is much to be learned, and much wisdom to be exercised, in dealing with the *mind.* And we are much surprised, from some little observation, to see how apparently heedless are many of the teachers in our schools for girls. The pressure for the last year at any rate upon the girls who are to graduate is such as imperils their health for life. We know of many young ladies who are exercised in study night and day with such unremitting severity, that it seems impossible that they will not be exhausted by it. We have known several instances in which years of feebleness and nervous prostration followed the graduating year. If teachers are so ignorant or heedless of the laws of health, what shall we expect of common people? Parents should look into this. Especially physicians, and gentlemen who are informed on such subjects, ought to exert an influence upon ambitious schools and seminaries. For an education that treads down the constitution of a child is a very doubtful benefit.

ON THE PLEASURES OF BEING A PUBLIC MAN.

LL men are, to some extent, *public men.* They have public duties to perform. As householders, voters, jurymen, in short, as citizens, they are public men. But some men are obliged to perform their professional duties in open publicity. They are always acting before men, and their daily life is upon exhibition. Now there are a great many persons in relatively private life who quite envy such persons as the peculiar favorites of fortune; and not a few make it an ambition to attain such conspicuity. Ah, to see themselves in a newspaper, placarded along the streets, advertised! To hear their names and deeds in men's mouths! — they think there would bo nothing like it! And, we assure them, that there *is* nothing like it.

From a public man, curiosity, sympathy, and antagonism shear off all privacy, and almost all true personality. Your affairs are everybody's business. Your movements are everybody's observation. What you do or say, or do not do or say; what you wear, where you go, with whom you walk, when you get up, and when lie down; what it costs you to live, and how you get your means to pay for your living; who makes your coats, or boots; who shaves your face, — all are diligently observed and reported. No privacy is allowed to a public man. Everybody uses him as common property. If a good story needs a known person to give it piquancy, his name is used upon it like a snapper on a whip-lash. Not only do people use him up in conversation, but it makes little difference at length whether he is present or absent. "O, he is a public man!" is excuse enough for saying the rudest things; and of all of them, none is so rude as blunt praise to his face!

Thus he is rained upon with himself. He reads about himself, runs over himself in the streets, finds himself figuring in the newspaper stories, and all beggars, and errand-hunters, and solicitors for public service, begin by setting him before himself in a public point of view. And, that nothing may be lacking, people wonder how it is that he is always contriving to get himself before the public!

One of the original faculties of the human mind, fundamental and universal, is the *love of other people's private affairs*. But strong as this faculty is, its action is somewhat guarded and concealed in the private relations of common citizens; but never in respect to *public men!* If he does not wish to be talked about, what is he a public man for? He must expect people to take an interest in him, and everything that belongs to him. How does he eat and drink? What is his income? Where does he get it and how spend it? The less proper it is that anything should be known, the more exquisite is the relish of knowing it.

It was Huber, we believe, who first constructed glass hives, through which bees could be seen at all hours and during every process of work. Public men are bees working in a glass hive, and curious spectators enjoy themselves in watching every secret movement as if it were a study in natural history.

Nor is it allowed him to seem to know all this. If

people stare at him in the street, or nudge each other in the ferry-boat and point at him, or if a bevy of young ladies whisper his name so that he may hear it at ten steps off, he yet must keep on a look of blessed unconsciousness! If he takes a lunch at the restaurant, and twenty gentlemen subside from their knives and forks, to watch, square-faced and staringly, what he orders, and what becomes of it; if he looks up and faces his spectators, of course they will not shrink or look down. One might as well try to make a battery of cannon wink with a look. At length a public man submits, and comes to think that he has no privacy. He is placed upon a pivot of observation, like a whirligig on a steeple, watched in all weather, for men's amusement or convenience. People expect him to be peculiar. They are waiting for something characteristic. They hope for some remarkable speech, some eccentricity, some oddity or striking conduct, or misconduct.

But all these things are only the fringe of the garment. Who can register the solicitations to which he is subject? Is he reputed wealthy, — men swarm upon him as summer flies upon honey. Is he "influential" and "popular," — who can enumerate the variety and number of "causes" that entirely live upon the help derived from the "influence" of those that are called to help them? He is assailed for autographs, for signatures to all sorts of commendatory letters. One man wants his name to a petition for pardoning a man who was sent to states-prison for arson, and who, having experienced religion, it is supposed would now be a useful member of society. Another man wishes his name to a recommendation of insect powders and rat pills, or to a good and pious book, or to get a man whom he does not know a place in a store of which he never heard, or to put a worthy man into the navy-yard or on the "watch," or "police," or into the railroad service.

But all these things are light in comparison with expectations of charity at his hand. For a public man is expected to pay liberally for all the annoyances which are heaped upon him. He is a kind of public fountain, and everybody has a right to fill his cup or bucket if he can. After he has given, and given, till the pump sucks, and the pocket-well is dry, he is gravely reproved for not filling another bucket by being told, "Persons in your situation are expected to be liberal"; or "Public men owe their standing to the public favor, and ought not be niggardly"; or, "Men are expected to pay a tax for their greatness."

Besides all this, there is the newspaper part of a public man's experience. It is so delightful to find your affairs arranged for you, and to learn for the first time, in the papers, where you have been, what you have said, and what has happened to you! A man finds that he has had many remarkable experiences, of which he was before quite unconscious. And then, if he be a "public man," in political affairs, he will have an interesting opportunity of finding out what people think of him! He will see himself flagellated through the land, his words distorted, his actions tortured and misrepresented, or, if his politics are theological, he will find great opportunities for self-examination in the religious newspapers.

At length, a man grows nervous. The sound of

his bell makes him start like a pistol-shot. He longs for rest. No luxury seems to him like that of being let alone. The very people whom he would like to have near him keep away through delicacy, and leave him a prey to the insatiate pursuers of "public men." Is there no remedy? Can we not devise a net, as we do for horses, to keep off gad-flies?

If we ever become supreme — an absolute monarch — we shall change things a little. When any public servant has done well and deserves reward, we shall say, "For your meritorious services to the state, we give you the privilege of four months' retirement." But when evil men shall be brought up for punishment, we shall condemn them to four or six months', or a year's "public life," according to the heinousness of their offence, and the severity required in punishment!

CHIMNEY-SWALLOWS.

VERY one knows, who lives in the country, what a chimney-swallow is. They are among the birds that seem to love the neighborhood of man. Many birds there are that nestle confidingly in the protection of their superiors, and are seldom found nesting or breeding far from human habitations. The wren builds close to your door. Sparrows and robins, if well treated, will make their nests right under your window, in some favorite tree, and will teach you, if you choose to go into the business, how to build bird's-nests, lay eggs, hatch out young birds, and feed the tenderlings. A great deal of politeness and fidelity may be learned. The female bird is waited upon, fed, cheered with singing, during her incubation, in a manner that might give lessons to the household. Nay, when she needs exercise and recreation, her husband very demurely takes her place, and keeps the eggs warm in the most gentlemanly way. This is equivalent, we suppose, to rocking the cradle.

Barn-swallows have a very sensible appreciation of the pleasures of an ample barn. A barn might not be found quite the thing to live in (although we have seen many a place where we would take the barn sooner than the house), but it is one of the most charming places in a summer day to lounge, read, or nap in. And as you lie on your back upon the sweet-scented hay-mow, or upon clean straw thrown down on the great floor, reading books of natural history, or sucking honey out of Keats, it is very pleasant to see the flitting swallows glance in and out, or course about under the roof, with motion so lithe and rapid as to seem more like the glancing of shadows than the winging of birds. Their mud nests are clean, if they are made of dirt. And you would never dream from their feathers what sort of a house they lived in.

But these birds have flown into this article unawares, for it was of *chimney-swallows* that we began to write, and they are just now roaring in the little stubbed chimney behind us, to remind us of our duty. Every evening we hear them. For a nest of young ones brings the parents in with food early and late, and every entrance or exit is like a distant roll of thunder, or like those old-fashioned rumblings of high winds in the chimney which made us children think that all out of doors was coming down the chimney in stormy nights. These little architects build their simple nests upon the sides of the chimney with sticks, which they are said to break off from dead branches of trees, though they might more easily pick them up already prepared. But they doubtless have their own reasons for cutting their own timber. Then these are glued to the wall by a saliva which they secrete, so that they carry their mortar in their mouths, and use their bills for trowels. When the young are ready to leave, they climb up the chimney to the top by means of their sharp claws, aided by their tail-feathers, which are short, stiff, and at the end armed with sharp spines. Two broods are reared in a season.

From the few which congregate in any one neighborhood, one would not suspect the great numbers which assemble at the end of the season. Audubon estimated that *nine thousand* entered a large sycamore tree every night, to roost, near Louisville, Ky.

Sometimes the little nest has been slighted in building, or the weight proves too great, and down it comes into the fireplace, to the great amusement of the children, who are all a-fever to hold in their hands these clean, bright-eyed little fellows. Who would suspect that they had ever been bred in such a flue?

And it was just this thought that set us to writing. Because a bird lives in a chimney he need not be smutty. There is many a fine feather that lives in a chimney-corner. Nor are birds the only instances. Many men are born in a garret or in a cellar, who fly out of it, as soon as fledged, as fine as anybody. A lowly home has reared many high natures. On these bare sticks, right against the bricks, in this smoky flue, the eggs are laid, the brooding goes on, the young are hatched, fed, grown. But then comes the day when they spread the wing, and the whole heaven is theirs! From morning to night they cannot touch the bounds of their liberty. And in like manner it is with the human soul that has learned to know its liberty. Born in a body, pent up, and cramped, it seems imprisoned in a mere smoky flue for passions. But when once Faith has taught the soul that it has wings, then it begins to fly, and flying, finds that all God's domain is its liberty. And as the swallow that comes back to roost in its hard hole at night is quite content, so that the morning gives it again all the bright heavens for its soaring-ground, so may men, close quartered and cramped in bodily accommodations, be quite patient of their narrow bounds, for their thoughts may fly out every day gloriously.

And as, in autumn, these children of the chimney gather in flocks and fly away to heavens without a winter, so men shall find a day when they too shall migrate; and rising into a higher sphere, without storm or winter, shall remember the troubles of this mortal life, as birds in Florida may be supposed to remember the northern chills which drove them forth to a fairer clime!

THE FARM.

T once befell me to buy a small farm. Compared with my wants, it was large; and yet larger, if compared with my ability to develop its resources.

There is a distinct joy in owning land, unlike that which you have in money, in houses, in books, pictures, or anything else which men have devised. Personal property brings you into society with men. But land is a part of God's estate in the globe; and when a parcel of ground is deeded to you, and you walk over it, and call it your own, it seems as if you had come into partnership with the Original Proprietor of the earth. Nothing removes your property from its firm foundations. No wind can wreck it, nor rains dissolve it, nor decay take it down. The sills will never rot, and nothing will ever sway or sag it. There it lies, firm, deep (a great deal deeper than you will ever care to go down), inexpugnable to summer or winter, with all their silent forces or their boisterous storms. And it is yours. Since the planet set up for itself, your land has been preparing. Innumerable myriads of leaves have grown and fallen, to form its soil. Grasses and roots, for whose numbers there can be no arithmetic, have helped on the culture. Rocks have slowly crumbled to form its loam. Insects have made laboratories of themselves, secreting and elaborating various qualities, which, at their autumnal death, have gone back to the soil to enrich it. Worms have bored and dug air-passages through it for ages before a plough was known on earth. Winter frosts have locked and unlocked its clay ; rains have brought down upon it from the air minute medicines. You stand upon a history without a record. You own that which, if you could trace back its changes, would carry you beyond the flood, beyond the garden of Eden, and a good deal farther on than that! God has had millions and millions of unhired, but not unpaid, laborers at work on this soil. It is burial-ground for minute atoms of former swarms and tribes beyond all stretch of numbers. Ages have shaken down their dust here. And my foot treads upon ten thousand buried years.

If I think downward, what is the mysterious interior of this silent earth? How far inward should we go before we felt the heat of that fire-pulse which throbs in the molten middle of the globe? And, if we look outward, what realms has not this farm traversed in its mighty rounds, turning its face in succession to every star in the solar concave!

But I cannot honestly say that it was the relation of this interesting piece of land to the stars, or to the centre of the earth, nor the force of any such romantic reflections upon bugs and decaying grasses, and air-tillage, and storm-washes, and all that, which led me to buy this farm. Nor was it that famous trees beckoned me. For, besides two noble hickories, one gigantic apple-tree (with which I defy competition on the continent), one tulip-tree (with a Latin name — *Liriodendron Tulipifera* — sweet enough for lovers' lips in twilight hours), and one venerable branch-broken and rugged old pine, that sighs and sings to the wind on the lawn, — there are none worth a thought. To be sure, a double row of maples lines the avenue. But though a maple-tree is a clean, useful, excellent tree, it has nothing in it that touches the imagination. It is a round, compact, and proper tree, like many excellent people of good sense and homely kindness, but without any grandeur or wildness of imagination. Maple-trees are the cows of trees (spring-milked), plain, good, useful, but not adorable.

I knew that the place was good for grass, for grain, and for fruits, of all of which I talked a good deal during the preliminary approaches to a purchase, but for which I cared about as much as I should whether the inside of my boots were red or yellow.

If the thing must be told, and I mention it, MR. BONNER, to you confidentially, it was the remarkable aptitude of the place for *eye-crops* that caught my fancy. It was not so much what grew upon the place, as what you could see off from it, that won me. It is a great stand for the eye. If a man can get rich by *looking*, I am on the royal road to wealth. And, indeed, it is true wealth that the eye gets, and the ear, and all the finer senses; — riches that cannot be hoarded or squandered; that all may have in common ; that come without meanness, and abide without corrupting. So long as it remains true that the heavens declare the glory of God, and the earth his handiwork, so long will men find both heart-wealth and strength, by a reverent admiration of the one and a sympathetic familiarity with the other.

THE HIGHWAY OF THE PEOPLE.

F popular rights and benefits depended upon the fidelity and honesty of political parties, we should have little faith in their long continuance. Men are both proud and selfish. Nor in public affairs has Christianity countervailed even to the small degree manifest in social affairs. As fast as men rise above the average of their fellows, they are apt to grow in self-importance, to look down upon those below them, first with pity, and then with some degree of disguised contempt. And the prosperous are always tempted to form themselves into a class, and rule the unprospered.

It is, therefore, a sign of good in our age, that the prosperity of the common people has become so associated with the very elements of convenience, that, whatever men do as classes to favor themselves, in the long run benefits the whole community.

Does a man wish to be a profound scholar? How shall he live, unless he make his learning of some use? The price which he pays for eminence is, that he shall enlighten the community as he goes up.

None of the liberal professions disdains the most comprehensive and profound learning; but it must be learning which shall bring a man into service and sympathy with the people, or he will walk almost alone. There is no government to patronize anything. There is no learned class in our midst. There is no sufficient number of rich men to hold out a hope to any that they may despise or neglect the common people. It is to the masses of the community that men must look for support.

When it was attempted, in New York, to establish music for the benefit of the rich, the opera failed. Nor did it succeed until it came within the reach, and solicited the sympathy, of common people. Lectures, literary enterprises, papers, books, all are obliged to ask the common people whether they may succeed. Even Science cannot refuse to come from her laboratory or descend from her observatory. It is found that a general, popular sympathy in scientific matters forms a public atmosphere in which philosophers thrive. The American Scientific Convention is eminently philosophical and wise, therefore, in opening its meetings to the community; in going from place to place; in making membership open to all. There is a Divine hand in this thing. It is not meant that men should separate themselves from their fellows as fast as they are prospered, and leave the poor, the ignorant, the rude, to herd together at the bottom. The nature of our institutions, the habits of the community, the very economic laws of society, compel men, in going up, to draw the common people up a little way too.

There was a time when Art looked, for patrons and support, to nobles and monarchs. And, of course, without the intention, it was obliged to express the ideas which the ruling classes favored. But now, happily, Art must draw its support from the favor of the common people. It is vain to look to governments, state or national. They are poor customers. Artists that wait for public orders will die in the poorhouses. It is to the intelligent and flourishing householder that we must look for any such encouragement of Art as shall make it flourishing. And artists must not demand that people shall take what artists like, unless artists are first willing to paint what the people like. It is all very well to rail at the want of taste and appreciation in the community. It is the artist's business to educate the community. Even in a commercial point of view it is necessary. He must prepare his market. Portraiture always thrives, and always will, as long as men are vain or their friends fond. But beyond this, Art will prosper in proportion as it speaks to the wants and feelings of common people. And long ago this truth has been seen and obeyed. Look at the fabrics sold for a price within reach of the poor. The finest forms in glass, china, wedgewood, or clay, put classic models within reach of every table. The cheapness of lithographs, mezzotints, etchings, and photographs, is bringing to every cottage-door portfolios in which the greatest pictures, statues, buildings, and memorials of past and triumphs of modern Art are represented. That which, twenty years ago, could be found only among the rich, to-day may be had by the day-laborer. This is the true levelling. Let knowledge, art, refinement, be brought down, as the sunlight is. The sun is no poorer, no darker, because the world has fed so many thousand years at his bosom. Down come the sheets of light, flaming through space, flaming over all the earth, enriching all things without impoverishing the source whence they spring. Let knowledge, beauty, goodness, shine down upon the path, and make the way plain along which the people are to tread!

ASKING ADVICE, AND OXEN.

MY DEAR SIR: I know that you are able to give good advice upon farm interests; at least, upon all that turns upon horses. But are you also posted upon other things? Do you know how to plough? to reap? to drain? to build walls? Are you skilful in compost? Can you throw light upon planting out strawberries? preparing the ground for a pear-orchard? Do you know how to lay down a lawn, to plant trees, to group them, with reference to their forms, their colors, and their effects at all seasons? Well; if you cannot help me on these momentous topics, can you give me any advice on the subject of *oxen?* Do you think oxen better, on the whole, for farm-work, than horses? You know, I suppose, the argument, — horses are quicker, and a little more "handy." Oxen are more patient, stronger, less expensive in their keeping, and, when they have performed several seasons' faithful work, they will, as disobliging horses will not, change into good beef. Now I seriously wish your advice as to which I had better have. For *I have just bought a pair of oxen*, and am, like most men, now ready to ask advice under circumstances which make it impossible for me to take it, unless it accords with a foregone fact. I shall, therefore, expect you to say that oxen by all means are to be preferred on the farm. I hope, also, that you will be of opinion that they ought to be about four years old, of a white color, except the head and neck, which should be roan; and that they should by all means be Durham grade stock, say three-quarter blood, and that it would be better to buy them in Jefferson County, say in the town of Adams. For, if you advise all these things, then you will be pleased to learn that such are the facts.

Of course, you will now imagine your worthy correspondent, with a long whip, bawling at every other step, at the top of his voice, whenever he wishes the least thing done, for that is the common practice. You will expect every order to be given in such a way, that not one man in a hundred could tell what is meant, let alone poor dumb brute beasts. For not a great way off I hear men now driving oxen. When they wish anything done, they give three separate orders, two of which always contradict each other. If they are to start, the man says, "Whoa, gee, go-long!" or, "Whoa, back, haw!" And generally every order is given with a smart cut of the whip. And whenever the creatures, a little perplexed or vexed, miss the command, then comes a roar of passionate ox-invective, accompanied with four or five whacks, together with some pokes and slashes; and, unless the driver belongs to the church, he almost always curses a little, and, in extreme cases, once in half an hour say, sends the whole team to — a place where good oxen never go, and bad men do. Now would it not do you good to see your virtuous and excellent correspondent, very red in the face, and laying it on to his cattle because they did not understand his absurd orders, or because he had lost his own temper?

But all this is not to happen, even if you advise it.

For my oxen are sensible, well-bred, and used to the gentlest treatment. They have always been spoken to softly; told gently just the thing that you wished them to do, and never struck. They drive out of the yoke just as well as in it. They stand or go at a word. They step quick and work as fast as a pair of heavy horses would do.

I have heard my father say that it was the oxen that sent him to college. He did not know at the time what it was that made farming so utterly unendurable to him. He was quick, nervous, restless; and to walk by the dull sides of slow-treading oxen all day long was a task beyond all endurance. He was determined not to be a farmer. His uncle, who brought him up, came to the same result by another way. For the boy could never be tamed so that, at sight of a squirrel, he would not leave cart, plough, or team, wherever they happened to be, and take after the bushy-tailed temptation, — down the rail-fence across the road, and into the stone-fence, when the squirrel, with a victorious *churk!* and a whisk of the tail, disappeared. Moreover, the lad had a marvellous gift of taking things out of their places, and never putting them back again (a trait which ought not to have been hereditary), and so, one morning, when the old gentleman went out early to the barn to fodder the cattle, and saw the saddle lying in the middle of the yard, bottom side up, and the bridle on the ground in another place, he was convicted on the instant, that "Lyman would never be fit for anything but to go to college."

It is partly with the hope of the same results in my own family, that I have concluded on oxen instead of horses. I have tried all sorts of teachers, but they always know too much and the boys too little. I mean to try a quarter's tuition under the judicious management of the new oxen, and after about six months, depend upon it, there will be work for Amherst or Yale. Driving horses does not seem to tame young bloods. If the horses are fast, the boys are faster. But try ox-cure. I never have learned an instance of a young man led into bad company by oxen. No sprees in winter, no frolics in summer, no racing, no wildness, is apt to follow the habit of driving oxen!

And now, my dear sir, will you not come up and see my new turn-out? I invite you, and the most enterprising publisher of a recent volume on farming, to come up and take a ride in my cart. The creatures are good, too, for single work, and a little practice, I am sure, will make them patient of the saddle, and then, what is to hinder our taking, some soft and gentle evening, a good, sensible, leisurely ride on ox-back along the shady roads? Besides, if either of us should ever make up our minds to go on a Foreign Mission, we should, if sent to South Africa, be already in the way of the riding generally practised there.

THE OFFICE OF ART.

OME incidental remarks, in a recent number, have called forth the following letter from a well-known artist, one of whose pictures, the sleepy head of a cud-chewing cow, hangs before us at every meal.

"August 25, 1859.

"Dear Sir: In the 'Thoughts as they Occur' of the last number of your valuable paper stands a paragraph not fully explained, I take it, by the author, and therefore liable to misconstruction. It runs thus: —

"'Artists must not demand that people shall take what artists like, unless artists are first willing to paint what the people like.'

"The author admits that 'it is the artist's business to educate the community.' As the community, then, has an interest in this question of Art, the community ought, as an intelligent pupil, to understand its true position. The artist also, as a modest and intelligent teacher, ought to understand his own.'

"Most true it is that the artist has to 'paint what the people like,' but only because he must live and satisfy necessities, not from an acknowledgment of the right in the people to dictate to him. He is the public servant in no other sense than is the poet, the man of science, the minister of the Gospel. If Art is something more than imitation; if it is even more than mere intellectual production; if it is a child of the affections, an emanation of the *moral* part of the man, modulated by his intellect, then it is as sacred and inviolate as his religion, and cannot be prescribed.

"Moreover, if the artist, like the poet, is a teacher of something, he must LEAD, not FOLLOW. He wisely adapts the lessons to the mind and capacity of his pupils, and thus far he may consult them.

"In the noblest degree the artist rises to be a prophet.

"Who is it that shows him the vision? Is it the people? Inspiration is of Divine source, and the man who receives it is commissioned by God, though for proclaiming this message the world should let him starve. He may, like St. Paul, labor with his hands to supply his own wants, but this 'tent-making' for a living, and the preaching of his heavenly message, will ever remain distinctly separated concerns, in no wise to be confounded.

"An Artist."

We regard Art, in its higher offices, as a LANGUAGE. And as a poet, an orator, or a writer employs words and sentences to convey thoughts and feelings, so the artist employs forms, colors, and symmetries to convey some sentiment or truth. Many pleasing pictures there are without much meaning in them, — pleasing, because there is a pleasure in mere color and in form for their own sakes; just as there is a charm in fine language, almost without regard to the thought conveyed. But such in literature, and such pictures in Art, are passing trifles. A book that is to live with you, to be a companion, an instructor, must have something better than polished words or well-wrought sentences. It must have thoughts and sentiments that touch the head and the heart. Then a book becomes a silent power more and more influential. In like manner a picture, if it is to live with you, to ingratiate itself with you, to become necessary to you, must have, not only color and form, but something under them. Something there must be that shall touch the secret chords of feeling. An artist who only *imitates* what he paints is like an imitator in oratory or in poetry. He must have some thought or some feeling, which he wishes to express, and his picture is first to be judged by the sentiment which it contains, and *then* by the color-mode and the form-mode of expression.

Now every artist, like every other thinker, has the most perfect right to think for himself, and express his thoughts as he pleases. He may select his subjects when he pleases, and in the manner of any school. No one can find any fault with him, until he turns around to the public and says: "You don't buy my pictures! You don't like them! But you ought to like them! If you are not educated up to them, you should be." The greater part of society will simply laugh, and let the poor artist starve. But would not the same be true of every preacher, if, instead of applying moral truth to the ideas and manners of the age in which he lives, he should dig up the controversies of Origen, and feed his people on the topics which were fresh a thousand years ago, but are now dry as those thousand-year-old mummies in their silent grinning rows in Egypt? What if a lecturer should give to the audience an able and learned account of things once good and vital, but which long since went to seed? Ought he to turn and say to the community, "You don't like me, because you are not educated enough"? Of course. If a man preaches Latin, and writes Greek, the reason why the community will not care for his prelections is, that they do not know enough. If he will be heard, he must speak to the people in their own language. This is the sum of what we say about

Art. If it will please, it must address itself, not to an imaginary taste, but to a real sentiment, in the public. Taste changes with every age, but the original feelings of the human soul roll on from age to age the same, unchanged and unchangeable. And a picture which addresses itself plainly and strongly to any of the heart's feelings will always have admirers. While we write, there hangs before us a fine engraving of Leonardo da Vinci's Madonna (*La Vierge au Bas-Relief*). When this was painted all men believed in the Virgin Mary, according to the reverential and half-divine estimate of the Roman Catholic Church. That belief has waned and gone out. And yet, in Protestant America, the picture, if less reverenced, would be as much loved as at the day and in the land where it was painted. For it is still *a Mother with Children*. As long as the world endures, a picture that fitly handles that subject will live in love that time cannot abate. As the "Mother of God" it was not so powerful as now it is simply as a Mother of Men.

And, in like manner, a picture that touches any affection or moral sentiment, will speak in a language which men understand, without any other education than that of being born and of living. If artists choose to paint scholastic pictures, they must not grumble if only scholars care for them. If they will paint classical pictures, they must go to a market where men want such wares. If they will paint mythologies, or court subjects, or any other subjects, that are beyond or above the people, they must not expect a market for them among the people.

We protest against the arrogance of those who say,

or think, that an artist condescends when he represents by his art the subjects which belong to the life of the masses. The life of the common people is the best part of the world's life. It will ennoble any man who reverently expresses those thoughts and feelings on which the race stands. This contempt for the common people is the worst fruit of debauched pride. Not their ignorance, their tastes, their deeds, their knowledge, their refinements, are always to be esteemed. But the loves, the hopes, the joys, the friendships, the aspirations, the sorrows, of the great human family are always to be revered. Art dignifies itself when it embodies them. No man is fit to be an artist of men who does not profoundly feel how sublime common human heart-life is beyond his own art. And he only will be a true master whose education or disposition leads him to love the things which the race loves, and to paint them, not in condescension, not for the sake of a market, but because in his soul he feels that the life of the common people is the life of God, in so far as it is revealed in any age.

FREE TOWN LIBRARIES.

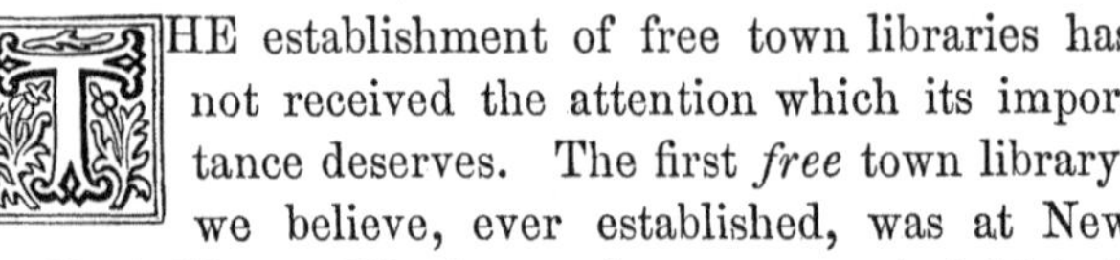

THE establishment of free town libraries has not received the attention which its importance deserves. The first *free* town library, we believe, ever established, was at New Bedford, Mass. We do not know upon what historical authority the statement rests; but we derived it from a gentleman connected with that library, whose intelligence and caution lead us to think that he could not be in error. If the facts are so, our country is honored in beginning so admirable an institution.

Libraries of every kind are multiplying with unexampled rapidity. The private libraries of New York will, for number, for the range of works, their great intrinsic value, their rarity, and costliness, astonish all who have not directed their attention to the subject. A series of papers last year appeared in the Evening Post, giving accounts of many of these noble monuments of private enterprise.

The libraries of colleges, of the various professions, law, medicine, &c., of literary societies and mechanical institutions, together with the state and national libraries, increase the growing supply of books for the universal reader. But all these do little or nothing for the smaller towns and the country proper. There is needed a class of libraries to which our young farmers and our country mechanics can have free access. Much as books are cheapened, a library is yet too expensive a luxury for private families, whose living depends upon their daily labor. Besides, in thousands of instances, even if the money were possessed, the disposition to own books is yet to be created. Now if in each town, and in thickly settled regions and smaller districts, there were a well-endowed free public library, those who hunger for books could be fed, and those who have never learned to love such food might be tempted, all the more easily because it would cost them nothing.

In such libraries it is desirable that those works should be stored which are important to all the different branches of industry, and to the learned professions, and such more expensive collections of history, travel, and art, as are not usually within the means of private purchasers. It is a great folly to fill up a public library with the evanescent trash which now too often encumbers their shelves. Public funds should make a more permanent investment, and young men and women should find here works not otherwise within their reach.

There are two points which ought specially to be considered. First, whether, with large and comfortable accommodation, both for quiet reading and for social intercourse, a free library may not afford a safe rendezvous for the young, for many hours that would otherwise be employed in places of temptation. And, second, whether, with suitable arrangements, one library may not be made to serve both men and women, avoiding all necessity of women's libraries, as such. The Boston free city library is one of the noblest monuments erected in that city of noble institutions. And there rooms are provided for men and women alike, where they may quietly meet, read, write, or pursue their intelligent investigations.

In several instances within our knowledge, these free town libraries have been established by the contributions of public-spirited citizens, and the town has afterwards voted an annual appropriation to maintain and increase the same. If every town would build a large town-house, with a hall, which, while it served for all ordinary meetings of citizens, should give ample space for public lectures during the winter, there might be established in it the alcoves of a free library. Then every town would have an institution for moral and intellectual culture, of incalculable value. Ten years will change the face of a town if a good school, or a good course of lectures, or a good free library be established in it.

But while the importance of free town libraries justifies the action of the towns themselves, these institutions give admirable opportunity for rich and benevolent men to hand down to posterity their names honorably distinguished in connection with noble institutions which they shall have founded and endowed. Every man ought to be his own executor in charitable gifts. While he is alive, and can superintend his own work, let him bestow his money. After his death his money may be applied to the purposes which he contemplated, or it may not. But if, while living, he establishes an institution for the diffusion of public intelligence, his work will be better done, and he will in part reap the reward of his liberality in the gratitude of his fellow-citizens.

HONOR YOUR BUSINESS.

T is a good sign when a man is proud of his work, or his calling. Yet nothing is more common than to hear men finding fault constantly with their particular business, and deeming themselves unfortunate because fastened to it by the necessity of gaining a livelihood. In this spirit men fret, and laboriously destroy all their comfort in work. Or they change their business, and go on miserably shifting from one thing to another, till the grave or the poorhouse gives them a permanent situation.

But while, occasionally, a man fails in life because he is not in the place fitted for his peculiar talent, it happens ten times oftener that results from neglect and even contempt of an honest business. A man should put his heart into everything that he does. There is not a profession in the world that has not its peculiar cares and vexations. No man will escape annoyance by changing business. No mechanical business is altogether agreeable. Commerce, in its endless varieties, is affected, like all other human pursuits, with trials, unwelcome duties, and spirit-tiring necessities. It is the very wantonness of folly for a man to search out the frets and burdens of his calling and give his mind every day to a consideration of them. They belong to human life. They are inevitable. Brooding, then, only gives them strength.

On the other hand, a man has a power given him to shed beauty and pleasure upon the homeliest toil, if he is wise. Let a man adopt his business, and indentify it with his life, and cover it with pleasant associations. For God has given us imagination, not alone to make some men poets, but to enable all men to beautify homely things. Heart-varnish will cover up innumerable evils and defects. Look at the good things. Accept your lot as a man does a piece of rugged ground, and begin to get out the rocks and roots, to deepen and mellow the soil, to enrich and plant it. There is something in the most forbidding avocation around which a man may twine pleasant fancies, out of which he may develop an honest pride.

We met, not long since, a fine specimen of just the thing we mean.

He began life a blacksmith. "I never wanted to be anything else than a mechanic," said he. He determined to make himself respectable and honorable, not in spite of his business, but by means of it. He entered with heart and soul and ambition into it. Little by little he improved it. Selecting a single line of articles, he began manufacturing them. "When I first entered the market," said he, "I found everybody trying to sell cheaper than his neighbor, and so making poorer and poorer articles, and running down the trade. I determined that I would not *undersell*, but *excel*."

In this spirit he entered heartily into his work, was proud of it, nursed and nourished it, and now he is, in his own department, almost without a competitor in the market. He has gathered riches, which he employs benevolently, and is respected and honored by all his townsmen. The good which this honest mechanic has done will not stop with himself. He will have made his business honorable to others. A man can impart to a business a flavor of honor by his own conduct, which shall make it thereafter more creditable to any one who enters it. Franklin left upon the printing-office an impress which has benefited the profession of printers ever since. Blacksmiths love to speak of the yet uncanonized St. Elihu Burritt.

Mr. Dowse, by tanning and currying, amassed a fortune, and bequeathed it, and its literary products, to the public in Boston and Cambridge; and we venture to say that, hereafter, that business will be easier and more encouraging to every lad that is bound apprentice to the nasty trade. Once let a man convert his business into an instrument of honor, benevolence, and patriotism, and from that moment it is transfigured, and men judge its dignity and merit, not by what it externally is, but by what it has done, and can do. It is better to stick to your business, and, by patient industry and honorable enterprise, crown it with honor, than to run away from it, and seek prosperity ready-made to your hand. It is not what a man *finds* that does him good, but what he *does*.

MOTHS, WINGED AND LEGGED.

Y DEAR MR. BONNER: As you are a business man, having always more to do than you can perform, I hope that you will sympathize with me in my abhorrence of *moths*.

I do not mean those beautiful winged fools that, in attempting, on summer nights, to put out our candles, only succeed in putting themselves out; nor those moths which use for food what we employ for a covering, who look upon an overcoat as we do upon roast beef, upon our furs as we do on chickens and wild game. It always seemed to me that, however mischievous to us was a moth's appetite, it must be a very dry and melancholy thing to him, to eat dry cloth, with nothing to drink, growing fat upon rubbish, and washing it down with darkness. I would not have you think that I am any more amiable than other people, when either of these moths assail my peace. I am nervous enough not to resist the sudden flap of a great winged miller in my candle as I am quietly reading, and his off-bouncing into my face, and fluttering over and around it with the most lively familiarity. Nor do I like in autumn to find my best coat eaten in holes all over, and my pantaloons looking as if I had been shot while running away from an enemy. Yet a little philosophy will teach us patience in such things, especially in contrast with the annoyances of other moths.

First, are those that anoint you with praise. It might have felt good to old kings to be anointed. We have never thought that a flask of oil poured on our head would inspire a sense of dignity as it went smoothly down the skin, dripping from the beard, and streaking the dress. But even though the oil were rancid, we think the operation more bearable than to be daubed with flattery. A friend who lives near your heart has a right to speak to you of that in you which excites his love. But a casual acquaintance, a stranger, a chance companion, have no right to insult you by supposing that you love flattery. This vice, which is inexcusable among ignorant and half-bred men, is utterly unpardonable among literary persons, who, as soon as you are first made known to them, begin to recall to you what they have read of your writing, or what you have done, or, if they can remember nothing of that, assume a complimentary reserve, and intimate the great delight which they have taken in your achievements. Is there no camphor, no ground pepper, no yellow snuff, for these moths?

Then comes the neighbor who has nothing to do, and means that nobody else shall do anything, who gets into your house, you hardly know how, and gets out you hardly can tell when, but drones and fatigues your ear with all the miserable tattle of the neighborhood. Would it be *man*slaughter to kill a *fool?* Ought not the law to give a man some discretionary power over the life of these mosquitos and gnats, that have, by some strange freak of nature, grown into the shape of men, without losing the propensities of insects?

Next, are men that never know when they have got through their business. They see by your look and attitude that they have caught you just at a moment of inspiration. Your fine thoughts are evaporating as they stand fuming about some errand that no more concerns you than do the domestic wants of a polar bear. Indeed, you feel not altogether unlike that savage animal. You answer emphatically, abruptly, perpendicularly; but there he is. No is no answer. You renew the answer, and fire into him with deadly aim, and he stirs no more than if he were a target, whose duty it was to stand and be shot at. One sweet fancy is gone already. The fine pulse of imagination is changing in you to the throb of vexation; and when, at last, you have got rid of the man, you have got rid, also, of your ideas, and sit down to your paper very much as a whipped schoolboy does who has a composition to write, and nothing in his head to write it with.

There is a kind of day-moth, an epistolary moth, of the same kind, who writes you a letter of business, or request, and begins it with excuses, and long-drawn apologies, or well-rounded complimentary reasons. You have to get into the letter, very much as a boy does into a blackberry patch. And the single, solitary berry hangs in the middle of a quickset hedge, and is not ripe when you get it, but sour and red. A man should deliver his letter as a sportsman does his shot. Let him glance at his errand like a rising woodcock, pull the trigger instantly, and bring him down without more ado.

There: I have expressed my mind, and feel better. After all, is it not wonderful that men do so well as they do? Consider how many men you daily meet, most of them with pleasure, and few of them with real annoyance. Common sense, at least in its lower forms, is more common than we are apt to think. And, on the whole, you need not do anything about these moths. Perhaps half of my impatience in such things is conceit. Am I too good to bear my part of life's vexations? Why should I not be annoyed as well as other people? How can a man be gracious, gentle, condescending, unless there is some occasion which requires such virtues?

Now that I think about it, is there not something said about patience in Holy Writ? Let me see. I'll search. Ah, here it is, in 1 Thessalonians v. 14: "Now we exhort you, brethren, warn them that are unruly, comfort the feeble-minded, support the weak, *be patient toward all men.*" On the whole, Mr. Bonner, if you have any impertinent, disagreeable, patience-trying people, send them to me.

BOSTON REMINISCENCES.

IN the opinion of unnumbered men, to have been born in Boston must be reckoned among the great gifts of fortune. Next to that is a Boston education; and next to *that*, is the beginning of a Boston education. In this third and humble estate we have the good fortune to stand; and although we cannot directly trace any part of the good fortune of our life directly back to this as a cause, it may yet be the occult and subtile influence which has breathed upon our years and spread our path with flowers.

However that may be, we love, always, to visit this curious old city. No other place has so many boyhood associations. A green, healthy, country lad, with a round, full, red-cheeked face, at about thirteen years of age we entered this city of marvels. We were dazed and dazzled with its sounds and sights. We had seen no larger place than Hartford. What was that to Boston! How fast our heart beat, on Sunday morning, to hear so many bells clamoring together and filling the heavens with calls to worship. One solitary bell had we been used to hear; one sweet bell, that rolled out its tones for a mile around and more, rising and falling as the wind blew or lulled, and having the whole air to itself, to make its own music in. This jangle and sweet dissonance of Boston bells was among the first things that touched the secret spring of fancy, and sent us up into dreams and imaginings. But the marvel wellnigh became a miracle. We had been told by some one, who loved to exercise the ears of right simple and all-believing country-boys, that there were so many bells in Boston that, when they rang on Sunday mornings, they almost played a tune. Judge of our amazement and breathless ardor of delight, when, on the very first Sabbath, we heard stealing in, in regular pulse of time, amid all the clanging and jangling that filled the air, the sweet melody of *Days of Absence* or *Greenville*. We could not believe our senses! Yet, yes! It was even so. Blessed city! in which dwelt so divine a spirit of harmony that some airy hand governed the widely scattered belfries, and taught the notes which each bell carelessly struck to come together in time and tune, and march through the air in harmony! Alas!

we had then never heard of *chimes;* and we were painfully disenchanted when the Old North steeple was shown to have played this tune all of itself; and the conviction came home, that every church preached and rung its bell "on its own hook."

Next to Boston bells were Boston ships. Here first we beheld a ship! We shall never again see anything that will so profoundly affect our imagination. We stood and gazed upon the ship, and smelt the sea-air, and looked far out along the water to the horizon, and all that we had ever read of buccaneers, of naval battles, of fleets of merchantmen, of explorations into strange seas, among rare and curious things, rose up in a cloud of mixed and changing fancies, until we scarcely knew whether we were in the body or out. How many hours have we asked and wanted no better joy than to sit at the end of the wharf, or on the deck of some newly-come ship, and rock and ride on the stream of our own unconscious imagination! We went to school to Boston harbor.

Next to the merchant marine was the navy-yard. We stole over to Charlestown almost every week. With what awe we walked past the long rows of unmounted cannon! With what exhilaration we looked forth from the mounted sea-battery that looked down the harbor, and just waited for some Britisher to dare to come in sight! We have torn any number of ships to pieces with those cannon, with imagination for our commodore and patriotism for our cannoneer. There have been great battles in Boston harbor that nobody knows anything about but ourself!

Then with what jubilant zeal did we climb all over the men-of-war building in the ship-houses, over the dismantled ships that lay at the pier-head! There is no gymnasium like a good ship and a parcel of fearless boys of robust strength in full chase of each other!

Wonderful to relate, also, would be the land engagements which took place in Boston. There were the Fort-Hillers, the West-Enders, the South-Enders, and, above all, the Charlestown *Pigs*. What patriotic North-Ender did not resent the indignity done to his side of the city by anybody that dared to live on any other side? When these external wars covered their glowing coals with the embers of a protecting peace, we always had a number of little neighborhood feuds which served to keep our hand in. The Prince Street boys, the Copp's Hill boys, the Salem-Streeters, the Sheafe Street heroes (we lived there), the Bennett-Streeters, and, above all, the Ann Street imps! Well, whole volumes would be required to perpetuate the fame which in these various fields will perish without a record!

It was in the Public Latin School of Boston that we laid the foundation of that classical lore that must have been, methinks, at the bottom of our prosperity! A little leaven is said to leaven the whole lump; and the same may be true of *Latin*, and in our case it was very little. It was in the days of Benjamin Gould that we made rabbits of our handkerchief, bravely took the rattan on our outstretched palm, and studied the grammar with a continual underthought of what we would do as soon as school let out!

But we are obliged to stop. If all the memorable events transpiring under the names of "One-lead-all," "Coram," &c., &c., were to be written, my brief chapter would become a whole book. The very streets where our life figured are no more. The canal is dry, and carts and drays pass where the old barges floated. New land, and whole neighborhoods have sprung up in places waste and void in our Boston boyhood. Even the Latin School is no longer to be seen in School Street. But, thank fortune, Dock Square is about the same, — as old, as shapeless, as crowded, and as dirty. But we must take another time to say other things of dear old Boston!

OBJECT LESSONS.

NE would almost think that *eyes* were an arrangement to prevent people from *seeing*. The same thought passed in the mind of the old prophet thousands of years ago: *Eyes have they, but they see not.* It is astonishing to observe, both what people do see and what they do not. One pair of eyes, for instance, will return from a crowded church, and will have seen (by an almost supernatural faculty, as it seems to us) every bonnet, every ribbon, every dress, every significant look, every posture or action, of a thousand people. Our own eyes, looking upon the same scene, would have seen not one of all these things!

One pair of eyes will go through the length of Broadway, and see only those who seem to look upon the owner of said eyes. Another pair will not have seen one *person* in that long walk, nor have missed one *horse* that walked, trotted, capered, or steadily pulled.

One man will see all the children, — the sweet, rosy-faced, clean ones, gladly; the ragged and keen-faced ones, sadly. One man will see all that Art can exhibit, and another nothing of it all. One man sees machines, and all mechanical contrivances; another sees only dresses and showy things. Now and then there is a rare head, whose eyes seem to take in everything, — from a mouse that scuds into a hole, up through all varieties of still or active life to the very top. And some there be who seem to see *nothing*. For all the effect produced upon them, Broadway is as empty as a street in Tadmor. Their eyes seem to have been made up with unprepared nerve; so that, like a daguerrean plate without chemical coating, nothing acts upon it, and no picture is burnt in.

It is a great pity that we are not taught, in our early days, *how to see*. It is more important than reading and writing, than arithmetic or geography. In a world of boundless treasures, above, beneath, on every side, we walk as if there were but few things worth seeing. And even these, when we have looked upon them once or twice, we exhaust, and suppose that we have really seen them!

A man shall pass and repass a *burdock* growing near the path which he daily treads going to and returning from his work. He would laugh if he were told that he did not know that familiar plant. And yet, in making it, God put upon it and within it a hundred things which are worth observation, but which this man never sees or suspects. The least things that come from God's hands are so full, so compact of qualities, that they will bear close scrutiny and long study. And we think that the chief advantage to be derived from teaching children *to draw* is not to be found in the pictures made, but in the new eyesight gained. This, however, implies that they are taught to draw directly from nature, and not from copy-books. Let a child study a plant, in order to draw it, and he will find out more about it in one day than otherwise he would in a lifetime. We only glance at things.

We overlook more than we see in the things which we see most thoroughly. It would be a good exercise for winter evenings for children, to have placed before them a rosebush in a flower-pot, and then let each tell what he sees, and keep the list; and then let older eyes do the same; and then, from all together, make out a more complete one; and laying it aside, every day whenever things occur afterwards, let them be put down. Thus, the bark, its color, texture, changes from youth to age; the branches, their relative positions; the sub-divisions, the angles at which they put off; the leaves, their form; the edges, their texture, color, size, number, health, thickness; the difference between the upper and lower surface, etc., etc. These and such like things will soon let one know how little the untrained eye sees, and how much there is to be seen!

The eye is susceptible of more training than perhaps any other of the senses. Fineness of sight, length of vision, comprehensiveness, or the number of things taken in at once, and rapidity, — these may be so far developed, that the educated eye is as far above the uneducated as a refined and cultivated mind is beyond a savage one. Houdin, the great French necromancer, relates the practice of himself and son, in preparing for one part of their jugglery. They trained their eyes to take in at a glance, from a shop-window, from a store full of varieties, from the face of books in a library, the greatest number of things. They came to such perfection, that in simply walking past a library-case they could, afterward, tell you nearly every book on its shelves, and its relative position. Their eyes seemed to be acted upon in a manner not unlike the photographic process. A picture was instantly formed. And, afterward, it rose up before their memories as if the original thing stood before them. Such incidents show how little use is yet made of eyes, how little we suspect their capabilities of education, and how little we know of the world we live in, even in its most familiar aspects.

CHARACTER AND REPUTATION.

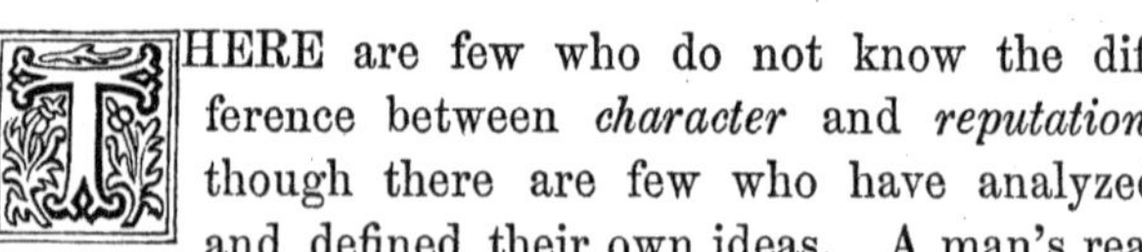

THERE are few who do not know the difference between *character* and *reputation*, though there are few who have analyzed and defined their own ideas. A man's real inward habits and mental condition form his *character*. This will work out to the surface in some degree, and in some persons much more than in others.

But the *appearance* which a man presents to the

world, the outward exhibition, gives him his reputation. A man's character is his reality. It is the acting and moving force of his being. Reputation is the impression which he has made upon other men; it is their thought of him. Our character is always in ourselves, but our reputation is in others.

It is true that, ordinarily, among honest men, the two go together. A man who lives out of doors among men, and who gives his fellows a fair chance to see his conduct, will find that he is accurately measured and correctly judged.

But it sometimes happens that men are much better than they have credit for being, and as often men are much worse than they appear to be; i. e. men may have a reputation either better or worse than their character. Thus, there are many men who are reputed to be hard, severe, stern, who at heart are full of all kindness, and would go farther and fare harder to serve a friend or to relieve a real case of trouble than anybody else around them. On the other hand, some people are thought to be very gentle, very sweet in manners; all smiles, promises, and politeness, but at heart they are cold and selfish. Character is bad and reputation good in such cases.

It is quite easy for a man to get himself a reputation. He has only to practise upon the imagination and credulity of the public. If he takes pleasure in being thought better than he is, if he chooses to live in a vain show, if he wears a mask, and his life is occupied in covering up his real feelings by feigned and false ones, he may have a measure of success.

But the same amount of labor and care which gives him but a flimsy credit, and which would fall before the least scrutiny or severity of test, would give him a substantial reality. He labors as hard for a sham as would suffice to give him a truth.

Indeed, it is easier to build a character than to sustain a false reputation. Once let a man's habits be laid, and solidly laid, in truth, honor, and virtue, and the more the man is tried, the more he profits by it. Such men are revealed to the world by misfortunes. The troubles which threaten them only end in letting people know how strong and real and good they are.

But when a man has learned to live upon a mere show, practising upon others with decent appearances, he will find that his reputation, good in fair weather, will be good for nothing in storms and trials. And then, when he needs most sympathy and respect, he will have the least. If it is a little harder to build up character than reputation, it is only so in the beginning. For reputation, like a poorly-built house, will cost as much for patching and repairs as would have made it thorough at first.

Besides, an honorable soul ought to be ashamed of credit which he does not deserve. One hardly knows how to interpret a nature that can deliberately take praises for things which he knows do not belong to him. This is particularly true of *young* men. A man may grow insincere through long temptation and the corruption of life. But what shall we think of a man that begins life on a lie? who deliberately sets out to build up a reputation without caring for his character?

GOOD-NATURE.

IF there be one thing for which a man should be more grateful than another, it is the possession of *good-nature*. I do not consider him good-tempered who has no temper at all. A man ought to have spirit, strong, earnest, and capable of great indignation. We like to hear a man thunder, once in a while, if it is genuine, and in the right way for a right man. When a noble fellow is brought into contact with mean and little ways, and is tempted by unscrupulous natures to do unworthy things; or when a great and generous heart perceives the wrong done by lordly strength to shrinking, unprotected weakness; or where a man sees the foul mischiefs that sometimes rise and cover the public welfare like a thick cloud of poisonous vapors, — we like to hear a man express himself with outburst and glorious anger. It makes us feel safer to know that there are such men. We respect human nature all the more, to know that it is capable of such feelings.

But just these men are best capable of *good-nature*. These are the men upon whom a sweet justice in common things, and a forbearance toward men in all the details of life, and a placable, patient, and cheerful mind sit with peculiar grace.

Some men are much helped to do this by a kind of bravery born with them. Some men are good-natured because they are benevolent, and always feel in a sunny mood; some, because they have such vigor and robust health that care flies off from them, and they really cannot feel nettled and worried; some, because a sense of character keeps them from all things unbecoming manliness; and some, from an overflow of what may be called in part animal spirits, and in part, also, hopeful and cheerful dispositions. But whatever be the cause or reason, is there anything else that so much blesses a man in human life as this voluntary or involuntary *good-nature?* Is there anything else that converts all things so much into enjoyment to him? And then what a glow and light he carries with him to others! Some men come upon you like a cloud passing over the sun. You do not know what ails you, but you feel cold and chilly while they are about, and need an extra handful of coal on the fire whenever they tarry long. Others rise upon you like daylight. How many times does a cheerful and hopeful physician cure his patients by what he carries in his heart and face, more than by what he has in his medical case! How often does the coming of a happy-hearted friend lift you up out of deep despondency, and, before you are aware, inspire you with hope and cheer. What a gift it is to make all men better and happier without knowing it! We don't suppose that flowers know how sweet they are. We have watched them. But as far as we can find out their thoughts, flowers are just as modest as they are beautiful.

These roses before me, salfataine, lamarque, and saffrano, with their geranium leaves (rose) and carnations and abutilon, have made me happy for a day. Yet they stand huddled together in my pitcher without seeming to know my thoughts of them, or the gracious work which they are doing! And how much more is it to have a disposition that carries with it, involuntarily, sweetness, calmness, courage, hope, and happiness, to all who are such? Yet this is the portion of good-nature in a real, large-minded, strong-natured man! When it has made him happy it has scarcely begun its office!

In this world, where there is so much real sorrow, and so much unnecessary grief of fret and worry; where burdens are so heavy and the way so long; where men stumble in rough paths, and so many push them down rather than help them up; where tears are as common as smiles, and hearts ache so easily, but are poorly fed on higher joys, how grateful ought we to be that God sends along, here and there, a natural heart-singer, — a man whose nature is large and luminous, and who, by his very carriage and spontaneous actions, calms, cheers, and helps his fellows. God bless the good-natured, for they bless everybody else!

APPLE-PIE.

HOW often people use language without the slightest sense of its deep, interior meaning! Thus, no phrase is more carelessly or frequently used than the saying, "*Apple-pie order.*" How few who say so reflect at the time upon either apple-pie or the true order of apple-pie! Perhaps they have been reared without instruction. They may have been born in families that were ignorant of apple-pie; or who were left to the guilt of calling two tough pieces of half-cooked dough, with a thin streak of macerated dried apple between them, of leather color, and of taste and texture not unbecoming the same, — an apple-pie! But from such profound degradation of ideas we turn away with gratitude and humility, that one so unworthy as we should have been reared to better things.

We are also affected with a sense of regret for duty unperformed; for great as have been the benefits received, we have never yet celebrated as we ought the merits of apple-pie. That reflection shall no longer cast its shadow upon us.

"Henry, go down cellar, and bring me up some Spitzenbergs." The cellar was as large as the whole house, and the house was broad as a small pyramid. The north side was windowless, and banked up outside with frost-defying tan-bark. The south side had windows, festooned and frescoed with the webs of spiders, that wove their tapestries over every corner in the neighborhood, and, when no flies were to be had, ate up each other, as if they were nothing but politicians, instead of being lawful and honorable *arachnidæ.* On the east side stood a row of cider-barrels; for twelve or twenty barrels of cider were a fit provision for the year, — and what was not consumed for drink was expected duly to turn into vinegar, and was then exalted to certain hogsheads kept for the purpose. But along the middle of the cellar were the apple-bins; and when the season had been propitious, there were stores and heaps of Russets, Greenings, Seeknofurthers, Pearmains, Gilliflowers, Spitzenbergs, and many besides, nameless, but not virtueless. Thence selecting, we duly brought up the apples. Some people think anything will do for pies. But the best for eating are the best for cooking. Who would make jelly of any other apple, that had the *Porter?* who would bake or roast any other sweet apple, that had the *Ladies' Sweeting*, — unless, perhaps, the *Talman Sweet?* and who would put into a pie any apple but *Spitzenberg*, that had *that?* Off with their jackets! Fill the great wooden bowl with the sound rogues! And now, O cook! which shall it be? For at this point the roads diverge, and though they all come back at length to apple-pie, it is not a matter of indifference which you choose. There is, for example, one made without under-crust, in a deep plate, and the apples laid in, in full quarters; or the apples being stewed are beaten to a mush, and seasoned, and put between the double paste; or they are sliced thin and cooked entirely within the covers; or they are put without seasoning into their bed, and when baked, the upper lid is raised, and the butter, nutmeg, cinnamon, and sugar are added; the whole well mixed, and the crust returned as if nothing had happened.

But O be careful of the paste! Let it not be like putty, nor rush to the other extreme, and make it so flaky that one holds his breath while eating for fear of blowing it all away. Let it not be plain as bread, nor yet rich like cake. Aim at that glorious medium, in which it is tender, without being fugaciously flaky; short, without being too short; a mild, sapid, brittle thing, that lies upon the tongue, so as to let the apple strike through and touch the *papillæ* with a mere effluent flavor. But this, like all high art, must be a thing of inspiration or instinct. A true cook will understand us, and we care not if others do not!

Do not suppose that we limit the apple-pie to the kinds and methods enumerated. Its capacity in variation is endless, and every diversity discovers some new charm or flavor. It will accept almost every flavor of every spice. And yet nothing is so fatal to the rare and higher graces of apple-pie as inconsiderate, vulgar spicing. It is not meant to be a mere vehicle for the exhibition of these spices, in their own natures. It is a glorious unity in which sugar gives up its nature as sugar, and butter ceases to be butter, and each flavorsome spice gladly evanishes from its own full nature, that all of them, by a common death, may rise into the new life of apple-pie! Not that apple is longer apple! *It*, too, is transformed. And the final pie, though born of apple, sugar, butter, nutmeg, cinnamon, lemon, is like none of these, but the compound ideal of them all, refined, purified, and by fire fixed in blissful perfection.

But all exquisite creations are short-lived. The natural term of an apple-pie is but twelve hours. It reaches its highest state about one hour after it comes from the oven, and just before its natural heat has quite departed. But every hour afterward is a declension. And after it is one day old, it is thenceforward but the ghastly corpse of apple-pie.

But while it is yet florescent, white or creamy yellow, with the merest drip of candied juice along the edges, (as if the flavor were so good to itself that its own lips watered!) of a mild and modest warmth, the sugar suggesting jelly, yet not jellied, the morsels of apple neither dissolved nor yet in original substance, but hanging as it were in a trance between the spirit and the flesh of applehood, then, when dinner is to be served at five o'clock, and you are pivotted on the hour of one with a ravening appetite, let the good dame bring forth for luncheon an apple-pie, with cheese a year old, crumbling and yet moist, but not with base fluid, but oily rather; then, O blessed man, favored by all the divinities! eat, give thanks, and go forth, "*in apple-pie order!*"

STRAIGHTENING THE LINES.

N the northeast side of our little pet farm there was, upon survey, found to be a jog, or angle. The line did not run from a given point straight through, but turned abruptly west, and then at right angles north. As soon as the plot of ground was mapped, we conceived a dislike to that corner. It looked as if the next lot was poking its horns into our sides. We did not fancy such an intrusive angle. The more we looked at it, the less we liked it. *How to straighten our line* became a very serious problem. To do it by cutting off any part of our own acres was not to be thought of. To buy more land, when you have enough, would be even worse. But who that owns an acre can resist the temptation of another acre? Whether we bought or sold is nothing to the reader; but that line *is straightened*, and there is no jog in our east line, and the map looks very well, and we have not lost any ground. And we have a little more room for our orchard!

Did anybody ever buy a farm without seeing some reason for adding a little more to it? If there is not a jog in the line, is there not one in the man's notions? The front is too narrow, and he would widen it; or there is a meadow that *ought* to belong to the place; or a bit of woodland is just the thing needed; or a muck-swamp would be so good for its contents; or the stock require that the lot with that ever-flowing brook in it should belong to the farm; or a pasture-range on the hill would be so good for the dairy; or that swale would form such a fine carriage approach; or the bit of a hill to the east has the very stone that you need for walls or buildings; or you have a shanty and a neighbor whose mind is too free and hands too loose in property-matters, and whom you can buy away easier than abate as a nuisance; or you want a little more garden, a little more orchard, a little more mowing-land or lawn or ornamental forest room, or you wish to secure a particularly fine prospect; — in short, you want a little more land. There is a mysterious law which makes twenty acres much less perfect than twenty-five, and twenty-five has a powerful attraction for thirty. A hundred acres are never content without fifty more. Five hundred acres complain for want of company, and regard themselves as lonesome without a few hundred acres more.

There are undoubtedly cases in which large farms are better than small ones. But there are twenty men who would grow rich on less than a hundred acres where there is one who would on more land.

A farm is only another name for a chemical laboratory. It is only another way of manufacturing, and many men can carry on a small, compact business, which their eye and hand can cover, who have no head to plan a complex one, and no skill to superintend its execution.

A small place thoroughly wrought is very seldom seen. There are very few acres that have ever shown what they can do.

There is one way in which men may increase the amount of soil with the utmost advantage, and that is *vertically*.

A man's lease runs from *nadir* to *zenith*. A man only sees the surface of what he owns. There is a great deal more down below than there is upon the top. Now, for many purposes, every inch a man goes downward, in cultivation, is equivalent to a foot on the surface. A vertical inch is worth more than a superficial foot. And it is lawful to increase the size of a man's farm by *going under* for the ground.

This is a point very little heeded, even by those who expend great sums of money in the improvement and ornamentation of their places. A system of drainage should be established at a depth of from three and a half to four feet. If, then, the ground be stoned and enriched to a depth of full three feet, it will be only in a good condition for till. Not only crops, but fruit-trees and forest and ornamental trees, demand at least such a depth. Then one will see the fruit of his labor in shrubs, vines, trees, and harvests, which will make his *luck* the envy of all lazy men in the neighborhood.

In short, let every man find the crooks in the bottom lines of his grounds, and spare no pains to take these out, and he may be sure that the side lines will not give him much trouble.

TALKING.

ALKING and laughing are distinguishing traits of the human species. No animal can laugh, nor, except as a mere mechanical imitation of sounds, can any animal talk. Neither bird nor beast uses articulate speech as a means of conveying thought or of expressing feeling. This is one of the prerogatives of man. But in no other one respect do men differ so much as in laughing or talking. Nor are we apt to consider how closely these acts are connected with, and the result of, the original organization, mental and physical. A secretive and cautious man neither talks fluently nor laughs readily. Some men's conversation is like the ticking of an old-fashioned clock with a long pendulum, whose measured beats are slow and solemn. Once started, they stop for nothing, but drop one word regularly after another, to the end of their methodical sentence. If you are yourself quick, versatile, and in a hurry withal, you grow intolerably restless under the conversation. Your tongue is horse-limbed, and their tongues are ox-footed. At the first half-dozen words you perceive their meaning, and then the slow-paced utterance of it is surplusage. Perhaps it is your minister. You cannot tell why he is so tedious. What he says is good, and it is well said; but you cannot refrain from wandering thoughts. You are mercurial and imaginative, and he is phlegmatic and literal. Perhaps it is your schoolmaster, and he bores you with his solemn and long-drawn repetitions. Or

you may be a bouncing boy, full of sparkles and quips, doomed to stand still and receive the slowly-poured admonition or advice. Your nerves rebel. You grow unreasonable. You inwardly mutter all sorts of harmless objurgations. But Nature is imperative.

Men of a cautious and secretive turn of mind are seldom talkers. And when caution is disproportionally powerful, a man will sometimes be unable to do more than issue here and there parts of sentences. He will begin, and stop; begin again, and soon tie up the sentence with a twist of interjected qualifying clause; then again, stopping as if to go back and look over what he has said, as a carpenter *sights* the edge of the work which he is fitting; and, finally, he will leave the sentence very much in the shape of a bushel of apples poured out in a heap upon the ground. And yet we have known such men to be very keen in perception, acute in thought, and shrewd in judgment. But it seems as if there were some break in the machinery which connects the thinking part and the language part of the mind. And their conversation resembles a tune played upon an old piano, half of whose keys do not connect with the wires, and give no sound.

Some men use words as riflemen do bullets. They say little. The few words used go right to the mark. They let you talk, and guide with their eye and face, on and on, till what you say can be answered in a word or two, and then they lance out a sentence, pierce the matter to the quick, and are done. You never know where you stand with them. Your conversation falls into their mind, as rivers fall into deep chasms, and are lost from sight by its depth and darkness. They will sometimes surprise you with a few words, that go right to the mark like a gunshot, and then they are silent again, as if they were re-loading.

In this class must be reckoned men who alternate between drought and freshet. Sometimes for days or hours they are all dried up. Suddenly they will send forth an immense tide of speech that quite sweeps you away. We have seen men like the far-famed Iceland Geysers, who never talked till they were mad, and then spouted terribly. It is said of these northern hot-springs, that if you throw a stone or tuft of grass into their throats, you soon bring up their torrents of scalding water at a most furious rate.

In strong contrast with such are the smooth, oily talkers whom we occasionally meet, whose voices are soft and sweet, and who have an inimitable talent in flowing on, without let or hinderance, in the most genial and soothing manner. They steal upon your ear and lull your temper; they come upon you with a kind of charge that resembles a May atmosphere after March winds. One cannot remember what they say, but at the time the charm amounts almost to a fascination. One word takes hold of another with such a soft touch, and one sentence moves into another, as drops of water in a stream move indistinguishably upon each other.

There seems no reason to doubt that a propensity to talk is as much a natural gift as a propensity to invent or to construct. We have known persons who neither cared whether you listened to them or heeded their utterances. A good woman, we once knew, who talked as rivers run, by the necessity of some inward gravitation toward outflow. She would begin with morning, talk, talk, talk, in a cheery, changeable way, branching off in this direction or that, running off on this analogy, or toward that suggestion all breakfast time, all the while the table was being cleared. One by one the people in the room — who had learned to listen to her no more than we hear the ticking of a clock or any other continuous sound — would go out, till the last one had left. It was all the same to her; a low murmur might be heard in the room, by those adjoining it, for the good soul was pleasantly talking all alone. When you entered again she merely continued, and so on all day and evening. It was a double mystery how she found strength and material for such a perennial flow by daylight. But, once impressed with the inevitableness of her tongue, you next wondered what miraculous power bound it to silence at night. It was like a brook from the glaciers, which flows all day while the sun shines on the ice, but is sealed up by frosts at night.

But the subject is vast. We have touched but the external edge. The tongue of man cannot be described in an article. It has deep inward relations. It has national and political bearings. It is the silver bell of the soul, or the iron and crashing hammer of the anvil. It is like a magician's wand, full of all incantation and witchery; or it is a sceptre in a king's hand, and sways men with imperial authority.

The pen is the tongue of the hand, — a silent utterer of words for the eye, — the unmusical substitute of the literal tongue, which is the soul's prophet, the heart's minister, and the interpreter of the understanding.

ART AMONG THE PEOPLE.

HE growth of good taste, the extraordinary facilities for obtaining art-creations in some form, and the amount of sound art-reading which has been spread into all society by the invaluable agency of newspapers, and which has educated and stimulated the feelings and judgment of the common citizens of our century, have begun an era of art such as the world never saw, and could never see in any other condition of society.

There has been a great deal said about the decline of Art in our age; a great deal of mourning after the great days of the masters of the sixteenth century, and a great deal of unwarrantable regret that governments do not more encourage Art.

We do not believe that Art has declined; we do not believe that the sixteenth century was any better served by the ministry of Art than ours is; and we do not believe that government should be appealed to to foster Art. Whatever incidental encouragement it can give should be freely and generously conferred. But it is the common people that must in our times be looked to. From them springs all political influence. We look to them for the maintenance of all our civil and religious institutions. We look to them for education, for reformation, for all civic public spirit; and it is the increasing faith of our times that an intelligent common people are better promoters of all the great interests of society than can be governments or hierarchies. This is just as true of Art as it is of Religion, Education, Commerce, or industrial pursuits. Governments may help. But the grand nourishing influence must come from public sentiment.

If Art be regarded as a mere decorator, to give us only grotesque or graceful arabesques, or close imitations of natural objects, or mere graded or contrasted colors, in Oriental profusion, it would be scarcely worth our while to inquire in what age it had flourished most.

There is undoubtedly a pleasure of the senses in the simple effect of form and color, and in adroit imitations. But it is a gratification in which the intellect and the higher feelings can scarcely participate. What would be the condition of learning and literature in an age in which the paper, the type, the binding of books, were deemed more important than the meanings and truths contained? But just that is done when pictures are valued for their mechanical dexterity and the impression on the senses.

But Art is a pictorial language. It must discourse in every age of the things which belong to that age, or to the purposes which a Divine Providence is developing in any period of time. In the far-famed sixteenth century, ideas found but a slow and very imperfect diffusion. The poet sang, the orator spoke, the churchman and professor taught. But there was no printing-press, no popular assembly, no common people reading daily newspapers, and made familiar with all that the noblest minds thought, or great hearts felt, or skilful hands executed. The most public things would seem to our day almost secluded.

In such a time, Architecture had a moral function

that it can never have again. We shall never have cathedrals, because we have better ways of expressing religious yearnings. We build up a great *Common People*, in thrift, honor, purity, faith, and piety, and they express the religious ideas of an age better than can the costliest and most skilfully wrought architecture. Meanwhile, Architecture occupies itself with another work. It now builds five hundred parish churches instead of one metropolitan cathedral. It builds fewer palaces, but more mansions. It builds fewer marvels, but more good houses. In short, Architecture is no longer in the hands of government, of the Church, or of mere wealth. It has become the servant of the common people. It has worked out the aristocratic idea, and is now working out the true democratic idea. And this work is in nature diffusive and detailed, not massed and magnificent. The world never saw so much architectural progress as now. Men fail to see it, because all men look at Art from the aristocratic stand-point, and do not sympathize with the moral element which it serves in our times.

The same thing is true of Painting. Once it was the creature of the state. This in Athens was so eminently the case, that not until after the decline of Greece began was Art regarded as permissible in the citizen's dwelling. It was a sacred language, used only in the temples of religion or in state buildings. The wealthiest men, the greatest statesmen, and the artists themselves, had neither paintings nor statues in their houses. Indeed, the private houses of Athens were small, stinking nuisances, long after the city was the admiration of the world for its public buildings.

In later days — those very days so much lauded, when Raffaelle, M. Angelo, Leonardo, Correggio, Titian, Paul Veronese, &c., lived — what interests did Art serve? It was aristocratic and hierarchic. It belonged to the palace and the church. It had almost no sympathy with the common people. It was large, noble, magnificent. It did a much-needed work. But it completed that work. It served one element as long as the world needed that it should. Its mission was then in advance. The earlier and ruder forms of society are the monarchic. The later and riper developments are republican in spirit, whatever be the form. Art was called down from great ceilings and vast walls, from churches and palaces, because the citizen was building his house, and it is a higher function for Art to serve the whole citizenship than to serve their rulers. The men governed are more noble and more valuable than they that govern them. Men are nearer to God than governments.

It is in this direction that Art has been steadily inclining. It has had less and less to do for exclusive wealth, for institutions and for governments, and more for the common people. And it is yet to perform its highest offices in this interest. There is a life to be expressed, there are truths to be represented there are exquisite experiences of joy and of sorrow, there is a whole realm of household life, of moral life, of common occupation, which, as yet, has been imperfectly served or expressed.

The true artist is he who perceives in common things a meaning of beauty or sentiment which coarser natures fail to detect. The artist is not an imitator who makes common things on canvas look *just like* common things anywhere else. Artist is Interpreter. He teaches men by opening through imitation the message of deeds, events, or objects, so that they rise from the senses, where before they had exclusively presented themselves, and speak to the higher feelings. A man who sees in Nature nothing but materiality, is no more an artist than he is a musician who, in one of Beethoven's symphonies, hears only noise.

And we deem this mission of Art as much more noble and morally grand than that which it hitherto served, as mankind are more noble and grand than their accidental rulers and their harnessing institutions. Thus far, we have but laid down the principal thought. Its applications would require a much larger space.

SLIDING DOWN HILL.

HERE is nothing in the tropics that can console a man doomed to dwell there for the loss of northern winters. Monkeys and humming-birds, gorgeous flowers and gigantic vegetation, insects, reptiles, luscious fruits which you cannot eat without a cholera, sweltering nights and roasting days! Deliver us from the intolerable delights of tropical luxury!

But a northern winter is full of bracing joys. Indoors all is ruddy and social, and out of doors all is energy and manly joy! A man who has blood and vital spirits glories in the cold of winter. But of all its sports, what one can claim superiority over *coasting;* or, as in our boyhood days it was called, sliding down hill!

Long before we attained the age of a sled, two barrel-staves, fastened together by the knowing workman, served an excellent purpose, and required no mean skill in sitting and steering. A slight mistake in balancing, and the boy and staves changed places, the boy under and the sliding machine a-top, — and then gradually rolling into a promiscuous heap, out of which came some ripping remarks — not made by the sled.

Next came the glory of full and real *sledship,* — a sled with runners, and iron or steel shod; a sled painted and lettered! With that we defied the thermometer, and set our faces against the north-wind! And how the long hill, a full half-mile, is sought, not all of a gentle slope, nor yet too steep, but properly made up, as all hills should be, with a fine gradual beginning, then a pitch quite steep, then another long middle slope, and a jounce here, a rullock there, a sweep yonder around a point, and a fetching-up place right along the river! On such a hill-top, with a glorious sled, well-muffled and mittened, the boy seats himself on his steed, prouder than ever sat king upon his throne! Away he goes, with nimble feet reaching out before him (for a sled carries its rudder at the bow), and whose heels, with skilful touch, steer the flying machine. See him make a leap over the rullock, lifted clear into the air, and coming down with a jounce that made everything crack — but the boy! Boys have springs inside of them, under every muscle, on all sides of each bone, and come down with a springy bound that cars and carriages may envy, but cannot hope to attain!

None of your belly-flounders! This lying down on a sled, like a buckwheat cake on a griddle; or that sideway sitting, on the hind end of it, with one leg cork-screwed out behind, for steering, are not the thing. They are not orthodox. They savor of a compliance with weakness and timidity. A real boy should sit upon his sled fair and square, with his face to his work, and ready to meet all difficulties with his breast to them!

Nor let any one decry the long tramp up hill that follows this fierce flight downward. What if it is long, the sled hanging behind, the way slippery, and withal some peril of those avalanches of other boys that come roaring and whirling down? The going up is still an indispensable part of the epic. It is the *dark* that gives power to the high light. The *up* makes, by contrast, the very glory of the *down*. Besides, as it is appointed to every hen, when she has laid an egg, to enter at large into the merits of the performance, and to tell the barnyard and neighborhood her opinion of that last egg, and, doubtless, if we but understood the true interior meaning of *cackle*, to say,—"Here's an egg for omelettes, omelettes, omelettes; good also for cakes, cakes, cakes; the very soul of custard, custard, custard; good raw, good roasted, good boiled, good fried. Good soft or hard;—good eggs, good eggs, very good eggs,"—so (let me see, that intolerable hen has confused this sentence so that we don't just see how to tie it together,—ah, here it is!) as this hen, having done all the above, discourses of it (as per above translation), *so* the boy occupies the long ascent in declaring the skill, speed, and wonderful daring of his descent, and is vehement in setting forth what *liked* to have happened, and the thing which he *almost* did!

We never see the snow on the ground, old as we are, that we do not feel the very spirit of the sled again! And now, an old man, we would if we could mount and plunge down the hill again. Though a man's hair is as white as the snow under his feet, he need not be ashamed of a voyage on a sled!

There is but one city in this nation, that we know of, that is civilized, and that city is New Bedford. One winter, not long ago, when we were there, we found a long street refused to horse-vehicles, and set apart to sleds. The Selectmen, or whatever their names were, at the public expense carted on snow where the track was worn; iced it by water thrown on overnight; stationed a band of music there; had torches lit and placed along the sides; and the generous people, catching the spirit, illumined their houses, and this preparation was then thrown open to men, women, and children. That city is civilized. That part of the millennium which consists in sliding down hill we believe will begin first in New Bedford.

GAMBLING.

THE universal prevalence of this vice is a reason for parental vigilance; and a reason of remonstrance from the citizen, the parent, the minister of the gospel, the patriot, and the press. I propose to trace its opening, describe its subjects, and detail its effects.

A young man, proud of freedom, anxious to exert his manhood, has tumbled his Bible and sober books and letters of counsel into a dark closet. He has learned various accomplishments, — to flirt, to boast, to swear, to fight, to drink. He has let every one of these chains be put around him, upon the solemn promise of Satan that he would take them off whenever he wished. Hearing of the artistic feats of eminent gamblers, he emulates them. So he ponders the game. He teaches what he has learned to his shopmates, and feels himself their master. As yet he has never played for stakes. It begins thus: Peeping into a bookstore, he watches till the sober customers go out; then slips in, and with assumed boldness, not concealing his shame, he asks for cards, buys them, and hastens out. The first game is to pay for the cards. After the relish of playing for a stake, no game can satisfy them without a stake. A few nuts are staked; then a bottle of wine; an oyster-supper. At last they can venture a sixpence in actual money, —just for the amusement of it. I need go no further — whoever wishes to do anything with the lad can do it now. If properly plied, and gradually led, he will go to any length, and stop only at the gallows. Do you doubt it? let us trace him a year or two further on.

With his father's blessing, and his mother's tears, the young man departs from home. He has received his patrimony, and embarks for life and independence. Upon his journey he rests at a city; visits the "school of morals"; lingers in more suspicious places; is seen by a sharper; and makes his acquaintance. The knave sits by him at dinner; gives him the news of the place, and a world of advice; cautions him against sharpers; inquires if he has money, and charges him to keep it secret; offers himself to make with him the rounds of the town, and secure him from imposition. At length, that he may see all, he is taken to a gaming-house, but, with apparent kindness, warned not to play. He stands by to see the various fortunes of the game: some, forever losing; some, touch what number they will, gaining piles of gold. Looking is thirst where wine is free. A glass is taken; another of a better kind; next the best the landlord has, and two glasses of that. A change comes over the youth; his exhilaration raises his courage and lulls his caution. Gambling *seen* seems a different thing from gambling *painted* by a pious father! Just then his friend remarks that one might easily double his money by a few ventures, but that it were, perhaps, prudent not to risk. Only this was needed to fire his mind. What! only prudence between me and gain? Then that shall not be long! He stakes; he wins. Stakes again; wins again. Glorious! I am the lucky man that is to break the bank! He stakes, and wins again. His pulse races;

his face burns; his blood is up, and fear gone. He loses; loses again; loses all his winnings; loses more. But fortune turns again; he wins anew. He has now lost all self-command. Gains excite him, and losses excite him more. He doubles his stakes; then trebles them, — and all is swept. He rushes on, puts up his whole purse, and loses the whole! Then he would borrow; no man will lend. He is desperate, he will fight at a word. He is led to the street, and thrust out. The cool breeze which blows upon his fevered cheek wafts the slow and solemn stroke of the clock, — one, — two, — three, — four; *four of the morning!* Quick work of ruin! — an innocent man destroyed in a night! He staggers to his hotel, remembers as he enters it that he has not even enough to pay his bill. It now flashes upon him that his friend, who never had left him for an hour before, had stayed behind where his money is, and doubtless is laughing over his spoils. His blood boils with rage. But at length comes up the remembrance of home; a parent's training and counsels for more than twenty years destroyed in a night! "Good God! what a wretch I have been! I am not fit to live. I cannot go home. I am a stranger here. O that I were dead! O that I had died before I knew this guilt, and were lying where my sister lies! O God! O God! my head will burst with agony!" He stalks his lonely room with an agony which only the young heart knows in its first horrible awakening to remorse, — when it looks despair full in the face, and feels its hideous incantations tempting him to suicide. Subdued at length by agony, cowed and weakened by distress, he is sought again by those who plucked him.

Cunning to subvert inexperience, to raise the evil passions, and to allay the good, they make him their pliant tool.

Farewell, young man! I see thy steps turned to that haunt again! I see hope lighting thy face; but it is a lurid light, and never came from heaven. Stop before that threshold!—turn, and bid farewell to home!—farewell to innocence!—farewell to venerable father and aged mother!—the next step shall part thee from them all forever. And now henceforth be a mate to thieves, a brother to corruption. Thou hast made a league with death, and unto death shalt thou go.

WINTER BEAUTY.

IT is the impression of many that only in summer, including spring and autumn of course, is the *country* desirable as a residence. The country in summer, and the city for the winter. It is true, that the winter gives attractions to the city, in endless meetings, lectures, concerts, and indoor amusements. But it is not true that the country loses all interest when the leaves are shed and the grass is gone. On the contrary, to one who has learned how to use his senses and his sensibilities, there are attractions in the winter of a peculiar kind, and pleasures which can be reaped only then. The disadvantages of wet roads, unpaved sidewalks, plashy fields, are felt more by an invalid than by persons of robust health.

It seems to me that winter comes in to relieve the year of satiety. The mind grows sated with greenness. After eight or nine months of luxuriant growths, the eye grows accustomed to vegetation. To be sure, we never are less than pleased with the wide prospect; with forms of noble trees, with towns and meadows, and with the whole aspect of nature. But it is the pleasure of one pampered. We lose the keen edge of hunger. The eye enjoys without the relish of newness. We expect to enjoy. Everything loses surprise. Of course, the sky is blue, the grass succulent, the fields green, the trees umbrageous, the clouds silent and mysterious. They were so yesterday, they are so to-day, they will be so to-morrow, next week, next month. In short, the mind does not cease to feel the charm of endless growths, but needs variety, change of diet, less of perpetual feasting, and something of the blessings of a fast. This winter gives. It says to us: You have had too much. You are luxurious and dainty. You need relief and change of diet.

The cold blue of the sky, the cold gray of rocks, the sober warmth of browns and russets, take the place of more gorgeous colors. If, now, one will accept this change in the tone of nature, after a time a new and relishful pleasure arises. The month formed by the last fortnight of November and the first two weeks of December is, to me, the saddest of the year. It most nearly produces the sense of desolateness and dreariness of any portion of the year. From the hour that the summer begins to shorten its days, and register the increasing change along the horizon, over which the sun sets, farther and farther toward the south, we have a genial and gentle sadness. But sadness belongs to all very deep joys. It is almost as needful to the perfectness of joy, as shadows in landscapes are to the charm of the picture. Then, too, comes the fading out of flowers, — each variety in its turn saying, "Farewell till next summer." Scarcely less suggestive of departing summer are the new-comers, the late summer golden-rod, the asters, and all autumnal flowers. Long experience teaches us that these are the latest blossoms that fall from the sun's lap, and next to them is snow. By association we already see white in the yellow and blue. Then, too, birds are thinking of other things. No more nests, no more young, no more songs, except signal-notes and rallying-calls; for they are evidently warned, and go about their little remaining daily business as persons who expect every hour to depart to a distant land. It is scarcely ever that we see birds *go*. They are here to-day, and gone to-morrow. They disappear without observation. The fields are empty and silent. It seems as if the winds had blown them away with the leaves. The first sight of northern water-fowl, far up in air, retreating from Labrador and the short Arctic summer, is always to us like the declaration: Summer is gone, winter is behind us, it will soon be upon you. At last come the late days of November. All is gone, — frosts reap and glean more sharply every night. A few weeks bring earnest winter. Then begin to dawn other delights. The bracing air, the clean snow-paths, the sled and sleigh, the revelation of forms that all summer were grass-hidden; the sharp-out-lined hills lying clear upon the sky; the exquisite tracery of trees; especially of all such trees as that dendral child of God, the elm, whose branches are carried out into an endless complexity of fine lines of spray, and which stands up in winter showing in its whole anatomy that all its summer shade was founded upon the most substantial reality.

In winter, too, particularly in the latter periods of it, the extremities of shrubs and branches begin to take on ruddy hues, or purplish browns, and the eye knows that these are the first faint blushes of coming summer. Amidst snows and storms and sharp severity of frosts, the lover detects the color of his coming mistress. Now, too, we find how beautiful are the mosses in the woods; and under them we find solitary green leaves, that have laughed all winter because they had outwitted the frost. Wherever flowing springs gush from sheltered spots looking south, one will find many green edges, young grass, and some few tougher leaves. Now, too, in still days, the crow sings heavily through the air, cawing with a pleasing harshness. For dieting has performed its work. Your appetite is eager. A little now pleases you more than abundance did in August. Every tiny leaf is to you like a cedar of Lebanon.

All these things are unknown to dwellers in cities. It is nothing to them that a robin appeared for the first time yesterday morning, or that a bluebird sang over against the house. Some new *prima donna* exhausts their admiration. They are yet studying laces, and do not care for the fringe of swamps, for the first catkins of the willow. They are still coveting the stores of precious stones at the jewellers, and do not care for my ruby buds, and red dogwood, and scarlet winter berries, and ground pine, and partridge-berry leaves.

There is one sight of the country at about this time of the year — the first of March — that few have seen, or else they have passed it by as if it were not worthy of record. I mean the drapery of rocks in gorges, or along precipitous sides of hills or mountains. The seams of rock are the outlets of springs. The water trickling through is seized by the frost, and held fast in white enchantment. Every day adds to the length of the ice drapery. And as the surface is overlaid by new issuings, it is furred and fretted with silver-white chasings, the most exquisite. Thus one may find a succession, in a single gorge, of extraordinary ice-curtains, and pendent draperies, of varying lengths, of every fantastic form, of colors varying by thickness, or by the tinge of earth or rock shining through them.

In my boyhood I used to wander along these fairy halls imagining them to be now altars in long white draperies; now, grand cathedral pillars of white marble; then, long tapestries chased in white with arabesques and crinkled vines and leaves. Sometimes they seemed like gigantic bridal decorations, or like the robes of beings vast and high, hung in their wardrobes while they slept. But whatever fancy interpreted them, or whether they were looked upon with two good, sober, literal eyes, they were, and still are, among the most delightful of winter exhibitions to those who are wise enough to search out the hidden beauty of winter in the country.

STREET CRIES AND ORATORS' VOICES.

OBERT BONNER:—I am reminded of my duty, by hearing the boys in the streets crying out, "NEW YORK LEDGER!" with a saucy tone, as much as to say, "Have you got your ears open, sir? D' ye see, sir?" Did you ever take notice of the voices of men and boys that get their living by their lusty crying? A public speaker may well envy them. Public speakers seldom have great advantage over other men in voice, power, or quality. It is rare, rather than common, among the tens of thousands whose offices require public speaking, to hear a man of a commanding voice, or to find a speaker whose tones are smooth, unlabored, and yet penetrating. Some men are boisterous and vociferous, that they may give force to their sentences. But that gun does not carry a ball the farthest that makes the most noise in going off. The crack of a rifle is anything but noisy. Such is the want of good voice capital, that men are always talking about good speaking-rooms, and the acoustic properties of lecture-rooms. But the best of all properties in a speaking-hall is, a man that knows how to speak, and has something to speak with! What does a rooster care for acoustic aids? He mounts a fence lustily, gives a preliminary flap of his wings, as if to say, "I could have flown twice as high," and then lets off a crow that rings and echoes for a mile around. A bull will sound you a bass note that would make old Westminister Abbey

shake. A crow will caw to you at two miles distance without the fear of bronchitis. A dog will bark to a whole town without the slightest inconvenience — to himself. And yet men who are brought up to speaking as the business of their lives cannot make themselves heard at a hundred feet distance, or, only by exertions that send them home for liniments, bandages, and caustic!

It does not follow because a bird can fly, that a man can, it may be said, and that the vigor of bird and beast in vocal organs is no fair analogy for men. But it becomes so, when it is observed that men who have vigor of body, who live much in the open air, and who practise their voice in the free, open outdoors, come to have the same resonance and almost the same power that is found in animals. A ploughboy can be heard over a whole neighborhood; an ox-driver of the old sort needed no horn to let people know that he was driving into town. Far off his coming *sounds.* Military men and shipmasters attain to great power of propagating sounds. It may be said, that, though such persons are able to eject single orders, or sentences, they could not sustain the fatigue of a continuous delivery for an hour.

But newsboys, old-clothes men, all street-cryers, and, above all, chimney-sweeps, have voices in exercise from morning till night, that are full, round, and often rich and melodious. There used to be in Brooklyn a chimney-sweep whose voice I coveted more than his trade or complexion. I was walking one day along Orange Street, toward the Heights, when the whole air seemed full and overflowing with a sound as smooth, round, and melodious as an organ diapason. It fairly rained down for abundance and universality. The houses reflected it. The streets were channels in which the airy stream flowed. I looked in every direction for the cause. No man seemed the author. I looked up and down the street, turned around to every quarter, — for the sound came equally from everywhere, — until at length, mounted upon the chimney-top of one of the highest houses, sat the fellow like a king on his throne. Astride of the stack, lowering or pulling up his scraping machine, he was perched like a blackbird indeed; but much more musical! Ah, did I not have to lay fast hold of the commandments, to save myself from coveting? This fellow, without doubt, if he ever lived in a pre-existent state, was an organ-pipe, and the divinities gave him life, and changed his bellows to lungs, as a reward of merit.

But to return from Ethiopia: —

These newsboys show what out-of-door practice will do for a man's lungs. Here is a lawyer who can hardly fill a court-room. What would he do if he had a long street before him? What would the pale and feeble-speaking minister do, who can scarcely make his voice reach two hundred auditors, if he were set to cry "New York Ledger"? These newsboys stand at the head of a street, and send down their voice through it, as an athlete would roll a ball down an alley. We advise men training for speaking-professions to peddle wares in the streets for a little time. Young ministers might go into partnership with newsboys awhile, till they got their mouths open, and their larynx nerved and toughened.

The great want of public speakers is *general vigor.*

They need open air, toughening exercise, practice of speaking under the skies, — *speaking*, not *bawling*. A man may tear his voice up by the roots, by too much of a gale. There is such a thing as *speaking at a mark!* With the same tone, let a man practise, removing the hearer step by step each day, till, with the same exertion, he can be heard at great distances. In this way he will develop *quality* of tone. For in speaking it is *quality* and not *quantity* that gives control of an audience.

BE GENEROUS OF BEAUTY.

IF there be one thing that marks the Divine benevolence in the administration of the natural world, it is the openness, and, if one may so say, the free benevolence with which *beauty* is made to be the property and solace of all men. It is provided above and beneath, in every form, in all substances, so that, whoever has hunger for it cannot well fail to find food for his want. Many desirable things are rare. Only skill can gain them; only great wealth can purchase them. The possession of libraries, pictures, sculpture, decorated grounds, must be limited to the few. They are a fortunate aristocracy. But, fortunately for the great multitude, the gifts of God in nature are without money and without price.

There is a duty implied in the possession of treasures of beauty. No selfishness seems to us so endless, and so peculiarly base, as that which refuses to men the innocent enjoyment of the treasures of beauty. It may not be wise to lend books, or to be free with things which, passing from hand to hand, may be lost, damaged, or misappropriated. We do not blame any one for making his library, museum, or picture collection *stationary*. But whoever has that which can confer pleasure and profit for merely the looking at it must be selfish indeed to hide it from hungry eyes. If it were money to be lent, raiment to be worn, food to be eaten, or any usage that wastes or diminishes the treasure, the case would be different. But what harm comes to garden, grounds, picture, or statue, by being looked at? The eyes wear out nothing! Ten million men have gazed upon Raffaelle's Sistine Madonna and Transfiguration, and soiled them not, nor chafed nor dulled their surface. Not half so softly does the dew steal upon the flower; not half so lightly does it rest there, as does the eye rest upon objects of beauty!

Nothing can make others so rich, without diminishing our own means, as generosity in the use of art-treasures, or materials of beauty. What then shall we say of men whose houses are stored with rare and curious books which they secrete? There are men who take a pride in owning works possessed by almost no one else, and then in hiding them from curious eyes. There are those who act as if things were unfitted for their own pleasure if they had also given pleasure to any one else.

What shall be said of a man who, by mere force of money, has come into possession of some picture, or other work of art, which embodies the noblest thoughts of an artist's divine genius, and then veils it from the world, locks it up for his selfish gaze, and virtually annihilates it?

It is creditable to our people that, generally, a man who has anything that is worth another's attention, is more than willing to throw it open to all proper and reasonable scrutiny. Many private collections of pictures in New York and vicinity are generously placed, on certain days of every week, before any that desire to see them. But exceptions there are. It is said that some of Turner's most striking pictures in New York cannot be seen; that curious and excessively rare copies of Bibles have been hidden up with a miser's greed, and that scholars and gentlemen seeking access to them have been rudely repulsed. A money miser is bad enough. A picture-miser, a book-miser, is yet more abject!

There is another thing worthy of consideration, and that is, a certain freedom *of private grounds*. Gentlemen's places are springing up in every direction. Great skill is employed in developing the finest effects in landscape, garden, bower, and shrubbery. We cannot be so unreasonable as to ask that one shall divest himself of all privacy and seclusion, and make his grounds a common; but a regulated liberty of courteous intrusion is peculiarly proper and graceful in the possessors of fine grounds.

But, whatever may be a man's judgment as to admission, he must be a curmudgeon who insists upon it that neither the foot *nor the eye* shall intrude upon the beauty of his domain. In planting one's grounds it is fair, by hedge or thicket, to shut out too much gazing, — all unsightly objects, noise, and dust, by thick trees or fences. But a system of seclusion, that yields no part of a man's grounds to the sight of passers-by, cannot be justified. It is a wanton selfishness. A lawn and garden lying upon the street, but separated from it by a high, close fence, or impervious wall, so that little children, the poor, laborers, common people of all kinds, cannot see the treasures within, ought to be made an offence against good manners. It is an immorality, to be abated by a public sentiment. Can anything be more charming than to see a child's face set between two pickets, like a sweet picture in a frame, wistfully looking at beds of flowers, vines, and trees?

Methinks the gentle thoughts and grateful silence of hundreds, every day, who pass open gardens, and cultivated yards, must be more pleasurable to the indulgent owner than the fragrance of all his flowers. Nothing can well redeem the possession of beauty in a large degree, from the charge of sinful self-indulgence, but such a use of it as shall confer pleasure on all those who need the solace and ministration of the divine element of beauty.

TRAILING ARBUTUS.

ON this tenth day of April I have been out on the hills near Elmira, to see what is going on among the citizens of the vegetable kingdom. A basket, a garden trowel, a pair of thick gloves, and a stout, seamless cloth overcoat were my outfit. The ground was white in spots with half-melted snow. A few whirls of snow had come down in the night, and the air was too cold to change it to rain. Some green leaves, in sheltered nooks, had accepted the advances of the sun, and were preparing for the summer. But that which I came to search after was the *trailing arbutus*, one of the most exquisite of all Nature's fondlings.

I did not seek in vain. The hills were covered with it. Its gay whorls of buds peeped out from ruffles of snow, in the most charming beauty. Many blossoms, too, quite expanded, did I find, some pure white, and a few most delicately suffused with pink. For nearly an hour I wandered up and down, in pleasant fancies, searching, plucking, and arranging these most beautiful of all early blossoms.

Who would suspect by the *leaf* what rare delicacy was to be in the blossom? Like some people of plain and hard exterior, but of sweet disposition, it was all the more pleasant from the surprise of contrast. All winter long this little thing must have slumbered with *dreams*, at least, of spring. It has waited for no pioneer or guide, but started of its own self, and led the way for all the flowers on this hill-side.

Its little viny stem creeps close to the ground, humble, faithful, and showing how the purest white may lay its cheek on the very dirt, without soil or taint.

The odor of the arbutus is exquisite, and as delicate as the plant is modest. Some flowers seem determined to make an impression on you. They stare at you. They dazzle your eyes. If you smell them, they overfill your sense with their fragrance. They leave nothing for your gentleness and generosity, but do everything themselves. But this sweet nestler of the spring hills is so secluded, half covered with russet leaves, that you would not suspect its graces, did you not stoop to uncover the vine, to lift it up, and then you espy its secluded beauty. If you smell it, at first it seems hardly to have an odor. But there steals out of it at length the finest, rarest scent, that rather excites desire than satisfies your sense. It is coy, without designing to be so, and its reserve plays upon the imagination far more than could a more positive way.

Without doubt, there are intrinsic beauties in plants and flowers, and yet very much of pleasure depends upon their relations to the seasons, to the places where they grow, and to our own moods. No midsummer flower can produce the thrill that the earliest blossoms bring which tell us that winter is gone, that growing days have come! Indeed, it often happens that the air is cold, and the face of the earth brown, so that we have no suspicion that it is time for anything to sprout, until we chance upon a flower. That reveals what our senses had failed to perceive, — a warmth in the air, a warmth in the soil, an advance in the seasons! Strange, that a silent, white flower, growing on a hill-side, measures the astronomic changes, and, more than all our senses, discerns that the sun is travelling back from his far southward flight! Sometimes we admire flowers for their boldness, in cases where that quality seems fit. When meadows and fields are gorgeous, we look for some flower that shall give the climax. An intensity often serves to reveal the nature of things in all their several gradations. A violet color in these early spring days would not please half so well as these pure whites or tender pinks. We like snow-drops and crocuses to come up pale-colored, as if born of the snow, and carrying their mother's complexion. But later, when the eye is used to blossoms, we wish deeper effects and profusions of color, which, had they existed earlier, would have offended us.

Flowers seem to have peculiar power over some natures. Of course, they gratify the original faculties of form, color, odor; but that is the least part of their effect. They have a mysterious and subtile influence upon the feelings, not unlike some strains of music. They relax the tenseness of the mind. They dissolve its rigor. In their presence, one finds almost a magnetic tremulousness, as if they were messengers from the spirit-world, and conveyed an atmosphere with them in which the feelings find soothing, pleasure, and peacefulness. Besides this, they are provocative of imagination. They set the mind full of fancies. They seem to be pretty and innocent jugglers, that play their charms and incantations upon the senses and the fancy, and lead off the thoughts in many a curious wondery, in gay analogies, or curious medleys of fantastic dreamings.

Well, I have much more to say, if I should say all that I have thought, and all that the arbutus said to me, this wintry spring morning. But, since I cannot bring you here, Mr. Bonner, to let you see the hill and all its little jewels, I send you one of the blossom clusters, to wear in your button-hole; and when you go home, and, very properly, are asked, "Robert, who gave you that token?" — don't you tell.

MORALS OF BARGAINS.

DID you ever hear a company of good people, as the world goes, recounting their adventures in the purchase of goods? They shall be persons who would shrink from untruth, and yet more from an overt dishonesty. Yet have you never witnessed the great delight and almost exultation with which they narrate the *cheapness* of their bargain? Is the fair market price of cloth one dollar a yard, they ask your congratulations because they bought it for fifty cents a yard! Is the rich figured silk worth two dollars, with a glow of undisguised pleasure they tell you that they paid but one dollar a yard! Is a horse bought for half his value, — a carriage for one third of what it cost but a week before, — a house for less than half it cost the bankrupt owner to build it, — there are few persons so honest as not to feel that the acquisition has an added worth by this very buying it for less than it is worth.

Now we do not pretend to say that one should never buy things for less than their real value; that one should never avail himself of depreciated prices. But what is the *disposition* which makes men rejoice in such bargains? Is a picture worth two hundred and fifty dollars, for which you paid but fifty? You have obtained goods *without paying a fair equivalent.* Every really honest man should always pay a fair equivalent for whatever he possesses. The wish to get property without equitable service, or full and fair consideration, is not honest. It is certainly true that property may lose its value in commercial fluctuations, and that real estate, personal property, and money itself, may from time to time change its value; and every man has a right to take property at the value which it has at the time of purchase, without regard to what a former value may have been. But this is very different from that spirit which seeks to beat down property below its value; to take advantage of temporary necessities, to *desire*, even, to get hold of another man's property without paying for it what it ought, in a given state of market, to command. *No man should wish another man's property without rendering for it a full equivalent.*

Now it is our impression that honest people (in their own opinion honest) do habitually desire to get more than they give. They wish to obtain *something* for *nothing*. They jew, chaffer, higgle, and manage, with that peculiar wisdom implied in the term "bargaining," to obtain goods without paying for them what they ought to pay. They glory in success. They narrate the steps by which they ensnare the bargain. They hunt for coveted goods as if they were wild animals, and to be obtained by adroitness and cunning, without any regard to justice and fairness. A merchant is a man who has goods. A customer is a man who wishes to get possession of them. And he seems to think it to be a mere trial of sharp practice between them, without any moral principle to govern the transaction. But if to desire a neighbor's goods without paying for them is *coveting*, why is not a wish to obtain them at less than a fair price, in its own degree, just as surely coveting?

There are few people who will not be benefited by pondering over the morals of shopping. The wish to get more than you have means to pay for is a wish to injure your neighbor, — to obtain his possessions without a just compensation. And although, occasionally, a thing may come into our hands which we could never have had had it not been cheap, yet the uniform *desire* to depress another's property for the sake of making it our own is dishonesty in disposition, whether custom sanctions it or not.

OUTLANDISH BOOKS.

IT is good to walk through an antiquarian bookstore. There is a great deal to be learned from books without reading them. The histories which books *contain* are, often, not half so interesting or so instructive as the histories which books themselves *are*. As often as the spring comes, and work is less imperious, and warmer days set loose the wild and yearning imaginations of the soul, as the air sets loose the roots and frees the flowers from their long imprisonment, we feel a roving mood. The fields are too far off, and a solitary sea-side is not to be found in the vicinity of this great commercial city. Picture-galleries are few, and the people in them many; and one scarcely knows where to find the quiet and the meditative incitements which he wants.

At such times I stroll into one of those establishments, now so numerous, that import and sell second-hand books. The moment that one is across the threshold he feels that he has changed worlds. All the clamor of the street, the ceaseless passage and clash of innumerable vehicles, the confusion of voices, seem smothered to a low and gentle hum, and even that is forgotten in a moment. Then one walks up and down the passages lined with books, the alcoves of books, the long tables thick with books, the corners stocked and heaped with books, as if this were a city of books, in ruins, like some Oriental city of desolation. All languages are here, and all of them are dumb. Their silent symbols hold up hieroglyphic significance to such eyes as may chance to know them. But as one might stand over a tomb, and muse who was laid therein, of what nature, disposition, history; of what experience of woe or joy in life; with what hopes, thoughts, ambitions, struggles, failures, or evanescent victories; so do we stand by the side of a book in an unknown language. What means this title-page? What are the words of introduction? Open to the middle: is this a story, an argument, a criticism, a history? Is it a grave affirmation of mighty truth, such as Bacon would have plucked down for heavenly thoughts? or is it some jester, that flashes his momentary say, and waits for an answering laughter? How causeless are causes here. These words that have fallen on many a soul like a bow on the violin, and caused vivid emotions to spring forth from their touch, are now reaching toward my eye, but without a response. They touch, but I do not sound. They are like winds blowing among petrified trees whose leaves are fast and whose branches are stiffened forever. But though their glory is gone, once they were sovereigns. This well-thumbed volume has once been a favorite. It has been the last thing consulted before sleep; a solace to lucid intervals; perhaps often a companion of journeys. Or when the new grass was soft to pavement-worn feet, and the solitary scholar has wan dered out to hear blackbirds sing by the side of spring-swollen streams, or to search for cowslips in the watery edges of the marsh lands, under his arm, but with affectionate care, goes this welcome companion. A book *is* good company. It is full of conversation without loquacity. It comes to your longing with full instruction, but pursues you never. It is not offended at your absent-mindedness, nor jealous if you turn to other pleasures, of leaf, or dress, or mineral, or even of books. It silently serves the soul without recompense, not even for the hire of love. And yet more noble, it seems to pass from itself, and to enter the memory, and to hover in a silvery transfiguration there, until the outward book is but a body, and its soul and spirit are flown to you, and possess your memory like a spirit. And while some books, like steps, are left behind us by the very help which they yield us, and serve only our childhood, or early life, some others go with us in mute fidelity to the end of life, a recreation for fatigue, an instruction for our sober hours, and a solace for our sickness or sorrow. Except the great out-doors, nothing that has no life of its own gives so much life to you.

And here are these uncomplaining favorites, now tumbled in heaps, or keeping dusty company in this great catacomb of literature! No gentle hand now fondles them, no eye searches them. They are foreigners, strangers in a strange land. But, peradventure, there yet shall come a dried and wrinkled man, poor in garb, as befits so poor a purse, and, wandering up and down among these silent souls imprisoned in ink and paper words, who, seeking this dusky volume, shall renew his youth of joy, greet a loving, absent friend, go and sell all that he hath to buy this pearl of price to him, and faintly kindle again in his heavy, dark heart the light of a long-lost treasure.

But really, Mr. Bonner, will you be kind enough to give me a nudge? Will you do me the kindness to tread on my foot, and tell me that I am wandering? In sooth, I have not said one of the fine fancies that led me to begin. So much the worse, you will say, for those that have the reading of them hereafter!

THE DANDELION AND I.

NOT the first blossom, but the first *dandelion* of the year came to us on the seventeenth of April! Golden-faced and most welcome! Not the earliest of flowers, for the woods are full of spring beauties, anemones, and others. The willow has put forth its queer, mulberry-shaped blossom. But there is something so bright and cheerful in the dandelion that its first coming is always watched and waited for with great eagerness, and greeted with enthusiasm. It is not a fragrant flower, neither is it often gathered for the house or hand. It soon shuts up when picked. But it is the first real democratic flower of our season. The field violets are yet reluctant. The wood flowers fight the lingering cold from behind fences, from leaves, and under partial protection. The sanguinaria, or Indian puccoon, is not yet sending its pure white blossom from its blood-red root, like a noble soul rising from a battle-stained body. The ground is too cold for the marsh marigold or cowslip of New England, far-famed as "greens."

The dandelion is the first conspicuous, hardy, wide-spread, and abundant flower of spring. It grows in all places; on hills, in the meadow, in town and city, as well as country. It gives one a sudden start in going down a barren, stony street, to see upon a narrow strip of grass, just within the iron fence, the radiant dandelion shining in the grass, like a spark dropped from the sun! It stirs up the thoughts and tells us what is going on in the heavens and on the earth, unbeknown to us who are pent up in cities. Why, if dandelions have come, then birds are mated; nests are repairing or building; swallows are coming, and wrens and phœbes have come! Bluebirds and robins and song-sparrows must have become familiar sights to country people by this time of the year. We reach our hand through after that solitary dandelion. It is too far off. All eager persons measure the length of their arm by their eye, and will not believe how short it is, under three or four tryings.

Is it stealing to take a dandelion through the fence? Then we have made a gap in the Commandments a good many times. But are ethical rules quite as rigid upon dandelions as upon ducats and dollars? At any rate, we have never had remorse for pulling the first dandelion — if we could reach it. There is a little ambition in the matter. Several pairs of eyes besides our own have a gentle rivalry and competition for the first golden disc.

People watch us, and wonder what we can be at. Two or three gentlemen, thinking there must be something important that attracts us, stop and look over, and seeing what it is, scarcely disguise with politeness their contempt for a man hunting dandelions. Newsboys edge up familiarly. "Wat ye lost, mister? — Sha'n't I jump over and hunt it?" It needs no hunting, lad, — here it shines in the grass like a golden eagle in a miser's eye. And as for picking it *for* me, that would just take away half the pleasure. I want to feel the moist, cool stem with my own fingers, — to slide down the touch to its very root, and with the nail gently to cut it, without prejudice to the half-dozen buds that nestle there like so many baby heads in a crib. I could reach it with a stick, but that would be profanation. A kind old gentleman passes, and smiles sympathetically, as if he would say, "Ah, — I understand all that, — I like you a great deal better for your enthusiasm," and he passes on, himself almost as handsome as a dandelion.

No. Though I reached at least two inches farther than before, I could only just touch, but not pluck it! Some chubby-faced children want to see what it is, and, a little shy of me, stand at some distance, with their sweet faces framed in between the iron pickets. Yes, dear things, that is just the way of the world into which you have entered. Flowers on one side, children on the other, and iron fences between! Yet you will find some flowers on *your* side of the fence too by and by, I hope.

I *will* try a forked stick! Where is there one? A stick! — stones enough, dirt enough, bricks, shavings, beams, and planks. But *sticks* are rare things in a city. O, the country is the place to live in. You can always find a stick! I am in two troubles. I cannot get my dandelion without a stick, and I cannot find a stick. If I go off for one, somebody will get my flower!

Some school-girls are going past, — one, two, three, four, five, the last one silent and alone; the rest like a tree full of birds, making a jargon of music, and cross-firing of sweet discordances. They look at me, and then at each other. The creatures see the ludicrous side of this affair! They hope for me, and really sympathize, I know. Yet witches, they scarcely care to hide their laughter, which, at half-a-dozen steps, breaks out like water pent up that has found a new channel to gurgle in!

Shall I climb this ailanthus-tree for a stick? I would in a minute if it were only in the country. That 's another objection to a city life. Nobody is surprised in the country to see a man up a tree. But in a city, a gentlemanly person making his way up into a tree would have a motley crowd around him in a jiffy! (Mr. Bonner, can you tell your readers, in your column of Answers to Correspondents, just the measure of time meant by "jiffy"?) And no wonder, come to think of it. The act of climbing is one of adroitness rather than of gracefulness. First, a jump and a good hug with the arms. Then, drawing up the legs, the knees clasp each side of the tree, the feet touching each other at a point that would be intersected by a line drawn through the spine and extended. You are in posture. You resemble a frog drawn up for a spring, and set up endways. Next, you straighten up and raise your arms a ring higher. Then holding fast by them, like an inch-worm, you bring on the other half. After two or three jerks, you will begin to put one leg around the tree, so that the calf shall clasp the back side and the shin scrape itself on the other. And as you go up, so do the legs of your pantaloons, which, at ten feet, are corrugated around your knees in a manner that will give your skin and the bark of the tree a fair chance to see which is toughest. And about this time it is a curious fact that most men begin to quirl their tongue out of the corners of their mouths, as if that were a great help to them. Now I decline doing all this in a city, with policemen musing whether I am to be arrested for insanity, and my neighbors laughing, and boys cheering me, and sundry unsavory jests broken on me,—not even for a *stick* will I so expose myself. Cities are hateful. Nobody can do anything but just walk up and down the streets; everybody afraid that everybody will laugh if anybody acts as he wants to! Ah, sweet herald of coming summer! there you nest yourself in the grass, unconscious of all this disturbance in my breast! The church over opposite, built high and grand of carved stone, with windows full of painted saints, throws its great shadow toward you; but tell me, dear little flower, did it ever say "God bless you!" to such a useless thing of God's making as you? Ah, dandelion, what do you think of those saints in the window? Do you hear or feel that organ whose solemn tones jar the very ground? Do you need priests and Sabbaths and choirs to help you worship Him that made you? or, with sweet-faced simplicity, is it needful for you only to open your bosom, and God is praised by your blossoming beauty? Yet do not deride the cathedral, O dandelion! Men need them, though flowers do not!

But what shall I do? Can I not throw a lasso at its neck, and noose it? To be defeated now would be ignominious indeed! Why not climb over? What if I should slip and get caught on the top of these iron spikes? A dainty spectacle! If only half-way over I should be no better off than on this side, and certainly no better *on*.

Must I relinquish the thing? What! baffled by a dandelion? I, a freeman, with pride of faculty, touching the stars by my reason and imagination, and not able to touch that dandelion! No. Have it I must!

Have it I did!

ORAL FARMING.

T is now May 4. Not only has spring come, but the full farming spring. And as your humble servant (as very proud people call themselves) is now a Peekskill farmer, living by the sweat of his (hired workmen's) brow, how can you expect anything from him except of crops, of sorts, of fertilizers? Indeed, sir, my grass-lands look remarkably well, considering the backwardness of the season. I have rolled them, top-dressed them, and given them the best advice in my power. Let the moss keep away! Away all thistles; and, above all, that thistliest of all thistles, which is, doubtless, the very one sent originally to sharpen Adam, — the Canada-thistle! Let no dock come forth; and, ox-eyed daisies, fair as is your great moon face, and beautiful as you certainly are to unsophisticated eyes, a mowing-lot is no place for you. Meantime, let the Timothy shoot up its stem, bearing a cat-tailed head, only less for horses than oats themselves! Prince of all grasses for fodder, may the season be propitious for thee! Let dews moisten thy cat-tailed head, and frequent rains thy roots, until July comes riding to thee in a mower. Then bow thy head, — die as meekly as thou hast gracefully lived; for is not glory before thee? Thy slender stem shall be changed to horses' legs; thy blades shall beam forth from the mild eye of my Alderney; thou shalt come forth white as milk, and thence, yellow as butter or rich as cheese!

But now, shall the mowing-lot rest? Is its work

done? Not if properly constructed. The Timothy will seldom give a second growth worth cutting. It ought not to be pastured, because cattle pull up the tufts by the root. But if a due admixture of other grasses has been made, no sooner is the first crop gone than four or five other kinds of quick-springing grasses will come again; and if the soil be in good heart, a second; and if irrigated or watered from a cart, a third crop may be cut.

But really, you will imagine that this is a communication from some president of an agricultural society! I am not a president of anything, — not even a member. But you know that I am in the first love of a spring farming campaign! It is not hot yet. I have actually been working with my own hands! O, the apple-trees set! the pear-trees — standards and on quince — that are prophesying to me from the side of the hill! Not a leaf is on them; and yet I see Seckels, Bartletts, D'Angoulêmes, and Rostiezers, (and Sir Seckel had better look out for its supremacy when such pears as the Rostiezer come along!) Will you not come up and eat pears with me? Not this summer! But when the trees come into bearing! What if the engagement promises to be some years hence? Shall we not both be a little older, and wiser, and, losing nothing of our relish for good fruit, shall we not be able to hold a more grave and profitable conversation while sitting on the balcony, eating?

But ah! the corn that I intend having! I have arranged to beat the field over the way all hollow. The fact is, I quite look down on the neighbor at the foot of my lane. He won't cut away the trees in his yard that hide from his parlor windows the broad Hudson! Can such a man raise corn? I have moved my corn-field right down to the road, so that everybody can see it, and especially the man over the way! It will not do for people that wish to thrive to lie awake mornings, looking out of their windows at woodchucks. Good corn can be had at Peekskill only by enterprise and industry. Now I have made an arrangement with my conductor, that if this crop of corn succeeds, it is to be my cultivation; but if it turns out indifferently, is to be *his* work. May cut-worms spare it! May all these loads of benevolence-to-grain, hauled with so much trouble and expense, lie low through the summer, under the roots, but shoot their vigor up the stem to the very tasselled top! Let no drouth come before mid-August, and then corn will laugh at it, and shake its jolly head in defiance. Shall I insert along the rows a few of those round-bellied pumpkins, — the genuine, old-fashioned Yankee pumpkins? Some say not, and some say, do. I hesitate. Ought the same soil to feed two crops at the same time? And yet, how quaint and pleasant, in autumn, as the blades of corn grow russet, are the yellow orbs that shine out! What instant thoughts do they suggest to the passer-by of pumpkin-pies, of Thanksgiving days, of old New England homes! But I must close, and it shall be with a story.

Good old Dr. Bigger (we will call him) was a Baptist preacher in Indiana, and never liked to have any one beat him in telling a round, full-proportioned story. A wag seeing him coming down the street, said to his cronies: "Now I mean to stump that old gentleman." So, on his approach, he says: "Doctor,

I really wish you had seen a piece of land I have on White River. I planted corn and pumpkins on five acres, and when I cut off the corn, the pumpkins were so thick along the ground, that I could step from one to another across the whole field!" The Doctor, nothing loath, drew up, and, eying him a moment, broke forth: "Why, sir, that was very well, but *I* had a ten-acre field this fall on which the pumpkins lay so close to each other that when I stood at one corner, and hit one pumpkin with my foot, it *jarred* the whole ten acres!" Can anybody around Peekskill raise better pumpkins than that?

DRY FISHING.

MY DEAR MR. BONNER: Allow me to invite you to go with me a dry-fishing. What is dry-fishing? Not one in a water-tight boat; nor on high-bank streams; nor on white, dry gravel along the edges of pools. I practise it in this wise. If you will come with me, you shall have your share. Let us go into Conroy's. Now don't strike out that name for fear the LEDGER will be thought advertising his establishment. I wish the name to stand. I repeat it, for I have many associations of pleasant hours there. Come, then, with me to Conroy's. A modest front! Only a net, a decoy duck, a few cane-poles, and some other fishing-stuff, to hint to you that April has come, and that every honest man is expected to do his duty. Enter.

Behold a long room, stocked on either side with things innumerable, needless and necessary for the practice of the royal art! On the right stand rows of trouting-rods, the best in their cases with the lower end of the cloth rolled up, like a boy's trousers in summer, revealing the polished brass or German-silver ferules and joints. Ah, what do *you* see? Only those cloth cases, and the half-concealed trouting-rods? But I see more. I see a boy, fresh, ruddy, unperverted, brave-hearted. If rude, only so from a frank, honest way of forethinking nothing for deceit. Him the benign father has promised on his thirteenth birthday a real Conroy's rod. He has dreamed of it. At length the day comes. It is his. The reel, the silk line, the fine leading lines, the hooks, the cunning flies, the basket, all are his! See the lad walk out into the street. Nobody can give him anything now! What are princes? Who are kings? Boys, undoubtedly. They are the only royal persons. Kings in empire, all the air and all the earth are theirs for enjoying! Kings without crowns or cares, they! He walks the street homeward, pitying beggar-boys that have no fathers to give them fishing-rods! He pities merchants and bankers that, having money, lack sense to buy rods and lines! He walks into the house before the admiring family, to display his treasures! I see him in the country. It is scarce four in the morning, but he is up. The east is beginning to turn white and red. He is off for the brook. It comes down from the far hills, and winds its way silently with many a twist and turn in the meadows. Ah, glorious morning on the meadows! Sleep on, lazy folks yet in bed; God reserves these royalties of the morning for honest work-folk that rise early, for birds that never sing as they do before sunrise, and for bold, truth-loving boys, that forswear sleep and forget food, that they may wind through these meadows in the light of sunrise! The rod is put together, the reel in place, the long line flashes in the air like a spider's thread, the daintiest bit of a fly at the end of it, portends mischief. My dear boy, tread softly. The very weight of your free foot will impart a jar to the earth that trout understand. The wise ones are always large and fat and shy. Give the grass a pressure, but not a stroke with your foot. There. See the light flash in that water at the turn. Something is tickling it, for see the ripples that smile over its face. Then the boy makes his first cast. He poises himself. Measures the distance. Dexterously swinging the long lash, he puts the fly pat upon the very spot. Another ripple flashes up. Our boy slings back the line, with a bright fellow shining and shivering through air, and flung a dozen rods behind him, where he flounces and squirms, vainly endeavoring to swim in the wet grass! Excuse the overeager twitch. The boy is nervous yet. He will sober down to his work, for he must fish a full two hours here, clear up to that bridge, up past that gaunt tree that is dead all but one branch, which holds a few leaves in its hands like a pocket-handkerchief, and up to the alder-thicket. By that time his basket will be full and his stomach empty, of which facts he will be more and more conscious at every step as he goes home. But who comes? The sun is driving its flocks up the mountain-side, which we should take to be mists, did we not know that those hills are the sun-pastures for aerial breeds of unsheared sheep, that feed of nights and are driven home of days! But come back, Mr. Bonner, to the store. In this glass case see the nameless traps and fixings for all manner of uses! Here are flasks, leather-covered. I never could imagine why it was necessary to cover flasks so elaborately for the purpose of carrying milk. Do you suppose that water is cooler or milk sweeter for it! But here, too, are eating arrangements for picnics, drinking-cups, and all manner of things that lift up before our eyes the vision of summer woods, of bonnets laid off, of merry, laughing people, among rocks and trees, by the side of a clear, bubbling spring, where youth and beauty spend a joyous hour!

Those spear-heads, too, — fish-spears. Did you ever go a suckering at night, Mr. Bonner? Then you have something good before you yet. We will have a burning torch in one hand, our spear in the other, and enter on a good wide, but not too deep river, about eight or nine at night. Begin below, and work your way up. You are dressed for wetting. Now step cautiously along, searching by your light for fish, which you shall see soon moving as in a dream, down below the water, along the stones, or pausing upon a few gravel spots, their mouths playing with a sucking motion, as if the whole stream were their mother, and they were feeding at the breast. These are true philosophers! How coolly they take life. No newspapers disturb their tranquillity. They sow not, nor reap. Plough and sickle are unknown below the water. No washing-days have they, nor hanging out of clothes to dry! No dust in their eyes, unless some impertinent mill lets sawdust into the stream! No insects buzz about them, neither do flies nor mosquitos annoy their sleep. Their beds are always ready, their raiment is always clean without washing, they spread no table and wash up no dishes. Combs are a superfluity. Books are never dry down where the fish live! Happy people! Your caudal fin is better than Ericsson's propeller up stream, and down stream the river itself bears you without toil. If I were a fish, I think I should take up a travelling business. But we must attend to duty. There is a call for that fish right under you! With a dull grating sound, down comes your transfixing spear, and he is fast in the middle, and very lively at both ends. Invert your spear. Basket him. And as you look up at the lifted spear, see the overhanging trees above you. No man knows what fairy trees are, until he has stood at night underneath them, with a strong light cast *up* into them from below. Stand a moment. There are oaks and chestnuts, vast and wide outstretching. Their roots drink here a full supply. Are not these fairy bowers? A breath of wind moves the leaves. They dance in the green twilight, up there, like sylphs. A moving leaf lets through a star, and another, as if diamonds hung in the tree. Out on either bank the air is dark. The stream gurgles and plashes about your feet. The torchlit tree overhead, the somnolent twilights down under water, all bewitch you from your work, and set you a fishing for other things than suckers. Your companions are shouting for you. No such romance detains them. They have caught ten fish to your one. But will your basket reveal *all* that you have caught? But, Mr. Bonner, I put my hand on your shoulder and give you a shake. See. We have not been out of the store at all. This has all been Dry Fishing! There is much more besides. There are shark-hooks, there are sea-gaffs, there are nets, all manner of lines, of cords. I could take you a Dry Fishing to Newfoundland Banks, away up to Labrador, or on the Thousand Islands, or the St. Lawrence, or along the weirs and herring of Eastport and Lubeck. But I forbear, lest some say that, if dry fishing is no better than dry writing, the less there is of it the better!

APPLE-TREES IN LOVE.

IT makes no difference that you have seen forty or fifty springs; each one is as new, every process as fresh, and the charm as fascinating as if you had never witnessed a single one. Nature works the same things without seeming repetition. There, for instance, is the apple-tree. Every year since our boyhood it has been doing the same thing; standing low to the ground, with a round and homely head, without an element of grandeur or poetry, except once a year. In the month of May, apple-trees go a courting. Love is evermore father of poetry. And the month of May finds the orchard no longer a plain, sober, business affair, but the gayest and most radiant frolicker of the year. We have seen human creatures whose ordinary life was dutiful and prosaic. But when some extraordinary excitement of grief, or, more likely, of deep love, had thoroughly mastered them, they broke forth into a richness of feeling, an inspiration of sentiment, that mounted up into the very kingdom of beauty, and for the transient hour they glowed with the very elements of poetry. And so to us seems an apple-tree. From June to May, it is a homely, duty-performing, sober, matter-of-fact tree. But May seems to stir up a love heat in its veins. The old round-topped, crooked-trunked, and ungainly-boughed fellow drops all world-ways, and takes to itself a new idea of life. Those little stubbed spurs, that, all the year, had seemed like rheumatic fingers, or thumbs and fingers stiffened and stubbed by work, now are transformed. Forth put they a little head of buds, which a few rains and days of encouraging warmth solicit to a cluster of blossoms. At first rosy and pink, then opening purely white. And now, where is your old homely tree? All its crookedness is hidden by the sheets of blossoms. The whole top is changed to a royal dome. The literal, fruit-bearing tree is transfigured, and glows with raiment whiter and purer than any white linen. It is a marvel and a glory! What if you have seen it before, ten thousand times over? An apple-tree in full blossom is like a message, sent fresh from heaven to earth, of purity and beauty! We walk around it reverently and admiringly. We are never tired of looking at its profusion. Homely as it ordinarily is, yet now it speaks of the munificence of God better than any other tree. The oak proclaims strength and rugged simplicity. The hickory grown in open fields speaks a language of gentility. The pine is a solitary, stately fellow. Even in forests, each tree seems alone, and has a sad, Castilian-like pride. The elm is a prince. Grace and glory are upon its head. In our Northern fields it has no peer. But none of these speak such thoughts of abundance, such prodigal and munificent richness, such lavish, unsparing generosity, as this samo plain and homely apple-tree. The very glory of God seems resting upon it! It is a little inverted hemisphere, like that above it, and it daily mimics with bud and bloom the stars that nightly blossom out into the darkness above it. Though its hour of glory is short, into it is concentrated a magnificence which puts all the more stately trees into the background! If men will not admire, insects and birds will!

There, on the very topmost twig, that rises and falls with willowy motion, sits that ridiculous but sweet-singing bobolink, singing, as a Roman-candle fizzes, showers of sparkling notes. If you stand at noon under the tree, you are in a very bee-hive. The tree is musical. The blossoms seem, for a wonder, to have a voice! The odor is not a rank atmosphere of sweet. Like the cups from which it is poured, it is delicate and modest. You feel as if there were a timidity in it, that asked your sympathy and yielded to solicitation. You do not take it whether you will or not, but, though it is abundant, you follow it rather than find it.

Is not this gentle reserve, that yields to real admiration, but hovers aloof from coarse or cold indifference, a beautiful trait in woman or apple-tree?

But was there ever such a spring? Did orchards ever before praise God with such choral colors? The whole landscape is aglow with orchard-radiance. The hill-sides, the valleys, the fields, are full of blossoming trees. The pear and cherry have shed their blossoms. The ground is white as snow with their flakes. But it is the high noon just now, on this eighteenth day of May, with the apple-trees! Let other trees boast their superiority in other months. But in the month of May, the very flower-month of the year, the crown and glory of all is the apple-tree!

Therefore, in my calendar, hereafter, I do ordain that the name of this month be changed. Instead of May, let it henceforth be called in my kingdom, "*The Month of the Apple-Blossom.*"

GENIUS AND INDUSTRY.

NDUSTRY is a substitute for genius. Where one or more faculties exist in the highest state of development and activity, — as the faculty of music in Mozart, invention in Fulton, ideality in Milton, — we call the possessor a genius. But a genius is *usually* understood to be a creature of such rare facility of mind, that he can do anything without labor. According to the popular notion, he learns without study, and knows without learning. He is eloquent, without preparation; exact, without calculation; and profound, without reflection. While ordinary men toil for knowledge by reading, by comparison, and by minute research, a genius is supposed to receive it as the mind receives dreams. His mind is like a vast cathedral, through whose colored windows the sunlight streams, painting the aisles with the varied colors of brilliant pictures. Such minds *may* exist.

So far as I have observed the species, they abound in academies, colleges, and Thespian societies; in village debating-clubs, in coteries of young artists, and among young professional aspirants. They are to be known by a reserved air, excessive sensitiveness, and utter indolence; by very long hair, and very open shirt-collars; by the reading of much wretched poetry, and the writing of much yet more wretched; by being very conceited, very affected, very disagreeable, and very useless: beings whom no man wants for friend, pupil, or companion.

The occupations of the great man and of the common man are necessarily, for the most part, the same; for the business of life is made up of minute affairs, requiring only judgment and diligence. A high order of intellect is required for the discovery and defence of truth; but this is an unfrequent task. Where the ordinary wants of life once require recondite principles, they will need the application of familiar truths a thousand times. Those who enlarge the bounds of knowledge must push out with bold adventure beyond the common walks of men. But only few pioneers are needed for the largest armies, and a few profound men in each occupation may herald the advance of all the business of society. The vast bulk of men are required to discharge the homely duties of life; and they have less need of genius than of intellectual industry and patient enterprise. Young men should observe that those who take the honors and emoluments of mechanical crafts, of commerce, and of professional life, are rather distinguished for a sound judgment and a close application, than for a brilliant genius. In the ordinary business of life, industry can do anything which genius can do, and very many things which it cannot. Genius is usually impatient of application, irritable, scornful of men's dulness, squeamish at petty disgusts; — it loves a conspicuous place, a short work, and a large reward; it loathes the sweat of toil, the vexations of life, and the dull burden of care.

Industry has a firmer muscle, is less annoyed by delays and repulses, and, like water, bends itself to the shape of the soil over which it flows; and if checked, will not rest, but accumulates, and mines a passage beneath, or seeks a side-race, or rises above and overflows the obstruction. What genius performs at one impulse, industry gains by a succession of blows. In ordinary matters, they differ only in rapidity of execution, and are upon one level before men, who see the *result*, but not the *process*. It is admirable to know that those things which in skill, in art, and in learning the world has been unwilling to let die, have not only been the conceptions of genius, but the products of toil. The masterpieces of antiquity, as well in literature as in art, are known to have received their extreme finish from an almost incredible continuance of labor upon them. I do not remember a book in all the departments of learning, nor a scrap in literature, nor a work in all the schools of art, from which its author has derived a permanent renown, that is not known to have been long and patiently elaborated. Genius needs industry, as much as industry needs genius. If only Milton's imagination could have conceived his visions, his consummate industry only could have carved the immortal lines which enshrine them. If only Newton's mind could reach out to the secrets of Nature, even his could only do it by the homeliest toil. The works of Bacon are not midsummer-night dreams, but, like coral islands, they have risen from the depths of truth, and formed their broad surfaces above the ocean by the minutest accretions of persevering labor. The conceptions of Michael Angelo's genius would have perished like a night's fantasy, had not his industry given them permanence.

NEW CLOTHES.

RE not *clothes* an evidence of sin, and a penalty therefor? When one considers the care, labor, mental trouble, and various degrees of discipline connected with clothing, it seems strange that it should not have been arranged for men as for birds and animals. What a large part of human industry is employed in the manufacture of fabrics; how great the number of persons who spend their lives in cutting, fitting, sewing, and otherwise preparing dress! Then, too, the time which every one of us must consume in thinking of dress; selecting and arranging; and the daily consumption of time in robing and disrobing! All this care and expense is spared to birds and beasts. It is said that they toil not, neither do they spin! So neither do they weave, cut, or sew! They have no buttons to put on, or grumble about when they come off!

There are my ducks: they have the most compact dressing-case ever invented. Do they wish to eat, — the bill is employed; do they wish to carve and cut their food, — the bill is case-knife, or carving-knife, and fork to boot! Do they wish to dress cloth, — the bill is better than teasels are! Would they brush their coat and pantaloons, — behold! the bill is brush too. Would they prepare themselves with a mackintosh, or india-rubber garment, against water and weather, — the bill goes to work, and, from a little private arrangement of their own, extracts the wet-repelling oil, and lays it on evenly all over their coat. Would they brush their hair, polish their boots, — again comes this facile instrument-of-all-work, the bill, and dusts the one and rubs down the other. Then, with inimitable simplicity, this important member turns to the dinner, and becomes, indeed, a bill of fare and food. How much would human life be simplified by some such arrangement!

There, too, is my friend the bobolink! He steps off his perch in the morning, finds a wash-basin in the dew on a head of clover, and makes his toilet with flowers for a looking-glass. He sings awhile, brushes his hair, sings again, takes a bite of breakfast, and eats, sings, and brushes, without fastidious suggestions of a ridiculous propriety.

My cows, too, have a very economical method of arranging their wardrobe. It is a wonderful convenience to have your clothes grow on you. In fact, a cow is preparing a coat and vest in the mere act of eating! Since hair and skin are formed from secretions, and these are supplied to the blood by digestion of food, the stomach turns out to be a great cloth manufactory. And while a cow, lying down at evening under a tree, seems the very picture of quiet, chewing her cud with half-shut eyes, she is, in fact, getting ready her clothes!

Only man is doomed to spend a large portion of his time in providing the materials and making preparation of his clothes. How odd it would seem to see a robin pull off its feather coat at night, and prepare for retiring!

How much stranger still, if respectable men had their clothes formed upon them! and vests, pantaloons, coats, secreted from their food! If a button flew off, lo, a button germ would at once begin to swell and grow! If a seam ripped, or some unlucky contact tore a hole, the parts would throw out new matter for repairs, and bridge over the gulf. Alas! it is vain to repine or speculate upon the probable convenience of a different arrangement. Here we are, just as we are! And sheep and flax and cotton must give us staple; we must dye, spin, and weave; measure and cut, fit and sew, put on and wear out, cast off and renew, to the end of the world. But one thing ought to be done. Every one who has made luxury a study, knows that the worst period of dress is when it is *new*. A new hat creases and hurts your head. A new boot fevers your foot. And though new clothes may fit you like a skin, yet because they *are* new, you are conscious of them. You are afraid to sit down then, lest the new clothes should be soiled.

Your coat must not be rubbed. At every step life has to serve your new clothes. This may do for Sunday. The greater leisure of that day gives unoccupied minds a welcome business in taking care of their clothes. And so we see men animating the centre of a well-arranged suit of clothes, and carrying them, with great care and painstaking, so that they are exhibited to the fairest advantage!

But to those who are a little nervous this first service in behalf of new clothes is annoying. We are never really happy till new clothes are *broken in.* Then we are their master; before, they were ours! Now, would it not be as well to have new clothes old at the start? Counterfeiters are said to put new bills into their boots and walk upon them, to give that worn and crumpled look that shall resemble well-circulated, lawful bills. Why should we not have clothes crumpled a little, and worn for us, as a part of their preparation? In short, as we have oxen trained before we buy them; as we have horses broken and drilled, so clothes ought to be broken in. Then we should have the luxury of an old coat, from the beginning! Then boots and shoes would embrace our feet, not as strangers, with cold formalities, but with that negligent ease of care which belongs to established friendships. But I barely make the suggestion. To others must be left the carrying out of a thing so important!

WORMS.

A YEAR with but eleven months must be lame. Yet Brooklyn has but eleven in her calendar. June is lost out. Eaten up! Worm-eaten! The fairest month of the year is June. Summer has not dried her soil, nor scorched the grass or leaves. They are in the earliest growth,—fresh, plump, and succulent. The air is tempered between extremes. It is the rose month, the lily month, the month of early flowers. And yet June is lost to us by the irruption and devastations of worms. It ought to be named the Vermicular month! The trees are stripped of their leaves, the air is full of webs, the pavement is covered with crushed or crawling worms, and, floating upon their silvery threads, worms so fill the space between trees and sidewalk, that one cannot pass under without carrying with him a retinue of worms! The air is full of their odor, the walks are slippery with them.

It is amusing to witness the various methods of locomotion and escape practised by those who are not yet hardened to this warfare. Ladies may be seen walking in the middle of the streets, or walking a zigzag course, now poking their parasols at some invisible enemy in the air, or dodging and winding around hither and thither; stopping occasionally to take account of stock and deposit superfluous additions to the wardrobe. Some, more nervous, on being enwebbed under some tree, utter gentle shrieks, and we have seen not a few turn back, and make a circuit of several blocks, rather than face these pendants of the trees! See that fair lady advancing serene and secure. With an earnest look she suddenly stops, glides to the right, only to recede yet more quickly. But forward, backward, right or left, up or down, it is all the same. The tree is a vast tent, and once beneath it, it matters little which course you take!

Individually, a worm is insignificant. But collectively, they defy a whole city. They are easily crushed, undefended, with no power of escape, universally detested, and yet they are invincible, and man, if not crushed, is defeated before the worm.

The greatest forces are made up of units of weakness. An engineer can pierce and tunnel solid mountains, build roads on the precipitous sides of cliffs, bridge floods, and rear up against the very ocean barriers which defy tide and storm. But a locust, a rat, a worm, an insect, simply by fecundity, is more powerful against skill, science, and every enginery, than the lightning or the floods of the sea. The wire-worm takes possession of the fields, and the farmer is in his power. The fly attacks the wheat, and no force can hinder his devastation. Your plum-trees may be planted around your house, and within reach of daily observation and protection, and yet, in spite of every precaution, the insignificant brown-coated *Curculio* will use every green plum for a nest for his baby-bugs, and then kick them off the tree before your angry eyes.

The Oriental hosts of *Locusts* are famous in history and in literature. Indeed, some of the most sublime passages of the prophets in the sacred Scriptures are those which describe the coming, progress, and desolation of locust swarms. A single example shall show. It is from Joel: —

"A day of darkness and of gloominess, a day of clouds and of thick darkness, as the morning spread upon the mountains: a great people and a strong; there hath not been ever the like, neither shall be any more after it, even to the years of many generations. A fire devoureth before them; and behind them a flame burneth: the land is as the garden of Eden before them, and behind them a desolate wilderness; yea, and nothing shall escape them. The appearance of them is as the appearance of horses; and as horsemen, so shall they run. Like the noise of chariots on the tops of mountains shall they leap, like the noise of a flame of fire that devoureth the stubble, as a strong people set in battle array. Before their face the people shall be much pained: all faces shall gather blackness. They shall run like mighty men; they shall climb the wall like men of war; and they shall march every one on his ways, and they shall not break their ranks; neither shall one thrust another: they shall walk every one in his path; and when they fall upon the sword, they shall not be wounded. They shall run to and fro in the city; they shall run upon the wall, they shall climb up upon the houses; they shall enter in at the windows like a thief. The earth shall quake before them; the heavens shall tremble; the sun and the moon shall be dark, and the stars shall withdraw their shining: and the Lord shall utter his voice before his army; for his camp is very great; for he is strong that executeth his word; for the day of the Lord is great and very terrible; and who can abide it?"

But to return to the beginning of these remarks, it is not all, and altogether an annoyance. There is an element of the ludicrous attached to this annual incursion of worms. Every man's first duty on coming into the house is to be picked. Among the kind offices of the church, the assembly room, is that of *devermicularization.*

Unconscious beauty sits tranquil, while a vast worm is looping itself on the bonnet, another is navigating the shores of the lace collar, and several are apparently following the steps of illustrious searchers for the poles.

On the whole, children set the best example. As a fair young mother was walking the other morning, she heard her little girl, not old enough to speak plainly, expressing her trouble: "I have lost my worm." She carried one in her hand as a pet, and mourned its loss.

If we were educated to look upon things with eyes of philosophy, how much annoyance we might escape! Is a gas-pipe repairing in the street? So soon as we know that the insufferable stench is sulphuretted hydrogen, it has a scientific smell much more endurable. If one will resolve noisome elements and disgustful odors into some chemical form, and regard them in their relations to the great economics of nature, it will aid their patience.

Nevertheless, after considering worms in the light of entomology, of benevolence, of utility, together with all manner of illustrations from literature and history, we are constrained to admit that we are so far uneducated as to regard their presence with some displacency, and to contemplate the early completion of their summer pilgrimage with an entire resignation. Meantime, our blessings on the ailanthus-tree! Let no man revile *its* odor, next month, without remembering that it was a bulwark against worms. Nothing can eat ailanthus,—nothing, we mean, except a well-practised tobacco-chewer. He could eat anything.

PLEASURE-RIDING.

IT is astonishing how much pains people will take to be *not-happy*. Great sums of money are spent on disconsolate hearts, empty heads, restless, nervous *indolents*,—to make them happy. But, unless there is the quality of happiness in them, it is as vain as to beat upon lead in hope of music. How much money is lavished upon horses and splendid equipages, and how many sunny hours are witnesses of the unhappy creatures who affect happiness in their ostentatious parade! If the heart be merry, it bubbles up and overflows with enjoyment without an effort. Did you ever take notice that unarranged and unexpected rides, uncouth and even ridiculous, are productive of more real enjoyment than the best that are sought and expected?

Fix up your boys, and get out your best carriage, and take a regular ride, and ten to one next time you offer the chance they will say no. But when did a boy ever refuse a ride in an ox-cart? When did a boy ever decline a ride to mill, on creaking cart, but above all, astride the plump bags of grain on horse-back? Away with your fine turn-outs for sensible boys! A lumber-wagon, an old cart, a stone dray, are better than any chariot. If a big brother or a kind "hired man" will give the boys a turn in a wheelbarrow, that will be superlative. There is an indescribable relish, too, in a pair of wheels, with two boys hitched on before, and one upon the bare axle-tree, occupied alternately in tumbling off and getting on. But who shall tell or imagine the satisfaction of riding upon a jack or jenny? It is plain that these creatures were created with special reference to boys' wants. They are tough, insensitive to the whip, self-opinionated, and in no danger whatever of being abused; having a way of using their heels and mouth that promotes humanity among boys. If the boys do not enjoy the exercise, every spectator *does.* The jenny on our premises is something larger than a rat, and of the same color. She goes where she has a mind to, stops when she pleases, throws the boys off when she is tired of them, turns around when they forbid, starts when they say, "Whoa!" and stops when they say, "Go 'long!" A whip seems agreeable to her hide, rather than otherwise. She is so short that a moderate boy has to hold up his feet in riding; and of course, in falling off, he has not so far to go as if on his own feet. It is amusing to see what an amount of work can be got out of a boy, for nothing, which would be considered a great hardship if applied to good uses. All the toil of riding Jenny applied to the garden would make almost a man's work for the day!

But we have reserved for the last the grand, triumphal ride! When the cart has been stacked with sheaves, or loaded with hay, and towers high in the air, then let the importunate boy be lifted to its top, and come home embosomed in clover and fragrant hay! No king has such triumphant entrances into rejoicing cities as boys have into barns, upon the broad backs of hay-carts! It makes one quite melancholy to see how much money is spent upon unhappy people to make them discontented! Strip off their gentility, send them into the country, give them a plain cart, an ox-sled, or a harvest-wagon, and they will have sensations of pleasure long strangers to them! Ah, Mr. Bonner, vainly do you drive forth behind the magnificent Lantern and mate, — flying through the air as if two stars whisked you at astronomical velocities! The thing may be well enough in its way. But when you have tired of this, I have in reserve for you a crowning joy! You shall mount my hay-cart; and drawn by my oxen, — upon a springing load, softer than stuffed cushion or cunning springs, more fragrant than the gardens of the Orient, you shall be seen with radiant face, coming up the field, for once a perfectly happy man!

SUMMER RAIN.

MEN begin to look at the signs of weather. It is long since much rain fell. The ground is a little dry, the road is a good deal dusty. The garden bakes. Transplanted trees are thirsty. Wheels are shrinking and tires are looking dangerous. Men speculate on the clouds; they begin to calculate how long it will be, if no rain falls, before the potatoes will suffer; the oats, the corn, the grass, — everything! To be sure, nothing is yet suffering; but then —

Rain, rain, rain! All day, all night steady raining. Will it never stop? The hay is out, and spoiling. The rain washes the garden. The ground is full. All things have drunk their fill. The springs revive, the meadows are wet; the rivers run discolored with soil from every hill. Smoking cattle reek under the sheds. Hens, and fowl in general, shelter and plume. The sky is leaden. The clouds are full yet. The long fleece covers the mountains. The hills are capped in white. The air is full of moisture. Rain, rain, rain! The wind roars down the chimney. The birds are silent. No insects chirp. Closets smell mouldy. The barometer is dogged. We thump it, but it will not get up. It seems to have an understanding with the weather. The trees drip, shoes are muddy, carriage and wagon are splashed with dirt. Paths are soft. So it is. When it is clear we want rain, and when it rains we wish it would shine. But, after all, how lucky for grumblers that they are not allowed to meddle with the weather, and that it is put above their reach? What a scrambling, selfish, mischief-making time we should have, if men undertook to parcel out the seasons and the weather according to their several humors or interests!

But if one will but look for enjoyment, how much there is in every change of weather. The formation of clouds,—the various signs and signals, the uncertain wheeling and marching of the fleecy cohorts, the shades of light and gray in the broken heavens,—all have their pleasure to an observant eye. Then come the wind-gust, the distant, dark cloud, the occasional fiery streak shot down through it, the run and hurry of men whose work may suffer! Indeed, sir, your humble servant, even, was stirred up on the day after "*Fourth of July.*" The grass in the old orchard was not my best. Indeed, we grumbled at it considerably while it was yet standing. But being *cut* and the rain threatening it, one would have thought it gold, by the nimble way in which we tried to save it!

Blessed be horse-rakes! Once half a dozen men, with half a dozen rakes, would have gone whisking up and down, thrusting out and pulling in the long-handled rake, with slow and laborious progress. But no more of that. See friend Turner, mounted on the wheeled horse-rake, riding about as if for pleasure. Up go the steel teeth and drop their collected load, down go his feet, and the teeth are at work again; and at every ten or fifteen feet, the winrow forms. It is easy times when *men* ride and *horses* rake! No more hand-rakes, and no more *revolving* horse-rakes!

Meanwhile, the clouds come bowling noiselessly through the air, and spit here and there a drop preliminary. But the hay is cocked, the sides dressed down, and all is ready — except the *hay-covers!* Alas for our negligence! The manufacturers had offered to send us some for trial, and we had forgotten to say, Send them along! And now, with our hay out and the rain coming, we mourned our carelessness. With good hay-covers, our two dozen little hay-cocks would have been as snug as if in the barn. Well, if one thing suffers, another gains! See how the leaves are washed, the grass drinks, corn drinks, the garden drinks, everything drinks. It 's our opinion that everything except man is laughing and rejoicing. Trees shake their leaves with a softer sound. Rocks look moist and soft, at least where the moss grows. Even the solitary old pine-tree chords his harp, and sings soft and low melodies with plaintive undulations! A good summer storm is a rain of riches. If gold and silver rattled down from the clouds, they would hardly enrich the land so much as soft, long rains. Every drop is silver going to the mint. The roots are machinery, and, catching the willing drops, they assay them, refine them, roll them, stamp them, and turn them out coined berries, apples, grains, and grasses! When the heavens send clouds, and they bank up the horizon, be sure they have hidden gold in them. All the mountains of California are not so rich as are the soft mines of Heaven, that send down treasures upon man without tasking him, and pour riches upon his field without spade or pickaxe, — without his search or notice. Well, let it rain, then! No matter if the journey is delayed, the picnic spoiled, the visit adjourned. Blessed be rain — and rain in summer! And blessed be He who watereth the earth, and enricheth it for man and beast!

MY TWO FRIENDS.

HAVE two friends whose habits illustrate two opposite principles. Both are ladies. Both have received the advantage of early education, and have moved in good society. The one is of a slender form, elegantly made, of exquisite taste in dress, and with a rare sense of propriety in all matters. There are few that would venture to wear the articles that she sometimes will, yet with unerringly perfect judgment. It is scarcely right to call it judgment, since that implies a process of deliberation. But in her case it seems rather an intuition. Like a bird, she seems to wear gay plumage unconsciously; as if it grew upon her. She is always dignified, and yet leaves the impression of always smiling upon you graciously. This is not that prepared smile of good society which, after a little, leaves a kind of threadbare kindness on the face, a seedy, lustreless smile. It is rather the shining out of unaffected kindness. If she meet you at church, in the street, at a party or concert, or in her own house, you feel that you have been shone upon.

This does not result from that easy temper that cannot help itself, nor from a moral constitution that has feeble discriminations and preferences. On the contrary, there are few persons more clear and positive in their likes and dislikes, and with better grounds. She is herself a person of truth, of fidelity, of honor. The want of these qualities in others acts upon her as a discord. She is not warped by her general kindliness to compromise her clear perception and calm judgment of what is right or wrong in the slightest degree. She is remarkably considerate, within her own thoughts, of the grounds of conduct and character in others, and is apt to be almost judicial in her deliberations about them.

But — and here is the element for which I have drawn this outline — meeting those whom she does not like, whose conduct she condemns, there is toward them a quiet, cheerful politeness, that conceals her repugnance, that confers happiness, that leaves them quite ignorant of the gravity of her moral dissent. She seems to say, within herself, and I suspect this is about her own way of reasoning about it, — "This person seems to me both wrong and disagreeable. But he is a human being. As such I owe a debt of kindness to him. I must not, by word or act, approve the evil. But within that limit I am bound to confer innocent happiness. The law of conscience does not exonerate me from the duties of benevolence. So long, therefore, as we meet only in general society, and I am not called to sit in judgment, my only business is to treat such a one as if I wished him well, and would contribute my share of making him happy."

I confess that I see nothing in this that is not just and Christian. It cannot be charged with insincerity. Every one is to feel and express kindness, even when exercising the functions of conscience, and much more under circumstances that call for the expression of no moral judgments.

I have another friend. She also has excellent taste. She is wise in selection of colors and in forms. I have never known her to wear a discordant article. And yet, such is the strength of her character and the energy of her nature, that one seldom thinks what she wears. The predominant impression which she leaves upon you is of character, and not of costume. You do not remember her presence as of a sweet bird, but rather with that awe which you have while standing before an eagle. You respect her. You might revere her. You would hardly think of offering her help, though you might homage.

This lady, too, has the most clear and positive opinions about those whom she meets. She likes no one, but loves many. She seldom dislikes any, but she abhors many. The doors of her heart are quite royal. Those who find them open are like a queen's guests, and are entertained with a very sovereignty of kindness. For their sakes upon whom she shines there can be no service too sacrificing, no deeds too onerous, no patience in their troubles too long-continuing.

To others those doors are like the portcullis of a king's castle in time of war. She will have no parley. They shall not come in.

There is seldom a doubt in any person's mind as to the ground they stand on. She makes people feel that she does not love them, nor like them, nor even tolerate them. She would not speak to them if she could help it. She has always seemed to me like some very noble hills that I have seen, whose approach on one side is easy, gradual, full of graceful lines, charming shrubs, and fine trees, but, on reaching the summit, the other side was a perpendicular cliff. For her friends she is a continuous garden, for her not-friends a precipice.

If she were to be expostulated with upon her resolute way of meeting disagreeable people, she would probably answer, "I do not think it honest to make people think that I like them when I do not. I cannot reconcile it to my conscience to play a part." Thus it is a duty which she feels bound upon her to let people understand that they are no favorites.

Is there, then, a judicial duty laid upon us, as members of society, to sit in judgment upon each other, and to execute the sentence of our disapprobation? May, or may not, a person make those cheerful and happy by personal graciousness whom one for many reasons condemns inwardly? Where is Addison? Where is Steele? Where is Dr. Johnson? I desire to lay before them this question,— Ought not a person's face, like God's sun, to shine kindly upon the just and the unjust?

EMBODIED JOKES.

HAS not Nature an element of the ludicrous in it? Are there no creations which may be regarded as mere quizzical oddities? What else can you make of the world-renowned Jack? Can any man look into his face without an irresistible temptation to laughter? Was ever anything more expressly made to be grotesque than a toad? What thing of all the barbarous inventions in Chinese pictures can surpass it in ridiculousness? Did you ever attentively study toad life and manners? You might do worse. At evening, when they begin to feel the inspiration of an evening meal, you shall find them awkwardly alert, and very entertaining. Their squat forms and ungainly movements, the very decorous and earnest sobriety with which they carry themselves, the peculiar wink with which they seem to intimate to you that they are keeping up a good deal more thinking inside than you might suppose, their imperturbable and unexcitable passivity, produce a comical result hardly equalled by any clown.

The bat is another jest in natural history. Its flight is the only redeeming feature of its ungracious form and manner. Even that has a capriciousness in it that savors of gambolling. Its voice is a squeak, its mouth a burlesque upon humanity.

The monkey has been set apart for ridiculousness the world over. He is an organized sarcasm upon the human race, with variations multitudinous.

But among insects, and among beetles especially, are found forms so singular, and manners so queer, that we never pass them without stopping to look; and we never look without a sense of the ludicrous.

But who ever saw, on land or in water, a crab, or a lobster, without being struck with their comicality! If these things address themselves to a feeling of the ludicrous in our minds, is it extravagant to suppose that they sprung from some such thought in the Creative Mind? It seems no more strange that God should create objects for mirth in the world, than that he should have placed the faculty of mirthfulness in the human mind. Is any faculty without provision for its enjoyment? Is it not rather to be supposed that, both in the vegetable and the animal kingdom, there are forms and processes which will never be fully appreciated until their relations to the feeling of mirth is recognized? We do not know that laughing philosophers are desirable: philosophers who do not know how to laugh are still less likely to be complete.

It is sometimes thought that there are no qualities of mirthfulness in nature; that it is purely in the mind of those who imagine it. Doubtless it is the mind that experiences the emotion; but so it is of color, of form, of grace. And these qualities will abound to those who are sensitive to their presence, and, on the other hand, will seem rare to those less admirably endowed. But no one, on that account, supposes that color is imaginary, — that there is no provision for it in nature. And because only the mirthful easily appreciate the ludicrousness of many parts of animated creation, it does not any more follow that the oddity is subjective, depending merely upon the observer, and not in the designed and real nature of things.

CHANGES.

UR days are a kaleidoscope. Every instant a change takes place in the contents. New harmonies, new contrasts, new combinations of every sort. Nothing ever happens twice alike. The most familiar people stand each moment in some new relation to each other, to their work, to surrounding objects. The most tranquil house, with the most serene inhabitants, living upon the utmost regularity of system, is yet exemplifying infinite diversities. And much more is the vexed and agitated flow of society but an ever changing, ever new complexity! The most familiar scenes are full of novelty to one who has an eye to see it!

But *we* are dozing, stupid, unobserving. We pass along in a waking dream. We look without seeing. We listen without hearing. Birds flit among the trees, a fly lights upon the page before us, and throws his thin shadow over the next word. Another comes to meet him, they meet with an enthusiastic buzz of satisfaction, and whirl off into the air with a delirium of gladness. We only brush at the intruder. The grass is twinkling with innumerous gems of dew. Every motion of your head is a new glory upon its shadow. The wind that just breathes around the corner, and shakes it, seems to come on purpose to show you the wreath of simple beauty!

The shadows all day long play at silent games of beauty. Everything is double, if it stands in light. The tree sees an unrevealed and muffled self lying darkly along the ground. The slender stems of flowers, golden-rod, wayside asters, meadow daisies, and rare lilies (rare and yet abundant, in every level meadow), cast forth a dim and tremulous line of shadow, that lies long all the morning, shortening till noon, and creeping out again from the root all the afternoon, until the sun shoots it as far eastward in the evening as the sun shot it westward in the morning. A million shadowy arrows such as these spring from Apollo's golden bow of light at every step. Flying in every direction, they cross, interlacing each other in a soft network of dim lines.

Meanwhile the clouds drop shadow-like anchors, that reach the ground, but will not hold; every browsing creature, every flitting bird, every moving team, every unconscious traveller, writes itself along the ground in dim shadow.

Nor are sounds less numerous, changing, and novel. At no instant, if one gives his mind to it, is there stillness or sameness. As I sit by my window, a door sounds, the gate rattles, a man's foot crackles on the gravel, a fly buzzes round my head, a song-sparrow sings sweet in yonder apple-tree, a whiplash cuts sharply through the air, a boy halloos at the team, another boy turns the rustling paper, and sings a snatch of song over and over with intolerable iteration, — a rooster crows, a bee hums under the window, saying grace before proceeding to breakfast. Now comes a lull. I listen for silence. No. A calf calls out for its mother, another answers it. A far-off rooster crows, and sets off a dozen more in various directions! The train roars with softened sound from the distance. New birds are discoursing: a plank falls down with resounding clap. A robin calls out, "What 's that?" The kingbird sings with a jolly noise, that sounds like a rich man shaking his pocket full of silver. The pigs are up and at it. An old hen is reading a barnyard homily to her unobservant attendants. Down goes a load of stones with a miscellaneous clash and rattle. The barnyard wooden-latched gate has a blunt snap. A chipping-bird flies down to a crumb of bread with a simple troll of exquisite notes. A wagon rolls along the road. A voice from the hill-side beyond comes soft and mellow hitherward. Should I write till the sun goes down, at every instant some new or changing sound would be recorded. And yet in the great room of Nature nothing is discordant, if we only are in tune. All harsh and grating noises, all low piping, all crack and crash, all piercing calls or bird warblings, all rustling sounds of leaves or dress, all slammings, rippings, jinglings, shouts, every plash and creak, are harmonious parts of one great orchestra, and when mingled in the multitude, they seem to wear each other smooth, so that the general hum of evening or the sharper sounds of noon fall upon the ear with a sense of harmony!

The endless variety and harmony of forms, the inexhaustible wealth of colors, the by-play of animal and insect life, the movements and industries of men, in the midst of this gorgeously decorated earth, these all fill up the tube and make each day but a rolling kaleidoscope, each moment brilliant with some new combination.

But few witness this perpetual wonder. The world is dull and life is tame to most men. Nothing has merit which does not in some way address the appetite, the feverish desires. Men are sotted with vulgar business. Nothing seems worthy that has not some relation to *them*. This egotism punishes itself. It separates between the soul and God's munificent provision for its satisfaction. We live in a palace, and call it dull. We have every delight for the senses, and yawn with *ennui!* We have myriad servants, each with some minute fidelity, yet we are always unserved! If one could but hold up the innumerable events of each hour in the golden light, — if the world were to them God's book, and each day an opening leaf, and every event a revelation, — no one would need to search for pleasure. To those who have susceptibility, an appreciation of things beautiful simply because they fall from the hand of God, and are significant of his taste or feeling, there is an unwasting satisfaction, placed beyond the contingencies of human affairs. When I am a bankrupt, and my creditor takes my property, he shall have the house, the ground, the furniture, the things on which men lay tax; but I shall laugh at him if he thinks he has touched my properties! Above my roof are finer pictures than are under it. In the trees and along the meadows I have winged instruments which a sheriff will hardly catch! Clouds are better property than lies hidden in the veins of the hills over which they cast their solemn shadows! My fancy is a plough that turns better furrows than the best inventor's, and sows the open soil of air with harvests more abundant than all that store the barns of the world. And these treasures for the finer senses are without cares, without envy, without taxes. Storms do not damage, and fires do not burn them. They never waste, they change only to grow better. They are young with my youth, young in my manhood, and young in age!

DRIVING FAST HORSES FAST.

Y DEAR MR. BONNER: You once promised me a ride with your never-to-be-excelled horses, and to-day is the very day for it. The sky is clear. It is a long while since we have had high, bright, clear days. They have been sad and cloudy. Sometimes snow, sometimes rain, sometimes a miserable compromise between both. But to-day is of one mind, and that a good mind. Nature is in her sweet and grand mood. It is the first day on which she has cared to have it known that her mind was made up to have spring weather. The secret is out now. Snow is melting. I saw grass with fresh growth of green this very morning. No birds yet. But the grass *said* birds as plainly as if it had spoken English. They cannot be far off.

Is not this a day for a ride? No mud yet. The road is hard and moist. Just the kind for a spin. For I do not want any of your lazy, jogging gaits. I am entirely of your mind, that, if a horse has had swiftness put in him, it is fair to give him a chance to develop his gifts. Of course there is a bound. Reason in all things. Even in trotting, it is easier and pleasanter for some horses to go twelve miles an hour than for others to go three. They were made so. Does it hurt a swallow to go swifter than an ox? Why not? Because he was made so. It is easy to do the thing we were *made* to do easily. And a good horse was made on purpose to go *fast*. He does it when wild of his own accord. He does not lose the relish of speed, even when domesticated.

Take a fine-fed horse, who in harness looks as if he were a pattern of moderation, a very deacon of sobriety, and turn him loose in pasture. Whew, what a change! He takes one or two steps slowly, just to be sure that you have let go of him, and then with a squeal he lets fly his heels high in the air, till the sun flashes from his polished shoes, and then off he goes, faster and fiercer, clear across the lot, till the fence brings him up. And then, his eye flashing, his mane lifted and swelling, his tail up like a king's sceptre, he snorts a defiance to you from afar, and, with a series of rearings, running sideways, pawing and plungings, friskings and whirls, he starts again, with immense enjoyment, into another round of running. Do you not see that it is more than fun? It is ecstasy. It is horse rapture!

I never see such a spectacle that I am not painfully impressed with the inhumanity of not letting horses run. Fastness is a virtue. Our mistaken moderation is depriving him of it. I drive fast on principle. I do it for the sake of being at one with nature. To drive *slow*, only and always, is to treat a horse as if he were an ox. *You* may be slow if you think proper. But your horse should be kept up to nature. He would have had but two legs if it was meant that he should go only on a "go-to-meeting" pace. He has *four* legs. Of course he ought to do a great deal with them.

Now why do I say these things to *you?* Not to convince you of *your* duty. But I feared lest, taking me out to ride, you would be disposed to think that *I* had scruples, and would jog along moderately, as if doing me a favor. Not at all. The wind does not go fast enough to suit me. If I were engineer of a sixty-mile-an-hour express train, I should covet twenty miles an hour more.

Let the horses be well groomed,—well harnessed. Let the wagon be thoroughly looked to,—no screw loose, no flaw just ready to betray us. Mount: I am by your side. The whip is not needed. Yet let it stand in its place, the graceful hint of authority in reserve, which is always wholesome to men and horses.

Now get out of town cautiously. No speed here. This is a place for sobriety, moderation, and propriety in driving. But, once having shaken off the crowd, I give you a look, and disappear instantly in a wild excitement, as if all the trees were crazy, and had started off in a race, as if the fences were chalk-lines, as if the earth and skies were commingled, and everything were wildly mixed in a supernatural excitement, neither of earth nor of the skies!

The wind has risen since we started. It did not blow at this rate, surely! These tears are not of sorrow. But really this going like a rocket is new to every sense. Do not laugh if I clutch the seat more firmly. I am not afraid. It is only excitement. *You* may be used to this bird's business of flying. But don't draw the rein. I am getting calm. See that play of muscle! Splendid machinery was put into these horses. Twenty horse-power at least in each! And how they enjoy it! No forcing here. They do it to please themselves, and thank you for a chance! Look at that head! Those ears speak like a tongue! The eyes flash with eagerness and will! Is it three miles? Impossible! It is not more than half a mile!

Well, draw up. Let me get off now, and see these brave creatures. What! not enough yet? No painful puffing, no throbbing of the flanks. They step nervously, and champ the bit, and lean to your caresses, as if they said: "All this we have done to please *you;* now just let us go on to please ourselves!"

FENCE-CORNERS.

IT makes a great difference whether we look at things with an exact business eye, or with the eye of poetry and beauty. If one sees a thistle in his mowing-lot, he runs at it as if it were a venomous animal. But if sauntering through the pastures, and in an appreciative mood he sees a thistle growing strongly where it will harm no one, and will scatter seeds only in the wild field, he begins to note more considerately its vigor, its stateliness, its robust health, and its regal blossom. It is, indeed, the very king of weeds.

And, like true royalty, it is guarded at every branch and every leaf by spines more efficacious in producing respect in those approaching it, than marshals' wands or guardsmen's halberts. For ourselves, we like a real thistle of the thistliest kind; none of your fine, lathy Canada-thistles, that grow in flocks, and have fecundity at the top and immortality at the bottom; but a real, rousing, stalwart, old-fashioned thistle two yards high, and of a spread that gives it some claims as a tree!

But all this is mere illustration. We were saying how differently things looked according to the spirit in which we look at them. And we were going to apply this to FENCE-CORNERS, or rather to the wild-weed hedges which form along old stone-walls or crooked rail-fences.

Now it cannot be denied, that, from the stand-point of clean and thorough farming, such hedges are disgraceful. They represent the carelessness or the indolence of the farmer. But if one will cease to be an agricultural critic, and allow himself some latitude of charitable complacency, he will find much to admire. Indeed, we may as well own it, we love wild, neglected, rampant-growing weed hedges!

One gets tired of too much regularity. Potatoes in rows, cabbages in squat rows, beans in rows, turnips drilled in rows, corn in rows, orchards in rows, everything in rows — one begins to feel the graceless stiffness, and to long for some irregularity and variety. This the eye gets abundantly in the weedy hedge. Here is no prim order. "First come, first served," is the only law here. "Blessed be the strong!" is the motto of the weed-row. And one will notice that nothing in all the fields is apt to be half so robust and healthy as are the heathen plants of the hedge. The plough of the careless farmer has, from year to year, thrown the furrow one way, and mould has collected near the fence. The flying dust, too, has been caught and washed down there. Then every year returns to the ground again the whole summer's deciduous growth, to decay and enrich the soil. Besides this, birds are not ungrateful for shelter and berries, and make their contributions of cheerful guano. And so it comes to pass that the richest part of all the field is its boundary.

Here, then, we shall find what vegetation can do. Great, rank weeds spread their succulent arms to point in pity at the starveling crops which the lazy farmer is eking out of the starved soil. Just so it is in towns and cities. You shall see mighty natures springing up in the hedgerows of society, and overtopping with their vigorous growth all the puny creatures that are faintly growing in feeble civilization.

There is a wild liberty, too, in the hedge, that excites pleasure. Here is no master. Everything thrives according to its own nature. No envious hoe decimates, no partial tillage cuts one and cultivates another. Everything is left to show its own force and nature, unhelped and unhindered. This would be distasteful in a whole field where we look for husbandry. But, as a contrast, it is all the more striking in the belt around the edges.

In this little forest you shall find often the fairest flowers. Here the golden-rod multiplies its roots and sends up its golden-branched tops in graceful profusion. Asters compete with it. The raspberry curves over in exquisite lines. And the creeping blackberry yields the most beautiful festoons of white blossoms mixed with exquisite leaves that you shall find in the whole world. The blackberry is a thousand times sweeter when eaten with the eyes, by its blossoms and leaves, than ever afterwards when it yields winy berries. Here, too, bindweed, ironweed, unsociable thistles, an occasional hawthorn, tufts of grass like a stack of spears, convolvulus, gold-thread, and I know not how many other graceful or graceless things, tower, or twine, or creep.

It is the very aviary, too, of the farm. Sparrows love the weedy thicket. Birds hunt through it, build in it, and find it both larder and nursery. Nor are they the only inmates. It is the very Jerusalem of insects. All nimble worms creep about in it. Long-legged spiders meditate profound metaphysics there, and express themselves clearly in cobwebs, and for amusement eat each other up. Crickets in their season abound. Every stone has under it a colony. Mice squeak in their little galleries. Squirrels dance along the top or move in and out of the chinks of the wall. And all manner of things seem to feel that here in this neglected place, where no law rules, no plough comes, no sickle, but only nature rules, there is for them a city of refuge, a dwelling of liberty!

Let others pish and pshaw! We shall still love the weedy hedge along the neglected fence. Nor will we forget, that chance-sown seeds have there brought forth some of the noblest fruits of the orchard and the garden! Out of the fence-corners of society, too, come often its very noblest men. It is a good soil to grow strong things in!

AGRICULTURAL PAPER.

MR. BONNER: You have sent me, on several occasions, parts of letters, from some of your innumerable subscribers, requesting sometimes one thing and sometimes another. Now, it is a correction of *fact;* then, a dissent of opinion. The last one, if I rightly remember, thinks that I am just the man to write some interesting articles upon agriculture! Let that discreet and virtuous man, and all who are of his sagacious turn of mind, now follow me! I shall go forth for my first article.

With our faces to the north, let us ascend the gentle acclivity. Pass by the strawberry-bed on the right, the grassy old orchard, with a few venerable remnants of trees, bearing apples in a state of nature, ungrafted, on the left, we come to the stone-wall beyond which lies the field and theme of our first paper on agriculture. And now, before proceeding, let me request you to send this paper to the various agricultural papers; to the several colleges in which an agricultural department is maintained; to Professor Liebig, Boussingault (if alive), Johnston (who published an admirable volume of lectures on agriculture, *without an index*, and where, in chase of a fact or statement, a man might as well run through all Oregon after an undescribed man or tree! Such books are a nuisance and an abomination, wasters of time, provokers of temper, and so wicked; now please help me over the fence of this bracket into the main-road of my remark, if you please), and to other eminent dignities agricultural, of whom my friend Saxton will give you a list. Now, then, for it. My subject is Pumpkins!

The spelling of this word is various. Pompion, Pumpkin, Punkin; Webster first gives Pompion. When I came to this, I had liked to have changed sides, and gone over to the Worcester man on the Dictionary question. For Webster was a Connecticut man, and to spell pumpkin pompion, could be nothing less than contempt for the usages of the community in which he was brought up. It was an act of orthographical treason Arnoldian. (Arnold, too, was a Connecticut Yankee. The fact is sometimes alleged against the virtuous fame of my birth-State. Just the contrary. Such men lurk in the blood of every State. But not every one, like Connecticut, has moral health to drive them out of the blood to the skin. The very appearance of a rogue in Connecticut is evidence of the purity of the blood that rids itself thus of disease.) But that word Pompion. Webster, sly and cautious man, instantly follows up that spelling with the true one, — *Pumpkin.* Have I not, a hundred times, stood up in the spelling-classes in the village school, where, drawn up in battle, in opposite ranks, sweet girls spelled the boys, and the boys misspelled the girls, and thundered out the right spelling, p-u-m-p — pump; k-i-n — PUN*kin*! On looking a second time, I see that Mr. Webster spells p*o*mpion with a *u*, p*u*mpion. This is an evasion, a disingenuous compromise. If one wishes to say pompion at all, let him say it boldly with full vowels. But to throw out the *o*, and give it a pumpkin flavor by inserting a softer *u* is a trick that will not succeed, and ought not.

But now notice his definitions. "Pumpion (Danish, *pompoen;* Swedish, *pomp*, a gourd). A plant and its fruit of the genus Cucurbita." This is all! Next, pumpkin is defined "a pompion," and that is every word that Mr. Webster says of this New England institution! Not a syllable of uses, origin, culture, nature, poetry, history, associations, relations, aspect; and not one word of that more than Olympic day, THANKSGIVING, when pumpkins were apotheosized! Why, on that immortal, gustatory day, Connecticut from time immemorial has stood, not like heathen Bacchus, wreathed with leaves of grape, and crowned with purple clusters, but like a Christian Puritan, as she is, with a pumpkin for her head, glowing with ripe yellow lustre, delightful and delicious to all devout boys! Let all that are interested in lexicography look well to such instances of concealed defection as this of Webster's. Would one trust a man with the English tongue, whose own tongue was so false to every syllable of his early experience, — pumpkin-pie, pumpkin-butter, pumpkin-molasses, and all other shades and forms of its benevolent existence? Until something is done on this pumpkin question, Mr. Merriam (not aqueous E. M., but bibliopolic G. M.) must not look to *me* for any further countenance. I will never support a dictionary that is false to pumpkins! It may be that the Quarto Pictorial Edition has both a picture and a definition worthy of my theme. If so, I am appeased. But a man that does not believe in pumpkins, must be a squash.

As to the derivation of this word, we need not go back to Danish or Swedish sources. If anything in this world is *English*, pumpkin is that thing! And it is not to be supposed that either the Danes or Swedes knew English before we did ourselves. No. The origin is on the very face of the word. The very family of words, immediately preceding this one in Webster, is *Pump*, defined to be a "hydraulic engine for raising water." That is exactly the function of pumpkin, and from that, without question, its name is derived. I know that in the Spanish *bomba* corresponds to the French *pompe*, and means a pump and a *bomb*. Some may think that the resemblance of a pumpkin to a bomb gave rise to its name. It *has* a formidable resemblance, and is filled, too, with seeds, that, when it descends from any height, and splits, fly about with much of the alacrity which belongs to the spices with which military bombs are stuffed. But this ingenious etymology cannot stand. Pumpkins existed long before bombs, and must have had a name. It is much more likely that the bomb was named from the pumpkin. Indeed, the bomb *is* a pumpkin of war, growing upon its lava soil, and filled with terrific seeds of ruin!

Having cleared away this rubbish, we are now ready for our pumpkins, which shall be served next week.

THE PUMPKIN FAMILY.—ITS RELATIVES AND RIVALS.

THE pumpkin is in the situation of a hero without a poet or historian. Its merits are worthy of renown. But it has found no worthy eulogist. Its vine indeed *is* a little coarse, as compared with the clematis, the honeysuckle, or the convolvulus. What great hands it holds up to the sun, broad, succulent, rough! And the leaf-stalk, is it not the trumpet, the cheap squirt-gun, the blow-pipe, and I know not what else, of ingenious boyhood?

The pumpkin-vine has a flowery and rhetorical way with it quite admirable. Other vines seem to require premeditation and a good deal of preparation, before they spread themselves abroad. But the pumpkin-seed may be dropped in any corn-field, or in a mere hedgerow, and it waits but a few days before it lifts up the soil, and emits two great, honest, spoon-shaped leaves, that stand looking about in simple surprise, as if the world looked greatly different from what they expected. But this pause upon the threshold of active life, this modest reserve, is becoming in both boy and pumpkin. Then it throws forth its vine, and runs boldly over the ground with a luxuriance comfortable to behold. No laggard is it; no stingy grower, needing to be nursed and coaxed and cossetted. You see vigor in the very seed. The first germ prophesies large growth, and every runner confirms and fulfils the prophecy. The blossom, too, is in hearty sympathy with the whole vine. It is no dainty thing, appealing to your admiration through a sentiment of pity; it is no pale, slender, fragile, city-bred beauty, that might blow away, or the sun drink up like a drop of dew. The pumpkin-blossom is large and buxom, open-hearted, a refuge for bees, that fly into it with open wings, and work around its nectaries in a golden dust, and so overload themselves with sweets as often to forget their homeward duties, and, like sailors in some tropic island, desert their ship to live in the luxury of overmastering sweets. And so you shall find dissipated flies and shrewish wasps and wanton bees intoxicated with the abundance, and even dying in an ecstasy of pumpkin-blossom.

But in due time behold the fruit. Even when green it is delightsome to the eyes. The unstinted fulness of the great, round, plump fellow; then the exquisite veining when the forces of Nature begin to change green to orange, and a network of green lines among yellow surfaces surpasses in ingenuity and frolicsome beauty anything that Raphael ever formed in arabesque, or Cellini traced upon his curiously wrought goblets. Indeed, every artistic goldsmith should attentively study the pumpkin. Its foundation color is quite in his way. Its lines are finer than he can fashion, and its meshes of green and gold, netting the great orb with an entanglement of figures that would have brought a Moorish artist to his knees in admiration.

Indeed, no one can have attentively studied Moorish architecture without perceiving that many of its principal features, its domes, its traceries, were borrowed from the pumpkin! What is the magnificent dome of St. Peter's but the highest development of that idea which you shall see expressed or hinted in every well-conditioned pumpkin! Thus a few acanthus-leaves, touched by human genius, gave us the Corinthian capital. The arches of the forest, we are sometimes told, are the primitive types of Gothic architecture. Do not leaves, stems, roses, fleur-de-luces, sunflowers, clover-leaves, and scores of other things, furnish to architecture its richest decorations? But it was reserved to the pumpkin to crown the whole, by giving to architects the conception of a ribbed dome.

Thus it is that modest merit often finds itself honored. And, much as the pumpkin is used as a term of ridicule, whoever saw a pumpkin that seemed to quail or look sheepish? How do they swell their great honest sides, warm with the autumn sun, as if they would say, As long as St. Peter's stands, and lifts the glorified and perfected pumpkin into the air, so long let every honest pumpkin hold up its head and be proud of its illustrious position! Who doubt, that the color, too, of the pumpkin suggested the practice of *gilding* domes? Indeed, architects awoke to the form and the color of magnificent domes when they intelligently studied the pumpkin. And one need not travel in foreign lands, to Mecca or Damascus, to see the mosques gleaming in the sunlight. Let him, when the corn has been cut from the field, and the whole expanse is aglow with radiant pumpkins, sit him down, and, like a true poet, letting the coarser substance of the scene subside, imagine himself gazing upon a city so far removed that its spires, minarets, and domes are in proportion to the objects before him. That single stem of corn is a spire, that clump of tall-growing reeds is a palace piercing the sky in many forms of tower, while golden domes glitter in wondrous magnificence as often as his imagination can transform a pumpkin into the ribbed orb of a stately mosque!

Among the ways which men employ to sustain their respectability, none is more common than an exhibition of their social connections. One whose cousin is a governor, whose uncle is a general, whose brother has been to Congress, cannot but stand well in society. Reputation is of the nature of a vine, and our reputable relatives are so much brush or trellis on which we run up. And every one knows how much more of a figure a blossom or a fruit cuts when lifted up in the air, than when lying half concealed in grass, or spattered on the bare ground. Now the pumpkin, had it no merits of its own, would yet hold up its head on account of its eminent relations.

The old family name, of great antiquity and renown, is *Cucurbitaceæ.* There were at least sixty branches of this family, and at least three hundred several special households with family names.

Who has not heard of the cucumber? All round the world it is used for pickles, for salad, and for exciting the ambition of gardeners. The first cucumber of the season, how many retired gentlemen, amateur gardeners, and regular cultivators compete for the honor of producing it! The excellent and amiable melon family, also known the world around. I refer to the *Cucumis melo*, or muskmelon, *alias* cantaloupe, *alias* nutmeg, *alias* Persian melon, which is a near kinsman of the pumpkin. So also is the *Cucumis citrullus*, or watermelon, a venerable relative. What living family of men can trace blood connections higher up the course of time than the homely relations of the melon? For is not the watermelon the very thing which brought tears to the eyes of the poor spiritless Jews, as they wandered in the wilderness? This is the record (Num. xi. 4, 5): "And the children of Israel also wept again, and said, Who shall give us flesh to eat? We remember the fish which we did eat in Egypt freely; the cucumbers, and the melons, and the leeks, and the onions, and the garlic."

But let no one severely reprove them. In a hot day, if you have been tramping along a shadeless road, until every drop of moisture seems to have run out of you, tired, dusty, hungry, thirsty, and faint, you sit down for a rest in some nook. The vision of your father's house rises,—first, the mossy well and dripping bucket, then the melon-patch, out of which your boyish arms used to bring, with much panting, early in the morning, the night-cooled, heavy watermelon, moist all over its black-green skin with dew; you remember the platter, the great carving-knife,—the crackle-slit of the knife, the two halves that, rolling each way, opened to your eyes the exquisite pink and red of the pulpy centre, whose vesicles of sugary juice glistened in the light with gentle invitation. Tell me, stoutest heart, did you not then involuntarily lick your own lips, and feel your whole mouth water? Then why should you revile the poor Jews, because the memory of melons made their eyes water?

And here, Mr. Bonner, although your paper is not

designed for Biblical criticism, I desire to express my conviction that the passage in Isaiah i. 8 is mistranslated. Zion is said to be left "as a lodge in a garden of *cucumbers*." They have confounded *Cucumis sativus* with *C. citrullus*. What boy ever was silly enough to rob a *cucumber* patch? No. It is the melon, the watermelon patch, that sends mortal heresy into boys' faith of property rights. And, without a doubt, human nature and watermelons were the same among the Jews as in our day. The *lodge* was evidently a place where the old gentleman hid himself with a long whip; and when the rollicking chaps, stealing along, looking on every side, peeping and spying, conclude that the dog is tied up, the old man asleep, and the whole coast clear, begin to spoil,—then out of his hiding-place he bolts, and comes down on them with such slashing welts, such piercing snappers, such lash-girders, and but-end thwacks, that the wretches, scattering with incredible speed, dive into the thicket, and bolt over the fence, as if each watermelon were a bomb, and with untimely explosion accelerated their retreat!

I ask you, Mr. Bonner, whether my view of this passage does not bear the truth upon its very face?

The squash family are of the same blood as the pumpkin. Indeed, this squash family have a sneaking ambition to supersede the pumpkin. Squash-pie and winter squashes take on airs at the table, and claim a seat much above their venerable predecessor. As for squash-pies, they are all very well for folks that have never eaten pumpkin. I must admit, that there are some members of this great family not presentable in good society. But in so large a connection is there not always some graceless fellow, some rogue, robber, or cunning swindler? There was Colocynth, and there was a Bryonia, and several other names of a bitter kind, who invariably cleared out any persons who took them in.

But if we were to come to the very marrow of this matter, what pen could recount the world's indebtedness to the pumpkin, for rich milk in pumpkin-fed cows, for pumpkin-sauce, for pumpkin-butter, pumpkin-molasses, and, above all, pumpkin-pies! But that is a subject too intimately connected with our patriotic associations, and with too many family scenes, to be treated at this end of an article. I prefer to meditate in expressive silence, or to be inspired with a separate article!

P. S. — This article is to be considered as my second paper on husbandry.

2d P. S. — I began by saying that the pumpkin had no poet. The following stanza may seem to disprove the assertion: —

"Peter, Peter, pumpkin-eater,
Had a wife, and could n't keep her;
He put her in a pumpkin-shell,
And there he kept her very well."

This beautiful scrap stands in our literature without a name. Whether part of a larger poem by some Tupper, or only the sport of the moment, is unknown. But it is plain the author meant to sing the domestic infelicity and victorious discipline of Peter, and not the merits of pumpkin. *That* is merely incidental.

AUTUMN COLORS.

HEN stone, timber, or muck are to be drawn, then a farm on a level plain is sighed for. But when one considers the enjoyment of the eyes, never let him settle on a flat. One should look down on the world. This I do. And this morning, O Mr. Bonner! and all ye who live in the crypts and passages of New York houses, how I pity you! This morning is one of the mysterious and bewitching days. Surely it is not that the summer is ended, the green year passing, the winter coming, that gives such peculiar influence to the days. Something has been poured out into the air from the land of magic. It has been steeped with atmospheric wine, and we drink by breathing a subtile and exhilarating elixir. The blue is tender and pale. The skies are full of clouds, white, thin, and full of business. This one opening, shutting, melting, reforming, and so through all the changes; this one making haste, as if called to some distant battle, and fiercely driving on in heat to the rendezvous; or if milder thoughts prevail, then they seem like mighty flocks of fleecy birds, gathered from the summer hatching haunts of the north, and borne southward by the annual impulse of migration. But such is the depth, the beauty, and the mystic influence of the heavens, that to look up long into its cope affects you with giddiness, such as men feel who look down from great heights. And then, too, the color of all things is changing, — not changed, but only hinting

color. We must except the maple-trees. Some of them are changed to a straw color. Yonder is one very green except one branch, which stretches up from the bottom nearly to the top, and that is of vivid scarlet. It looks like a tree with a great bouquet of flowers in its bosom. But along the fences are crimson leaves; the autumn yellows predominate. The corn is cut up, and stands out on the hills around here in shocks to dry. The emerald grass was never more tender in its green. The orchard is waiting to be relieved of its burden. All summer long it has eased itself by throwing down a part of its fruits, worm-picked or storm-gathered; and now those apples that remain, full grown, plump, ripe, look wistfully at you, as if asking your care for winter. And the birds, — how they do behave! What is the matter with them? No one of them frolics. They have lost all their gamesome ways. They collect in mown field for seeds, they hover about orchards, exchanging remarks among themselves in low tones, like well-bred people, but none of them boisterous, frisky, or songful. Bluebirds, robins, and such sorts, abound; sometimes scores flock about, then trios and fours. It is plain that they are done with summer. They have no nests now. Their children are all grown up. The birds all belong to the old folks' party.

I wandered out this morning under the trees (the good lady had gone to the village, and her daughter too, and I was quite free, and was shirking all work, and having a good time on the grass). That, you know, is a good way to write an article. It is bad to go out and look at things if you wish to write about them. You must let them look at you. You must show yourself to nature; walk about confidentially and lovingly; gaze at just those things that have magnetism in them, or sympathy, or influence, or whatever you choose to call it. Then, after an hour or two, if you wish to write, go to your desk, and whatever has had a *real* hold upon you will then come vividly up like pictures, — just as it does to me, now; and I should give you a sparkling, glorious article now, were it not that at this very nick of time I am interrupted by the word, that if I send in time for this week, I must send this minute. O, what you *have* lost! It was very fine, — very, — the thing I was about to do!

OUR HOUSEKEEPING EXPERIENCE.

EN are naturally either proud or conceited, and sometimes both. This appears in many things, but in nothing more than in the supercilious airs in which they indulge about *housekeeping*. Every well-bred woman has had occasion to lament the ignorance in which men live, without shame or self-reproach, of the commonest elements of domestic economy. How often does the skilful wife lecture the discontented husband about the impossibility of getting a breakfast in ten minutes, or of always having things up to an imaginary perfection; or of doing as well on washing-days, or when the cook is sick, or has broken her temperance pledge, or when there has been an insurrection among the help. Only the constant reminders of the excellent women at the head of the bureau of domestic affairs can keep men from presumptuous remarks and ignorant complaints. It would be well if men could sometimes be left to do their own work. We have an experience to relate.

Our summer vacation was ended, but the family were to remain in the country until the frost opened chestnut-burrs and nipped the boys' fingers. We concluded to board ourselves for the day or two. It was Saturday. We began to reflect upon the stores to be laid in for Sunday, and the method of preparing them. We have a little gas-stove, invaluable for sickness, for pet suppers, and for returned gentlemen disposed to make their own tea. With it we could boil and bake. To *broil* was beyond its skill — or, at any rate, beyond our knowledge of its capacity. We rummaged the shops and alighted upon a gas-broiler, to be described hereafter.

We proceeded next to our grocer's, ordered six cantaloupes, as many tomatoes, and bread. On reaching home, it occurred to us that butter was sometimes used with bread, and that had been forgotten. We went back for it, and also procured half a dozen eggs. On reflecting how the eggs were to be eaten, pepper and salt came to mind, and not a particle of either could we find in the well-cleaned castor. We looked into the store closet, behind all the bottles, tore a little hole in every paper package, found sage, summer-savory, catnip, empty spice-boxes, salt-bags used for corks, and nests of boxes of all sizes, some with a smell of allspice, some with odor of cinnamon, and others fragrant of nutmegs, ginger, and cloves; but no salt, — pepper likewise. After wasting time in order to save it, back we go a third time to the grocer for salt and pepper. A few crackers, also, and a few herrings.

Next, we reflected upon the proper elements of a solitary gentleman's dinner. Soup was out of the question; roast, boiled, and fricassee were rejected; fowls and fish were marked out; and only porter-house steak and mutton-chop remain. The quantity staggered us a little. But, to err on the side opposite famine, we ordered two beefsteaks and five pounds of mutton-chop. (Let the sequel be noted.) As there was nobody in the house to receive them, we raced home to 'tend the door! We waited a full hour, and when at length the things came in, our patience had gone out.

Next, we found that coffee must be bought, then tea (English breakfast tea, of course, real Souchong, — the only tea of thorough refinement, green teas being for unlearned drinkers). These we brought home in our own hands. At length our labors of preparation seemed over, and we began to contemplate results, — when it flashed upon us that there was neither milk nor sugar in the house! These caused another journey. We hunted up a kitchen knife and fork, for every available instrument had been carried away, and the silver was all locked up in somebody's safe. Thus nothing was left for burglars, and — nothing for us. In this round of investigation we gained an acquaintance with our own house which forty years of common life would not bestow. We found out all about the sideboard, its spoon-drawer, its napkin-drawer, its closet, and that secret drawer on each side, so cunningly arranged that no thief would ever suspect its presence until he found it out. Then the china-closet was a perfect novelty, and held us in long investigation. We climbed to the top shelves of the store-closet, saw fragments of dishes,— various old acquaintances that disappeared long time ago. We searched the hall-closet, and the kitchen-closet, the closets between the two rooms, full of drawers; we got down on our knees to look into lower closets tucked in under suites of drawers, and we mounted up on barrels to peer into high nooks and shelves, and, in one case, the barrel playing us a mean trick, we came down both sooner and faster than we had intended.

But how shall we describe our experiences when all these preparations resulted in an actual meal? A long flexible tube was brought from the central gas-fixture, and connected with the pet stove. To boil the water for tea or coffee was easy. We had often done that. But we had forgotten just how much tea should be put in for a drawing. And the quantity was certainly enough. We diluted and diluted, and were prodigal of milk and sugar, without being able to cover the prodigious bitterness of the draught. We note that the two principal faults of tea-making were too much tea and too long steeping. It took us yet longer to drink it, and longer yet to get over it, and into sleep.

But this was all commonplace compared with our meat history. The broiler was very much like two iron pot-lids soldered together, with a hollow handle attached. The gas came through the handle into the space between, and the lower section being perforated with a multitude of gas-holes, when gas was let on the lower surface was covered with blue jets. The meat being placed on a tin dish, this blazing cover was placed on proper supports just over it, and shot its heat downwards. It is a capital contrivance. The juice, the odor, and the fragrant fumes, attempting to escape, were driven back into the meat, and in my own case, such was the force of repression, that they were driven out of the plate and over on to the dining-room carpet (for all our exploits took place there). Just as the meat began to sizzle and sputter, and while we were delightedly gazing at the process, the tube slipped off the handle, the flame went out very suddenly over the meat, but not till the escaping gas from the liberated tube had caught fire and shot a flame across our hands, that caused us to drop broiler, knife, and everything else, with astonishing celerity. We had no idea before how spry we could be. The evil was soon repaired, but only to play off again the same trick, till we held the tube on to the broiler with one hand, and manipulated the meat with the other. We salted it, we peppered it, we turned it twice, the first time on to the floor, the next time on to the dish, but with the same side up. The fork was a four-pronger. It could not get hold, or only just so far as was needful to effect a deception and a disaster. At length we put out the gas, uncovered the meat, took both hands, and triumphantly reversed the obdurate steak.

It was with some pleasure, but not much pride, that we sat down, at length, to the repast. The bread was baker's. Of course it was dry, tough, and tasteless. The tea we have spoken of. The meat was the grand dependence. It was serviceable. We could hardly cut it, and could not chew it. The tomatoes were good. The melons were not. But the whole dinner agreed with our theory of moderation in appetite, and the satisfaction which we lacked in eating we sought to gain by profitable meditations.

Facilis descensus Averno; sed revocare gradum, &c., — "It is easy to get dinner, but to wash up the things, this is the burden and toil!" Virgil never spoke a truer word.

The water was hot. We found it out the moment we put our hand in the dish. It was the same hand that the gas had flamed on. We reflected on the difference between dry heat and moist hotness.

We could find no dish-cloth. The grease would not come off the plates. There was no soap. We rubbed with our hand, which only gave the grease a circular form on the plates. At length we got a newspaper, and by vigorous rubbing, got the ware into a presentable condition. The tea-cups were better served. We found a napkin on the bottom of the spoon-drawer. It was a mercy!

There was no swill-bucket, and nowhere to throw the slops, and nobody that came for these superfluities in summer. The melon-rinds, the tomato fragments, the inexorable meat scraps, and the unmentionable sundries of a man's cooking were heaped into the dish-pan. There they stood. Another newspaper served to rub down the table. It was our last solitary meal. A week afterwards the fragments were found standing on the table where we had left them; the lamb-chops we had left and forgotten in the cupboard, and they had a way of making their presence and exigencies known. Indeed, our whole procedure in this case met with the disapprobation of the powers that be, nor can we say that they exactly suited us.

But we have, now, a profound sense of a man's dependence on women for domestic comfort. Instead of thinking that housekeeping is easy, — a mere nothing, we admire and revere the genius that conducts so intricate a campaign as must be every single day's housekeeping.

SOLITUDE: WASPS.

UCH company prepares us to enjoy solitude, and being alone fits us again for society. There is a longing for rest which grows upon us in the throng, not merely from fatigue, but from a subtile action of pride and self-respect. In society men are like threads, woven in and out, and composing a fabric of many colors. They tend to lose their personal distinctness. One wishes to separate himself from all influences about him, and see just what is left of himself. Our life runs hither and thither as the Croton water follows the plumber's pipes. It is no longer a river flowing at its own will, between its own banks, with its own pools and shallows, windings and shoots, depths and breadths. We escape from multitudes with a sense of intense gladness.

The quiet, the unquestioning silence, the absence of watching eyes, the subsidence of vigilance, guard, and circumspection, on our own part, the gentle rise of liberty in all things, the release of the nerves, the unvexed placidity of the disposition, — these are the first-fruits of solitude.

Now, if one has sought rest in the country, he will be conscious of the distinct luxury of sounds in distinction from noise. The city is a vast mill. It crashes, jars, rattles, grinds. The houses shake. There is not an hour of the day, and scarcely one of the night, in which your nerves do not quiver to the heavy roll of burdened vehicles. At a little distance the sound of the city is like the roar of surf on an exposed seashore. All individuality of sounds is merged in the great battle of noises which fill the air and shake the ground. After an hour's dash upon the express, we land forty miles away. Soon we are walking a silent path along the hill-side. A few crickets chirp. A chipmonk half whistles, half barks, as he dives into the chinks of the stone-wall. It is an upland path along which you walk, stopping often, gazing now at the great cloud-fleets that voyage through the sky without pilots or crew, forever sailing, but never accomplishing their voyage; now at the hills, scarped and moulded to every form and with every variation of line. The Hudson lies like a lake before you. It is a charmed world! Your cares forget you. A soft sadness mellows every feeling. Out of sadness, if it be a right one, grow the sweetest flowers of gladness. You take hold of God's thoughts in nature, and are sure that his realm is wider than the human kind.

Man is master. But there is a great deal in this world besides man. Nature takes a thousand darlings to her bosom. Every evening motherly darkness puts to bed myriads of unnamed children of the sod, of the leaf, of tree, bush, moss, and stone. Every morning she sends again to awaken her brood, and troops them forth to their dewy breakfast. "The eyes of all wait upon thee, and thou givest them their meat in due season. Thou openest thy hand and satisfiest the desires of every living thing." We sometimes get nearer to God in proportion as we get far from men. These neglected treasures of Nature are a book of Divine things, and if we do not read, the Creator does.

* * * * *

The wasp is always well dressed, and always ready for company. A nimble creature, exquisite in every particular, — trig, polished, burnished, elegant in form, — what single thing can be alleged against him except that little stiletto which he carries in a terminal sheath? Yet he is not to be blamed. He did not put it there. All that in reason can be required is, that he use his concealed weapons in a manner conformable to justice and good morals. And this I believe he always aims to do. At any rate, if men would use their tongues with half that discretion which belongs to the walk and conduct of wasps, the world would gain at a great rate.

If anybody has reason to avenge himself upon them, I am he. When October days come, and sad thoughts invade the bosoms of wasps, they gather themselves around the house and barn, on sunny days, to make ready for winter.

Now, for a gentleman at leisure walking up and down, soliloquizing good-will to all creation, it is a very awkward thing to have a wasp creeping up between his boot and pantaloon, and he be ignorant of the fact!

The poor insect is unconscious of any impropriety.

He has no suspicion of the scenes which you will soon enact. It is not until he has ascended above your knee that some motion constraining the cloth presses him close to your warm flesh. The contact is a terror to him. It may be the bosom of a devouring enemy! Like a hero, he will die fighting. He thrusts out his sword in a manner that dispels every poetic dream, and brings you to the realities of life with such a clutch at the spot as no man can give except one who has once had a wasp between raiment and body. You have got him! To do it you have taken a large grasp, that he may be encompassed with thicknesses of cloth impervious to the longest sting. But the act and attitude are not favorable to grace. You rush toward the house or barn, careless of pace or dignity, and eager only for deliverance. Now, unless one has been drilled, it is difficult to disrobe while you are bent half double, and with only a left hand at liberty for use and an enemy in the rear. As the cautious work goes on, some luckless fold loosens, and the enemy is at you again, this time in good earnest. Strange that so small an instrument can put a brave man into such ecstatic haste. But there is many a man who could firmly face a cannon, who could not stand for a moment with a wasp under his garment!

The fact is, you do not know where he is — or will be. He may be in your hand, or he may be just in the act of lancing you, here or there or anywhere. And the expectation is dreadful. We know that it is. An enemy in the dark is always powerful through fear.

I consider one wasp under our dress as more terrible than nine hundred and ninety-nine in a fair fight in the open field!

Bad as this scene is to a proud nature with delicate susceptibilities, there is a disgrace even worse; for, within a few days, and while your flesh creeps with the remembrance, you are walking your garden with a few friends, picking flowers for one and another in turn, and nourishing the hours with genial converse, when in the very middle of a sentence you seize yourself with a desperate clutch, and without word or bow you race and hobble toward the house again. You have but one single comfort, — that you are not stung yet. With utter expedition, you come down to the root of the difficulty, and find that there was no wasp at all, only a leaf tickling your skin! In fact, you are angry now to think there was no wasp. If one must go through the fear, the march, the fumble, the search, he ought at least to be rewarded with a wasp!

Now, whatever may have been the sentiment, the tenderness, the sobriety of the former hour, such an experience tends to dissipate it; and so, Friend Bonner, the mere writing about it has so put to flight all my pretty fancies and conceits about solitude, that I think it best to reserve them for a time when solitude shall not be so sweetened.

FOOD DISCOVERIES.

ID it ever enter your mind to inquire how certain articles of diet were first introduced? Much speculation has been indulged in respecting the origin of language: how men began; whether the first parents were born already talking, language being a part of the machine, just as striking is of the clock; or whether they first began by interjections and grunts, which in time worked out into words and syllables, until in time language *grew.* Such researches are very profitable, without doubt.

But will it be any less so to inquire into the steps by which the first eaters advanced, the progress of discovery and the eras of invention? It takes no deal of practice to set a child in the line of eating, now that everything is in working order. But how about the first men? Did they go about tasting everything that they saw? or were they instructed? There seems to be no positive evidence that they were, and analogies are against it. I can imagine Eve experimenting upon peaches, whose color invites, whose flavor provokes, a further trial. Strawberries and grapes, — how could a hungry soul do less, having smelled of them, than taste? But chestnuts, cocoanuts, and many other things, must have had a history. A chestnut-burr does not reward the handling at first. Perhaps these do not grow in regions first populated, or frosts may have had the first handling of the burr, and opened the silk nest in which the nuts had lodged, and then some wind served a writ of ejectment on them. Then the all-devouring pig might have experimented upon them. Or squirrels may have been pioneers, and men, observing the satisfaction manifested by their inferiors, may have concluded that it was worth their trial.

But the difficulties do not chiefly lie in the direction of nuts and flavorsome fruits. When was the transition made from cereals and fruits, from roots and leaves, to *flesh?* That must have marked an era.

Is it Charles Lamb that gives the account of the first roast pig? He has not mentioned, if I recollect aright, the authorities consulted, though his known sobriety of judgment and carefulness of statement lead us to conclude that he had satisfactory data for the statements made. But his theory or history does not seem to indicate so much the origin of a general use of flesh, as a local and special taste which sprung up for pig. When did men begin to slay cattle? to dare to eat meat red with its blood? When did they discover that water contained food? Was it not a bold man that first ate fish? But when we come to crabs and lobsters, the case becomes wonderful! Can anything be more abhorrent to the first impressions than those sprawling, many-legged, hideous-eyed, nimble, flat dragons of the deep? Suppose a storm to have thrown one upon the shore. How dared a man to touch it? He must have been drunk and reckless. But an oyster, that marvel of delicacy, that concentration of sapid excellence, that mouthful before all other mouthfuls, who first had faith to believe it, and courage to execute! The exterior is not persuasive.

One would be as likely to gather stones for a luncheon, as the oyster, shut fast in his shell. Imagine one opened. The long shell contains this armless, legless, eyeless pulp, without skin, hair, or bone, without motion or sense. What does it most resemble? Every one will have his own imagination. But each one of them, we dare to say, will be something repulsive to taste. Even to this hour, the first acquaintance with oysters is with much hesitation and squeamish apprehension. Who, then, first gulped the dainty thing, and forever after called himself blessed? I have my own theory.

Some adventurous sailors, probably, were driven ashore, their boat swamped, all their provisions sunk, and half their company drowned. Unable to find root or acorn on the barren shore, afraid to venture back into the country, where, perhaps, they might have been served up for food themselves, they sat upon the beach, disconsolate. Some dry sticks, which the waves cast up, lay near them. By rubbing they kindled a spark, and built a fire upon the sand and stones. They saw oysters lying about, cast up by the violent waves which had been so disastrous to them. Some lay underneath the wood, some at the edge of the coals. The oyster, surprised at such a warm reception, opened his mouth, and could not shut it! From that moment the world was richer. The hungry men believed the benignant gods had wrought a miracle for their salvation. The morsel looked unsavory. But if the divinities had wrought food out of stones, what were they, that they should be afraid to eat? No sooner had they tasted than they were confirmed in their superstition. This was the very food of the gods. A portion had been dropped down for them!

But, now that men have learned to eat such uninviting, and even repulsive things, why should they, with ill-timed prejudice, turn away from other morsels and delicacies? Why is not a rat as good as a rabbit? Why should men eat *shrimps* and neglect *cockroaches?* In other words, why eat the white shrimps and reject the black ones? Why, in short, should not every plump and well-conditioned insect be turned to good account, some for stews, some for soups, and some for garnishes? A boiled ham, ornamented no longer with useless cloves, but with grasshoppers and roaches! Vermicular soups, as well as Vermicelli? The French eat snails, and have snaileries. Saint John lived on locusts. Spiders taste like walnuts. There are stores of luxuries yet in reserve. Instead of taxing our wits to find how to exterminate the insect creation that invade our dwellings, prey upon our harvests, and mar our fruit, let us exchange our tastes, lay aside our prejudices, and attack them with our palate. Once let it be put in full activity, and there is nothing can stand before the human mouth. French *savans* are attempting to introduce horse-flesh to the tables which long have flourished beef. Why not next invade the long-neglected list of delicacies, hitherto despised as luxuries, and made to live a useless life, or even a mischievous one?

GOOD-NATURED PEOPLE.

R. BONNER: It is a great pleasure to write a paper upon *good-nature*, to a good-natured man, just as it is fit to speak of justice before a just judge, or of art before a refined person. Are you not good-natured? Then the handwriting on the face is not spelled rightly. The form, too, and all the personal circumstances, agree! There is something in breadth of body and largeness of countenance that always suggests generous and good-natured disposition. Good-nature seems to require some space on which to unroll. Lines and angles are for wit. A smooth brow and corrugated cheek indicate thought. This matter of the cheek, however, is purely stomachic, and not cerebral. A sunken cheek and thin face under a large brow show that the brain cheats the stomach of good digestion.

Good-nature is, for the most part, among the young a matter of *temperament*. Bilious temperaments are not apt to be cheerful. They are grave and stern, or sad. Nervous temperaments are not equable. They are excessively happy or intensely unhappy. They are quick for joy, and as quick for sorrow. A man of nervous temperament, in good health, in prosperous condition, in peaceful circumstances, may be cheerful and good-natured. But excitements and disappointments go hard with him. There are some men whose nerves seem not to have been covered up. They lie out to the weather.

But phlegmatic persons are good-natured from a want of sensibility. They are not affected by troubles, because they live under bomb-proof roofs.

The sanguine temperament affords the genuine good-natured disposition. Here it is natural. Everything conspires to produce cheerfulness, hopefulness, and ardor of sentiment.

But while good-nature in youth is largely a matter of nice organization, it becomes in age a result of will and of habit. Many men are drilled to it by their experience; some come to it by the force of religious motives; and some because, in the decay of forces, many of the unruly or discordant elements of their nature are weakened and subordinated.

But, however it may come, or upon whatever terms it may exist, how blessed are good-natured people! They only, of almost all mankind, have invariable good luck. They convert trouble into amusement. Or they meet it with such cheer that its power is broken.

Good-nature disarms enmity, allays irritation, stops even the garrulity of fault-finding. It more than half overcomes envy. A real good-natured man is the most troublesome morsel that the malign passions ever attempt to feed upon. He is the natural superior of irritable persons. He that can govern himself can control others. An irritable man, whom any one can excite, is like a horse kept at livery, ridden by every one, and spurred by each rider. Nobody is so little his own master as he who can be stirred and provoked at another's will. Anybody can eject him from his castle.

There is high eulogy pronounced in Sacred Writ

upon good-natured men, for such I take to be the meaning of the passage in Proverbs, "*He that is slow to anger is better than the mighty, and he that ruleth his spirit than he that taketh a city.*" It is harder to keep your temper than to take a city! It shows more skill, foresight, courage, and good engineering, especially in their cases who are naturally irritable. They have to provide beforehand, to make battle against subtle enemies, and often under desperate conditions. But it is worth all it costs.

Ought there not to be associations for the promotion of *good-nature?* Ought not premiums and testimonials to be given? No branch of education stands more in need of culture. None will be at once so much of utility and accomplishment together! And if some movement can be made, will *you* consent to preside at some meeting for such a purpose? In the earlier meeting none but men of known good-nature should be called together. Atrabilious reformers would ruin us. No man who cannot keep a smile on his face as long as the dew rests on clover in a cloudy summer morning ought to be intrusted with making the constitution and by-laws. After we have secured a proper organization thus, we might admit others to our good-natured influences. Something ought to be done.

There are a great many cross men about now-a-days. People are fault-finding. Indeed, I have been grumbled at myself. Can anything more be needed to show the need of reformatory measures?

STRAWBERRIES AND CREAM.

HOW sweet is the air! It is full of moisture, smell of new leaves and earth-odor. The sky does not scowl! Neither does it smile. It has a grave and reverend aspect. And yet clouds are frolicking like kittens, running in and out, whisking and scudding as if sent forth on purpose to play. There is a deal of waggery in a spring rain. It seems to enjoy the untimely spirts which it makes upon men and beasts. To catch a man under an umbrella, — to push him hither and thither, to swing sheets of rain underneath his protection, and finally to turn his umbrella inside out, wrest it from his hands, and then to pelt down upon him in unmeasured generosity, appear to give a spring rain the utmost satisfaction. Another trick is peculiarly pleasing to the moist divinities that spy and play in the clouds.

A wagon full of unprotected people, seeing the shower, make desperate speed toward a shed or shelter. A race is fairly set. The rain scuds after them, but holds off until they are within a few rods, then down comes the torrent, and wets them as thoroughly as if they had travelled at their leisure, instead of blowing their horse with tantalizing speed. So, too, a weather-wise eye scans the clouds from the place of refuge where he has lurked snug and dry, and declares the rain over, — ventures forth, and gets well on to the road, when, whish! dash! the cunning shower pours all over him! Water will put out fire. But it has kindled temper a good many times, or made it burn the fiercer when already kindled. And yet how inexpressibly balmy, and how full of mysterious influences is one of these changing, multitudinous days in early summer!

Well, you will ask me, "What of all that?" Why, that I have been up to Peekskill; that the hills are all clothed in green; that birds have improved since last summer, and can sing at least one note higher on the scale; that frogs are practising on one string in all the solitary pools; that squirrels are wide awake, and crows as solemn as ever. The moss on the stone-wall has been well kept through the winter, grass is almost fit for the scythe, daisies are winking at you all over the mowing-lot, wrens are gibbering, hens cackling, ducks waddling, calves frisking, as if all the world were at peace. Little seeds are sending up little stems; and little stems are rocking little baby-buds, which in a few weeks will open forth into beauty. The crops are giving glorious promise. There are my strawberries! — ah, sir, it would do your benevolent heart good just to look at the generosity of these plants! The leaves! — how large, what healthy green! — how they hold themselves, like a roof, over the young berries! Every day the hens go up and explore the chances. But they shall not have any! They shall all be shut up!

And this harvest of strawberries, — what visions of bliss lie in the near future! They shall be picked in great, cool dishes, before the sun rises, with dew fresh on their blushing cheeks! They shall be pulled by delicate fingers; heaped up in saucers forever too small, — great berries, — each one a mouthful, — some to be eaten just as they are, while the red multitude are to be overpoured with cream. Cream! what is that? A pasture, knee-deep with clover, with blue-grass, with orchard grass, and red-top; spring water gushing cool close by; a pail, large, scoured white, and brimming full with milk crowned with foam; pans, bright as silver, in a cool, sweet cellar, through which the air circulates, carrying off every gas or odor; and then, after twelve hours, do not be too particular, but take that which comes first on the pan,—not too long kept and clotted, not too soon skimmed and thin, but cream that is neither young nor old, but a term midway between both,—take this, O inquisitive reader! and let your hand be liberal toward the saucer-full of Jenny Lind, Triumph de Gand, Bartlett's Seedling, or Lanier's Madison, and then, with sweet bread and butter, and your friends around you, eat, and pity the gods that sit above the clouds where they can't have cows or strawberries!

But let not those despair who have no cream. Put ripe berries in a dish, add a little *cold water*, break them down with a spoon (a silver spoon will do) to a jelly, adding just enough water and sugar to make them half liquid, and you shall find many another dish less delicious than strawberries and water! But who can depict the comfits, the strawberry tarts, the pies, the puddings, jams, and preserves which they form? And yet, preserved strawberries are but a mockery. The flavor, the spirit, the aroma, cannot be kept by fire or sugar. The strawberry was born to bless us in its lifetime. Its posthumous honors are, like those of many others, but dim and fugitive memories of something that was, but is not.

And now, having suitably opened this subject, I am prepared to say, that I defy you to a trial of endurance and capacity in a strawberry-feast. You shall not return without a strong battle. We will so fill you, pelt you, stain you with strawberries that for a month thereafter you shall imagine yourself to be a round, red, juicy, fragrant strawberry!

P. S. — Do not publish this. I have no objection to its going into the LEDGER in a confidential way. But it is a family matter addressed principally to your eyes.

THE LIFE OF FLOWERS.

IT is conceded now, by vegetable physiologists, that plants have a real *life*, — not by a figure of speech, not a slight analogy of life, but a real vegetable life, which connects them with the long chain of more perfectly developed life above them. This it is a great comfort to know. Life without passions! Life without selfishness, envyings, jealousy, supplantings, or hatred! It may to some seem a little tame to have such an incompetent life. And, without a doubt, it would be a poor substitute for the higher animal life. But, with it, and as one department in the great realm of organic life, it is intensely interesting to see a development, if not of beings, yet of living agents, without wills, affections, or passions, producing such a round of magnificent effects as is found in the vegetable kingdom.

But to a sensitive imagination, the belief of this life-principle works increased tenderness toward flowers. They are now relatives,—if not country cousins, yet remote kindred. We plant them with some sense of the dignity of seeds! We nurse and tend them as if they were infant children. We begin to transfer to them the experience of human life. They must eat. They must drink. They must perspire. They must be kept clean. They must sleep, breathe, excrete, and, in short, perform all functions of supply, repair, and development.

But may we not imagine, now, that as there is a vegetable life so there is a vegetable soul, which bears to our higher human soul about the same relation that the vegetable life-principle does to the animal life-principle?

Is it so difficult to imagine (for we suggest it as a mere fancy) that flowers represent different dispositions? In human experience disposition springs from affections or sentiments. But flowers do not think or feel. Beauty seems the end of their life. Their souls, if they have any, must be regarded as a modification of this element of beauty. And as, when we speak of a person's disposition we think of conscious and voluntary feeling, so, when we speak of a flower's disposition, we should think of some tendency or active reaching toward beauty, in some of its innumerable combinations.

What the range of such a life is, it is impossible for one to conceive. It must not be measured by *our* estimate of beauty, nor by analogies with our sort of life. Men are supreme egotists. They regard nothing as of value that does not in some way measure itself by *them*. But beauty has relatively but a small function in human life. It would seem to play a higher part in the economy of the universe. If the profusion of things beautiful, the varieties of beauty, the creation of beauty outside of all human recognition, — as in shells under the wave, in fish, in insects that live in wood or earth, in tropical life, where the most gorgeous displays are least witnessed, in hyperborean beauty, in crystalline snow-forms and frost-etchings, — be considered, it is plain that beauty is developed in this world on account of the taste, or want, or love, of the organizing and creating mind, rather than for the immediate necessity or use of the human race. Thus, a civilized man, living among Indians, might sit for years, occupying his leisure in writing his meditations and observations, and pouring out the elements of a noble life, without its having relation to the consciousness or occupation of those among whom he outwardly dwelt. So God may be pouring out a noble life, written in elements of beauty, beneath, above, around, and within human life, and yet, in so far as we are concerned, little or not at all recognized.

In such a view, flowers may be said to live to God more than to men. And if they are effecting a divine mission, and having a relation to the Divine mind, they may have more of a soul-life than we think or dream of. Judged by our standard, birds have very poor language. But is the human idea of language the fit one by which to measure bird-language? Is there no listening except through our ears? Is there no back-realm, no invisible sphere through which musical sounds move and beauty gleams, more freely, easily, and copiously than through the opaque elements of human life? And precisely the same thought applies to form, color, and odor in flower-life.

How easily, then, may we imagine that flowers are set to develop, in this world, another and entirely different experiment of life, having its peculiar elements, its relations, more directly with God and spirits than with men, and discovered to men only so far as our gross senses can recognize them. Flowers, as such, can present themselves to only two doors of the mind, — to sight and smell. The ear has nothing to do with them. Touch and taste are related to them in no way that discriminates them from everything else. The eye and the nose at once, and they only, recognize the flower as differing from other objects.

In short, these most exquisite organizations, that have so very slight a hold on human life, have been created and spread, with a Divine care and wisdom, in such profusion, and are so full of creative thought and taste, as to compel us to infer that they answer a purpose quite beyond the ordinary ideas of men. Other beings are being ministered to besides men. As our eye glances over a meadow purpled with June, it does not follow that all this gorgeous life rises and expends itself for us, alone or chiefly, or *that there is no more life in it than so much as our coarse senses perceive.* Flowers have a life that ministers chiefly in another direction. They are sent to do God's work in unrevealed paths, and to diffuse influence by channels that we hardly suspect. A lighthouse upon a promontory jutting far out into the sea, cannot tell its keeper what it has been doing all night. While he slept, it burned on. It flashed its beams far out along the beaded crests of waves, and fell upon the eye of the watcher, — on an Indiaman, returned from months of sailing out of sight of land, — to tell him where he was, and how near to his port. It cheered some storm-tossed mariner that had lost his reckoning, and at its flash first knew, for many days, where he was. It warned many a sail, that then stood off from perilous shoals. It confirmed and cheered many a navigator, who, as it sent its beams forth to him, knew that his calculations were right. And so all night long, its long silent beams shot forth into the darkness, conveying mute lessons and tidings to a hundred ocean craft, and yet it kept no journal, and made no report of its doings; and when, in the morning, the keeper arose to trim his dying lamps, he knew nothing of all the mysterious signallings that had been going on, — messages of life and death, sent on beams of light through the darkness, to passers-by on the far-off sea.

Has God no lights and signals? Has the unkindled glow of Beauty no relation to those that pass by us through the invisible realm? Do we that look upon the kindled flowers, imagine what they have done, or are doing, to eyes that watch from afar? Because their life is not one fitted to commune with us, have they no life and communion the other way?

Flowers may beckon toward us, but they speak toward heaven and God!

CHILDHOOD AND DISENCHANTMENT.

HE progress of disenchantment marks the advance and decline of age. Our youth occupies itself unconsciously in surrounding all things with the hues and proportions of the imagination. Mountains will never again be so large as in childhood, nor roads so long, nor stones so heavy, nor colors so bright, nor distances so limitless. When the ripe man, after years of absence, revisits the scenes of childhood, he is disappointed and surprised. Is it possible that this little stone, which was a landmark in our games, ever seemed so vast as it did?

Is this the *river*—this thread of silver water—from whose edge we used to look fearingly into the current? And those immense trees, in whose tops winter winds roared, and summer birds sang, can it be possible that they were so small as this? Once we thought it a feat to throw a stone up to the middle branches; now to jerk one over the top is a mere trifle. The well is not so deep as it was, the pasture is not so large, the road to Aunt Bull's not so long, nor to the brook beyond where we watered the horse every day, nor to the orchard, nor to Mr. Bidwell's, nor clear round to the pond!

In like manner do our wonderful books and wonderful heroes diminish in interest and importance. Robinson Crusoe and Pilgrim's Progress alone hold out, and are as engaging in later years as in earlier. But even that incomparable marvel and soul-stirring repository of wonder, the Arabian Nights, has lost its wonderfulness. We read it with sadness to find that we are so little interested where once we were intoxicated with excitement. Meanwhile the witch stories, the children's tales, the Jack the Giant-Killer and his compeers, are gone forever.

If we could array before our judgment now the wits, the skilful men, the strong men, that excited our youthful admiration, it is very probable that we should turn them all off as worth scarcely a thought. It is said that *the strong man* of the town could lift a barrel of cider and drink from the bung. We used to imagine what a time Samson would have had with such another giant! And it is to be doubted whether Samson, with all his strength, ever lifted a barrel of cider and drank out of its bung.

In these degenerate days of railroads, stage-coaches are no longer the important things they were in our childhood. When the horn sounded, far up the street, where the road comes into the village, no matter where we were, nor at what play, we ran and tumbled into the front-yard to see the wonder of each alternate day. There came the four horses, and the swinging, round-topped stage, — and that great man, the stage-driver!

If he had commanded us, we verily believe we should have raced and chased the town over, on his errands, enough compensated by being under the command of a man so wonderful. Not Solomon in all his glory was ever arrayed like one of these, or drove such horses, or had such supreme influence upon the children! And then, to go down to the stage-yard, where Parks kept his horses; to walk reverently about the new, red, magnificent stage, to look in at the stable-door and see a long row of hind legs, and half as many long tails whisking around them, and to wonder what was outside of the door beyond, and take to our heels with desperate fear when the hostler, in imaginary anger, roared out, "Clear out, you rascals! what are you doing here?" — these experiences weighed on our after thoughts, and formed a part of our boyish conversations, and were of as much relative importance to us then as now revolutions and battles are.

But there are some things that lose nothing, and gain much. Those yearning thoughts toward the Infinite and the Eternal, — those solemn and trembling moods of veneration in the presence of evident manifestations of Divine Power, — those heart-lovings toward noble friends who were worthy of all that the soul could give them, — these suffer no declension and no diminution. Age deepens veneration and love. Our riper judgment approves the heart's experience, and adds new impressions. Thus, it would seem as if all experiences that are nearly related to the senses and the body wane as we grow old, while those that spring from the soul inherit something of its immortality, and neither fade with years, or fall away, but, like all the nobler faculties of the mind, grow brighter as they advance toward the gate at whose threshold all weakness ends, and perfectness begins.

MY PICTURE-GALLERY.

I HAVE seen the principal galleries of pictures in American cities, and a few of the eminent collections in London and Paris. It may seem to some like vain and foolish boasting to say that I have a collection of pictures far surpassing any at home or abroad. Yet I conscientiously affirm it. Of course, it would be the vice of a curmudgeon to shut up such a collection. I keep it open through the day, and often far into night. No fee is charged for admission. Entrance is permitted at all times, even when a new arrangement of pictures is going on, — for I have so many pictures that all cannot be exhibited at once, and every day I make some fresh dispositions. Although figure-pieces largely outnumber all others, yet there are admirable sea-pieces, ships, bits of landscape, fine cloud effects, very well executed trees, fruit-pieces, animals of many kinds, true to life. Great pains has been taken with costume. It would be difficult to find any disposition of cloth, from the out-blossoming of a beggar's coat to the heavy folds of velvet and satin, or the fine plaits of linen and lace, that I have not on exhibition. Will you walk with me and take a mere cursory view?

Let us go out the front door into the street. There! see that sad face coming. The artist undertook to depict the expression of one who had been well bred, whose thoughts and feelings were refined, who had for years passed from reverse to reverse;

by turns sickness, or watchings for the sick; poverty without sordidness; neglect of friends borne without bitterness of spirit; and at length age with sharp ills that cripple the limbs and make walking a slow torture. See how gentle and even tranquil the face is! Cheerfulness, patience, and divine trust overlie the sharp features, as gold is put along salient edges of great rooms to catch the light, and take away a sense of heaviness and gloom. Frère never painted such a head. It is a noble study, — within and without.

Just beyond, and in admirable contrast, see that group of little girls. There are six of them. The eldest is ten years old. They are full of life and motion. Just a shade of consciousness is falling upon them, but no regulated vanity as yet. Their hair was well brushed, but the wind has been brushing it again, as it does leaves and tall grass, into the beauty of negligence. Their cheeks are flushed with running. Would you see how sweet and loving they are? Let us walk along past them. Here they come, running, free, eager, without rudeness. They seize me by my hands, by my arms, by my skirts. They look up with pretty questions in their mouths and innocence in their eyes, while one or two, less acquainted or more shy, hang just on the edge of the group, wistful but unventuresome. I never tire of this picture. And such has been the matchless skill of the artist that it never looks to me twice alike.

Walk on. Look down at your feet. Do you see those exquisite effects? The shadows of leaves and branches are cast upon a golden ground of sunlight, and, most wonderful in a picture, they *move*. These long films of shade that shift hither and thither are willow spray. They seem like shadows of spirits. How unlike the rigid forms and positive motion of the leaves of the linden, or fern-leaved ailanthus, that much-abused, beautiful tree. This is an endless picture. Walk where you may, and as long as you will, filmy shadows, mottled with gold, move in a dreamy maze upon the cold, gray stones. We *walk* on pictures. The most delicate etchings, the most exquisite pencil-sketches, cannot compare with these leagues of frescoes under foot.

Stop. Look up at that window. Set as in a frame is a child's face, looking for some expected father, and just behind the young mother. They do not know what a rare picture they form. Neither do others. For, while half behind a tree, to shield my curiosity and interest, I look at them and at the passers-by, scarcely one looks up, and then but a single glance; and yet Reynolds never composed so sweet a figure, in such exquisite color, with such beautiful expression. Notice, by the curbstone yonder, that German woman with a cart drawn in part by two dogs. The hand-cart is full of half-burnt coal and cinders. What grizzly dogs, fierce and harsh to every strange comer; but how lovingly do they spring and tug to reach their mistress as she comes out, dusty, grimed, weather-tanned, with her fragments of fuel! And she! Five hundred people will go past her, and she will not know it. She is as separate from this crowd of life as if she were a carved stone, or a growing tree. Her thoughts and theirs have no more acquaintance than have the birds in the air with the fish in the sea. And yet there is a voice at home that will call out to her, and, with strange resurrection, up from this hard exterior will come the glow, the love, the yearning sympathy of motherhood! In the streets, dogs, dirt, and woman; in the house, mother and babe! and the difference is that of before and after resurrection!

Here go the misses to school! In twos and threes the street is lighted up with faces and beautiful colors! If I were a rich man, I would build a mansion, and have never less than a thousand children under care. To pass the age of twelve should be the fault for which expulsion should be visited. But there falls a broad shadow on the street. Look up. It is one of those unfolding banks of white, full of lines and cinctures of gray. Is it a tabernacle holding spirits within? Or is it some island floated off from ethereal realms? Or is this a caravan such as move through the highways of the air, freighted with treasures to some provincial star, in which odors and essences have given out? The shadow moves slowly down the street, colors fade out, the tracing of leaves on the path is effaced, grays gain ground and white vanishes, until that yellow flood behind, following close, pours the tide of sunlight again on all the street!

There moves a funeral, — twenty carriages; and, except in the first, all seem to take a cheerful view of death — in others. The sexton and undertaker is in his glory. He rides in front, as if he returned in triumph from the war. To him death means fees, gloves, scarfs, and a spectacle arranged in the very best taste for grief. Vanity and money go up to the very gates of immortality. The doctor had professional curiosity in the act of death; the nurse is vain of the number whom she has laid out, and this is only one more! The man that made the coffin is vain of the work; the sexton is vain of the whole job; the grave-digger looks with complacent eye on the grave, dug, he assures you, better than by any other operator in that line, and in half the time. There was much meaning in the Apostle's sentence, "It is sown in corruption and in dishonor and in darkness."

Here comes a nurse, with a plump babe in a little carriage, — another sort of procession, from death to life this is going. Five steps behind, the young mother, herself fair and but a girl; yet would you please her? Look at her child, and look again.

But you grow tired of looking at pictures? Well, it is tiresome. There are too many for once. Let's go back, forget what we have seen, look on some paint and canvas, and be filled with enthusiasm! For men admire men and their works more than God and his works. It is but a part of human egotism.

FAIRY MUSIC.

MOSQUITO has an intense individuality. Others of insects there are that love plunder, that will shed blood to secure their ends, that are prowlers in the night. But this only of all these adventurers commits indecent depredations under the color of the *Fine Arts*.

Gnats, fleas, bed-bugs, chiggers, and other things that shall be nameless, make a business of supplying their hunger, without refinement, without the accompaniments of conversation, or any refinements whatsoever. It is mere appetite. But a mosquito will not gorge himself for the sake of eating. He first offers you a song. He will exhibit you many feats of dexterity. He is a good gymnast, and nimble enough. Your first intimation of his presence is the finest of audible sounds, as if he had strung a gossamer upon his violin, and was sounding the scale far up in those tones which end the earthly scale and join on to the ethereal sounds too fine for gross mortal ears. It draws nearer. It is not a dull monotone. His swift flight and a habit of excursion give to his music the variable and intermitting effects noticed in an Æolian harp, — now loud, now soft, now near, and now far distant. It is this variety, among other things, that gives such effect to his music. Many persons that do not listen to common music listen instantly whenever they hear his. Persons without any natural musical ear can detect to a nicety every note of this airy musician, and often he sets them to beating time for him.

Some have supposed that the mosquito was of a devout turn, and never would partake of a meal without saying grace; but that can hardly be, so long is the ceremony, unless he be imagined a Puritan, addicted to excessive length of service. Others suppose him a gallant, out on a serenade, singing gayly to some fair one; or some roysterer, returning home from too convivial a meeting, and singing ditties and snatches as he goes. But no one who will examine this gentle creature can hold these theories. He is spare, which indicates temperate habits. He is slight and slender, and may be a little vain of his figure;

but the sober gray of his dress shows that he is not a vain beau.

I am, upon profound meditation, satisfied that the mosquito has a natural voïce; that, like the nightingale and whippoorwill, he sings of preference at night; and that blood-sucking is but an accident, while the fine arts are the true aim of his being. The great populous world of mosquitos never touch meats. They are born to vegetable juices. They are a refined and tiny species of vegetarians.

We all know that a mosquito is born in the water. He is not of a turbulent disposition, and does not affect unquiet waters, but still pools and stagnant reservoirs. Here he first appears as a horizontal wriggler. Shortly he mounts to the surface, to see if he can in some way get ashore. In lack of better means, he strips off his skin, tucks it under him as a float, pulls out from their folds a nice pair of wings, for which he had no use when under water, and holds them up to dry in the sun. This is the crisis of his being. Before he got at his wings, before he stript off his water-proof garments, he was nowhere so much at home as in the water. But now, while he is sailing on its surface with his skin-boat under him, should a puff of wind upset him, all is over. The element that nourished him an hour before would now drown him. His whole success in life depends upon a still and dry hour, in which to get his legs stretched and his wings ironed out. But once let him rise, and now "the world is all before him where to choose"! His first preference, next of course to music, is vegetable juice. He banquets on the sap of tender herbaceous stems. He seeks the shadows of underbrush, of weedy nooks, of forests; and here, for the most part, he passes his tranquil life in airy music.

As there are some adventurers even in the most moral societies, so there are some restless mosquitos, who disdain advice, breaking from the traditions and customs of the fathers, and wander into by and forbidden paths. Such enter houses without leave, go without knocking into chambers, and spy out other people's business. But, even then, a mosquito cannot forget the elegance of his native tastes. His flute, if it be a flute that he blows, or viol, if it be stringed music that we nightly hear, is his constant companion. Some rude and indiscriminating people have called him the pirate of the night. Whenever did a pirate preface his deeds of blood with music? No. My own impression is, that the mosquito comes on a serenading errand. He brings you music. It is benevolence, it is a love of harmonious numbers, that inspires him. And yet old harpers, after their strains, expected a full cup of ruby wine. And our tiny singer, being thirsty, alights upon the first succulent thing to slake his thirst. But that is a mere accident. That, after drawing blood, they may be perverted, I do not deny. There is much blood in the world that would turn the head of stronger creatures than mosquitos.

But, my dear Mr. Bonner, mosquitos cannot be treated fitly without some allusion to the conduct of persons visited by them. Admit that they are disagreeable; what do you think *they* would say of *us*, were they to write for the LEDGER? Let my next take up this subject again. Do you object to mosquitos in the LEDGER?

MOSQUITOS. No. 2.

THE day has been too hot. The night is sultry. You are nervous and restless. No place so good as the bed, and to the chamber you repair, hoping soon to lose all remembrance of your cares and troubles in sleep. The light is extinguished, and you resign yourself to the pleasing sensations of approaching rest. When lo! a thin, piercing sound salutes you! It needs no interpretation. It is a mosquito come a-serenading. Is there any trumpet that can wake a nervous man more quickly or more entirely? Every sense is attent. Now the sound comes near, now recedes, now it is lost. It soon comes again, and, watching your opportunity, you give yourself a broad slap upon the face, hoping that the mosquito shared it with you! For a moment he seems dead. You experience a minute satisfaction of petty revenge. But soon the inevitable sound comes again, but with a hither and thither motion. You are acutely attentive. This time, to make sure, your hand is disengaged, and lies outside of the coverlet, ready for a surprising blow. He alights. You feel his delicate touch upon your forehead. Quicker than winking, your hand follows him with such a slap as makes the room echo. But he is quicker than you are, and besides, sees in darkness much better. He is off like a sprite, and sings and pipes in a distant corner. By this time you are quite excited, — you discourse: "The thief (some men put naughty adjectives before the noun), if he would hold his peace and come and eat his fill, and be off, he should be welcome. But the intolerable piping is worse than a surgeon's lancet." Suppose, my friend, that you should get up, light the gas, hunt for him! You had better close the blinds, for, however suitable your condition may be in itself considered, yet, if seen from a neighbor's window, a night-capped man in search of a mosquito, at twelve at night, *en dishabille*, must subject himself to some ridicule. There, now, return to your work. You cannot find him? After all, perhaps that last slap did the business for him. It certainly did for *you*. See how red your much-abused face is! Why not let him take a little blood out of it? It would be improved.

The hero returns to his couch, and the tiny foe returns to the hero. Again the horn sounds, again he strikes out at him, and again misses. At length, tired out, the victim falls asleep. The little trumpeter draws near and sounds a challenge. He circuits all about, and sings every note in his serenade. At length he alights upon a chosen spot, and having satisfied his hunger, retires to some dark corner, overswollen, to collapse and die.

All this would not be worth telling but for its application. I see on every hand men engaged in beating themselves on account of fears, cares, frets, and petty annoyances.

The mother sits by her child slightly ill. She imagines all possible evils, — she torments herself for hours and days at possible, but improbable results. It is a mosquito game. The real evil is petty, and if quietly taken would soon cease of itself. But she must punish herself by every ingenious imagination. Love has its mosquitos. How many sounds does jealousy hear. How many dreads does anxious love breed. How many nameless fears, and how many "what ifs."

Much of the anxiety of business is mere musquito-hunting. When I see a man pale and anxious, not for what has happened, but for what may happen, I say, "Strike your own face, do it again, and keep doing it, for there is nothing else to hit."

Everybody has his own mosquitos, that fly by night or bite by day. There are few men of nerves firm enough to calmly let them bite. Most men insist upon flagellating themselves for the sake of not hitting their troubles.

BOOK-KEEPING.

SOMEBODY has sent to me a very nice book *on Book-keeping*. And no book could have been more timely. There is no other point on which I have a more lively interest than that of keeping books. In fact, I have found it very difficult to get them, and still more difficult to keep them. There seems to be no conscience formed as to *book theft*. It is doubtful whether any indictment could be made to lie against a man for such an act as borrowing and keeping your book. It is rather a mark of confidence. He thus says, "Ah, he is my friend, and he will not expect me to carry the book again to him. When he wants it he will come after it. We always have things in common." Pencils, umbrellas, canes, and books are not property. They cannot be appropriated by one man as owner. They belong to the category in which is included air, light, water, and fire; who wants them may have them. I will not say that this is yet the written law. It is the common law.

Books? The only bodies are they for noble spirits, that have no ailments or annoyances. Books talk to you, not through the ear, but another way. They shout their silent meaning at the soul through the eye. They never importune, and are never reluctant. They are always full without eating. They are still, but never sleep. They grow old without infirmity. They are neither sick nor weary; they outwatch the watcher, and greet the morning, and wait for the stars at evening. For every other guest we make a couch and spread a table. But strange are the manners of books and pictures, that bring rest to our perturbations, and are guests that perform all the offices of hospitality for the host.

Why should *they* be singled out for theft? When my spoons disappear, there is at least a pleasure in saying, "A thief has got them." But even that pleasure is denied me when books appear no more.

Once there came an artist with letters of renown from a friend. He needed help. A fine copy had I of "Stuart's Athens," uncut, large paper, early impressions. So gladly and greedily did he devour the matter therein, that I was beguiled, tempted of the Devil, to offer to let him take the precious volumes to his room, the better to ease his tasks and help his toil. He took them. He thanked me much, and his face glowed. The volumes were large — three — and heavy; — they ought to be, since they had the Parthenon in them, and the whole Acropolis, and many temples to boot. He went, they went, four years went, and he never returned, nor have the books returned! They are gone! That thief of an artist — I sigh for revenge. Could I have and hold him, he should be shut up in a book-case for indefinite years, and be sentenced to read Tupper or Wise's Letters. No. I relent. Not the last. Punishments may be severe, but should never be cruel.

How many first volumes are gone? What is a widowed volume? O that they would take the set if they will take any! The surprise of their "taking off" comes to you too at unexpecting moments. You are discussing with a friend of some matter; there is illustration or proof in Kugler's Handbook. You run for it, and then first learn that it is gone! That gem from Didot's press, — all that you know of it is, it was here, it is not here, and it never will be here. That last clause is the result of long experience. If a book is poor, it is not worth the trouble of returning; if good, it is too valuable to be returned.

When we are Pope, we intend to make great changes in the Creeds and Articles. Stealing books, i. e. borrowing them, shall be put among the mortal sins, and private revenge upon stealers of books shall be venial, under a very slight tariff.

Then, when we are Emperor, we intend, every year, to require each man in the empire who can read and write, to make solemn search of his household, and to file an affidavit that there is not remaining with him a borrowed book! Thus I would reinstate the old Jubilee; only for men, it was once in seven, and once in fifty years: but for books it should come as often as Thanksgiving, Christmas, and New Year's come!

My dear Mr. Bonner, you will now understand how delighted I was to perceive that this subject was attracting attention and that treatises were written upon it. "*Book-Keeping*"—for schools, too, it says. That 's beginning at the right place! I have not read the book yet; but any attempt to rectify this great evil of books that cannot be kept must do good. I commend them to Sabbath schools. "Practical Book-keeping." Admirable theme! Much-needed reform! "Embracing," saith the cover, "single and double entry." This is obscure. "Entry?" does this refer to the act of entering once and twice for books? Why limit it to *single* and *double;* why not say ten and twenty times entry? Men that will take one volume would take twenty if they could; if they come once, they come twenty times.

But perhaps this is explained in the book. I shall read it soon. No doubt it will be another excellent moral aid to weak consciences. The work that will teach *me* BOOK-KEEPING, will do what nothing has done before. I cannot *keep* money. I cannot *keep* books. Blessed is he that shall teach me how!

SPEAKING-HALLS.

LARGE rooms, or halls, for public meetings are not to be regarded merely as conveniences; they are institutions of instruction. And that quite independently of the mere knowledge that is dispensed in them. Our system of government demands of its people the habit of *conference*, of frequent assembly for consideration of common interests. Whatever tends to bring people together in peaceable ways, to elicit their thoughts, to move them with common sentiments, or to inspire them, even for an hour, with feelings common to them all, alike and together, confers a great benefit. It is on this account that convenient and inviting public halls are a means of education. They furnish also places of entertainments, for fairs, social assemblies, for the meetings of societies, lodges, and associations. Whatever brings our people peaceably together does them good. In our climate, and with our national habits, the open air meetings of Southern Europe, the *fêtes-champêtres*, cannot be expected, and provision must be made under shelter.

Churches and town-halls were the earliest provisions for popular gatherings. Pleasure next opened ball-rooms and concert-rooms. But it is to the lecture system that we are indebted more than to any other influence for the rapid progress made within ten years in building spacious and elegant public halls. Ten or fifteen years ago, and, except in a few of the principal cities, no hall could be found which would now be deemed respectable. Now, in all the larger towns, and in many villages even, we find large and convenient audience-rooms. And much more attention is every year bestowed upon warming, lighting, and ventilating them. As yet but few answer all the prime conditions of a good hall. These indispensable conditions are, — strength of structure, ease of entrance and exit, abundance of light, that yet does not dazzle the eyes, the means of regulating the temperature, good speaking qualities, and, lastly, but eminently, *ventilation.*

It is simply a piece of wantonness to build an entrance-way so small that, upon alarm of fire, the audience could not easily clear the hall without crushing and trampling each other. In no other thing is economy more culpable. Every hall should have an exit and vomitory at each end, and, if large enough to hold two thousand people, there should be side openings also. Even in times without alarm, the jamming and pushing of people wedged together in narrow passages is an outrage, not only upon convenience, but upon propriety. It ought to be made a matter of legislation. The law should require a definite relation between the containing power of the hall and the passages and vomitories.

The lighting needs less reformation, since in all large rooms gas is introduced. But much improvement may take place in the disposition of the flame. When the jets are lifted up toward the ceiling, arranged either along the cornice or in central clusters, with suitable openings for the passing off of heat and smoke, they afford the most agreeable light. But when this cannot be done, all strong lights at the end where the speaker stands should be avoided. They are a source of great suffering to many, and of annoyance to all.

It is the practice, frequently, to place on the lecturer's desk an Argand lamp, or a camphene lamp, or other intense flame, as if the only thing required was, light enough. These glaring and intense lights put out the speaker's eyes, and the hearers' too. They are intolerable. It is literally true, that they prevent one's seeing his manuscript; for, by dazzling the eye, and heating the head, they produce indistinctness of vision. The best of all lights are simply a pair of *sperm candles!* They give abundance of light, they throw it just where you need it, they do not blear the speaker's eyes, nor dazzle the audience; they require no snuffing, can be moved easily, and may be procured in any village.

Of ventilation we almost despair. What good will words do, when stench, stupidity, fainting, and half-suffocation do not avail? Only this week, on the 10th of December, we spoke in the hall of one of our best old New England towns, where every person in the room was poisoned by the foul air. Nothing fresh could get in, and nothing foul could get out. It has been so for several years, and will continue to be so. People in other things sensible, and public-spirited, seem to be infatuated on this subject. Bad air seems to be, if not a luxury, a necessary of life.

Even when ventilation is attempted, it is often with an ignorance that is ludicrous. We once were gravely pointed by a committee-man to the efforts made for ventilating a hall capable of holding twelve hundred people. And what was it? A round hole not above eight inches in diameter! This was expected to change the air for twelve hundred people.

Perhaps, at another time, we will mention some of the best speaking-halls in the country.

CONVERSATIONAL FAULTS.

VERY child is early admonished of the rudeness of interrupting a person while speaking. But why this caution should be confined to children we cannot imagine. Their rudeness is the least provoking of any. It is the exhibitions that we meet in genteel society that mar our comfort most and excite our surprise. And among adults we learn to be patient with impetuous natures, whose strong and ungoverned feelings, touched by some spark in your words, go off like bombs, past all power of restraint.

But the aggravated offenders are those who interject your conversation with comments and hints, or vexatious corrections, or meddling smartness, and so take from you all pleasure of fluency. Just as you are coming to the nub of a story, they quietly drop a sentence which tells the whole, and leave you with only the mortifying remnants. Is it a jest that is loaded and in your hand? They slyly step behind you and pull the trigger, leaving you empty as an exploded gun-barrel.

Sometimes a single word, like a drop of ink in a tumbler of water, will change the color of a whole statement. You cannot repel it, nor answer it, for it attacks nothing, says nothing positively, but only fixes in the mind certain suggestions.

There is an inflection of this evil, equally vexatious. It is when a shrewd lip comments in your ear, whisperingly, or aside, upon the remarks or address to which you are listening. It may be that you are not of a retentive countenance. A ludicrous word, dropped just right, sets you into a laugh, irresistible just in proportion to its impoliteness. *You* seem to mock the person speaking, while the arch-whisperer sits demurely, without blame, as innocent as a dove.

Yet less bearable are the comments of conceited persons, upon some performance to which you wish to give your attention. While a symphony is performing, they interpolate it; "Sublime," "Fine, very fine, don't you think so?" "Rather dull, that." During a discourse they are perpetually setting their remarks upon your ears, bringing you back to consciousness, and to contempt. They sing in your ears like mosquitos, they alight upon you as flies in summer-days, only you are debarred the pleasure of aiming a good slap at them. It is seriously to be considered whether this is not a case where a hearty box on the ear would not be entirely proper, moral, and reformatory?

But there is another rudeness which, if less frequent, is equally annoying. It is the rudeness of the talker and not of the interrupter. Many will ask you a question and answer it themselves; they will find fault with you, and race forward with remarks so as to prevent any explanation; nay, they will aggravate the matter by putting stupid replies into your mouth, and then answering *them.* "Don't speak, — I know what you are going to say, — but it is not so, for," — &c., &c.

Many persons have a very cool way of seeing what you think, and insisting upon it; — they saw it in your eyes, or in your face, and will permit no denial. Sometimes you are caught upon a turbulent stream of talk which sweeps you down in the most ludicrous way. You are whirled round, and soused, and overwhelmed with the rushing talk, which you cannot answer or get rid of or modify. At a table, or in car or boat, a man of opposite politics pours at you for a half-hour, misstating your position, charging you with all manner of absurdities, exaggerating facts, and abusing you and your friends and your party, and all the world generally, while you are like a man being played on by a fire-engine, — dishevelled, soused, half-smothered, and rolled up into a ridiculous heap.

Ought not some mark to be put upon such men, to warn every one of their danger? We mark dangerous places on the highway; we put up a sign on a broken bridge; we warn people from a dangerous ford. And yet these are lesser dangers! Why should not men wear some badge significant of their propensities? We put buttons on oxen's horns as a hint. We put a board on a cow's face intimating her dangerous propensity; we put a shackle or a poke upon a horse that is addicted to extending the area of his freedom. Why not put signs upon dangerous people?

BOOTS.

THE difference between 7 and 8 is not very great; only a single unit. And yet that difference has power over a man's whole temper, convenience, and dignity. At Buffalo, my boots were set out at night to be blacked. In the morning no boots were there, though all the neighboring rooms had been served. I rang. I rang twice. "A pretty hotel, — nearly eight o'clock, going out at nine, breakfast to be eaten, and no boots yet." The waiter came, took my somewhat emphatic order, and left. Every minute was an hour. It always is when you are out of temper. A man in his stocking-feet, in the third story of a hotel, finds himself restricted in locomotion. I went to the door, looked up and down the hall, saw frowzy chambermaids; saw, afar off, the master of the coal-scuttle; saw gentlemen walking in bright boots, unconscious of the privileges which they enjoyed, but did not see any one coming with *my* boots. A German servant at length came, round and ruddy-faced, very kind and good-natured, honest and stupid. He informed me that a gentleman had already taken boots No. 78 (my number). He would hunt him up; thought he was breakfasting. Here was new vexation. Who was the man that had taken my number and gone for my boots. Somebody had them on, warm and nice, and was enjoying his coffee, while I walked up and down, with less and less patience, who had none too much at first. No servant returned. I rang again, and sent energetic and staccato messages to the office. Some water had been spilled on the floor. I stepped in it, of course. In winter cold water feels as if it burned you. Unpacked my valise for new stockings. Time was speeding. It was quarter past eight; train at nine, no boots and no breakfast. I slipped on a pair of sandal-rubbers, too large by inches for my naked foot, and while I shuffled along the hall, they played up and down on my feet. First, one shot off; that secured, the other dropped on the stairs; people that I met looked as if they thought that I was not well over a last night's spree. It was very annoying. Reached the office, and expressed my mind. First the clerk rang the bell three times furiously, then ran forth himself, met the German boots, who had boots 79 in hand, narrow and long, thinking perhaps I could wear *them.* Who knows but 79 had my boots? Some curiosity was beginning to be felt among bystanders. It was likely that I should have half the hotel inquiring after my boots. I abhor a scene. Retreated to my room. On the way thought that I would look at room 77's boots. Behold, they were mine! There was the broken pull-straps; the patch on the right side, and the very shape of my toe, — infallible signs! The fellow had marked them 77 and not 78. And all this hour's tumult arose from just the difference between 7 and 8.

I lost my boots, lost the train, lost my temper, and, of course, lost my good manners. Everybody does that loses temper. But, boots once on, breakfast served, a cup of coffee brought peace and good-will. The whole matter took a ludicrous aspect. I moralized upon that infirmity that puts a man's peace at the mercy of a Dutchman's chalk. Had he written seventy-eight, I had been a good-natured man, looking at Niagara Falls in its winter dress. He wrote seventy-seven, and I fumed, saw only my own falls, and spent the day in Buffalo!

Are not most of the pets and rubs of life as undignified as this? Few men could afford to-morrow to review the things that vexed them yesterday. We boast of being free, yet every man permits the most arrant trifles to rule and ride him. A man that is vexed and angry turns the worst part of himself out to sight, and exhibits himself to the pity or contempt of spectators. Who would put on a buffoon's coat and fool's cap and walk forth to be jeered? And yet one's temper does worse by him than that. And men submit to it, not once, but often, and sometimes every day! I wonder whether these sage reflections will make me patient and quiet the next time my boots are misplaced?

COMPLIMENTS.

HOW far may one consistently with truth and honor employ *compliments* in his intercourse with society? This question requires us to fix the meaning of a compliment. Is it anything different from *flattery?* Flattery may be given by means of a compliment, and yet there are many compliments that are true, well deserved, and sincere. Both compliment and flattery belong to the element of *praise*. Every one holds that it is right to praise, if it be rightly done. But when one is praised for things not meritorious, or which the person has not performed, or for qualities not possessed, or when the praise is out of proper proportion to desert or fact, it is flattery. And yet this does not hit the precise moral element that determines it. Violation or exaggeration of the truth of facts may be an indiscretion only. It must be done intentionally, it must be done insincerely, and for a purpose. Flattery is praise insincerely given for an interested purpose.

A compliment is usually praise delivered in some unexpected and beautiful form. A compliment is praise in an art-form. It may be a mere intimation; a graceful comparison, an illusion, or an inference made or implied. It is praise crystallized. It bears about the relation to praise that proverbs do to formal philosophy, or that form does to poetry.

Compliments may then be Christianly honest. Several exquisite instances are to be found in St. Paul's letters and speeches. That men employ them deceitfully, flatteringly, affords no just reason against a sincere and honest use of them. On the contrary, there is all the more need of showing by their wise use that a perversion is unnecessary.

But there is a benevolence in compliments. It tempts one to look for agreeable traits among his friends, and not for faults. There is among the young of our time an impression that caustic and critical things are smart and genteel. It is supposed that dashing wit, unscrupulous cuts, and sometimes an abrupt and rude demeanor, are signs of gentlemanly freedom. This is a sad declension from the polished and kind gentilities of former schools of good manners.

But a habit of saying agreeable things in an elegant way, if it does not degenerate into falseness, will work benefit upon the speaker; sweetening his mind, turning him back from bitter and hateful things, and inclining him to the way of kindness. It will confer great pleasure on the object, since nothing can be more agreeable in the minor scenes of life than suddenly to receive praise for well-doing, in a form that pleases at once both the moral sense and the taste. A man, however, must be kind, of good taste, and thoroughly honest, to use compliments without danger — to himself.

SMELL AND PERFUMERY.

THE sense of smell is perhaps the lowest of the senses. Its range is least of all its importance and its pleasures. It would be a curious problem to determine the relative amount of pleasure which men derive from the *ear* or *eye*. Upon the ear is based the science of music; upon the eye the fine arts of painting, sculpture, &c. By the eye we derive all pleasures of form, color, proportion; by the ear come the delights of converse, the benefit of discourse, the pleasure of music.

There is no such range to the sense of taste. With this sense is connected the whole sustenance of human life. It is by food that the body is every day rebuilt, and tasting has much to do with food. But, as compared with these major senses, smell has but a limited function. And, as the world is constituted, it is doubtful whether we do not derive as much pain as pleasure from the sense of smell.

Civilization or barbarism are alike full of bad odors. Nature for the most part is sweet-smelling. When it is considered that universal death is followed by continuous decay, in the animal and vegetable worlds, it is surprising that there is so little evil odor in the air. The woods are fragrant, the fields are of a wholesome smell. Whatever decays is soon resolved to inodorous elements, and the exhaling gas is swept off into the great purifier, — the atmosphere of the globe.

If one lives in the country, it is his own fault if his nose is not at peace with all things. Winter is pure and inodorous. Summer is full of balmy leaves, sweet-smelling fruits, and perfumed flowers, and a man may surround his dwelling with beds of fragrant plants that shall fill his house with pleasure whichever way the wind blows.

But what can we do in cities? In the first place, it is almost impossible to keep our dwelling sweet. Even if the sewers work, the kitchen does too. Three times a day we have our food sent up in a spiroteal form. However good a mixed dinner may taste, it seldom smells agreeably in the parlor. Coffee smells gratefully even from afar, and better and better till smell is lost in taste. But ham and eggs, waffles, griddle-cakes, send up a faint, greasy stench through all the house, — pah!

Then comes gas. Can human imagination conceive of odor more utterly abominable? And yet how few dwellings have not a leak somewhere? In June come worms. The whole air reeks with sickening, vermicular stench. No sooner does this begin to abate before the ailanthus-tree sheds its heavy, noisome odor that fills the streets and penetrates the dwelling past all escape.

But what shall be said of a human being that, amid all these grievances, deliberately adds to the army of stenches that of voluntary perfumes? Under the plea of pleasing smells, men and women contrive to fill their hair, their dress, their handkerchiefs, with all manner of odors except agreeable ones. The hair is rancid with bear's grease, with ox-marrow, with pomatum, with named and unnamed oils, and they all stink!

Every time the handkerchief comes forth, a gust of musk is wafted into your face, warm, fainting, sickening! There are five hundred named odors, more or less, sold in bottles, that are only so many different ways of trying to hide the universal smell of *musk*. Is it apple-blossom? It smells musk. Is it mille-fleurs? It is musk. Is it geranium? It is musk again. Orange smells musk. Violets, heliotropes, roses, fade away to their base, the inevitable and universal musk. The gloves smell of it, the silks, the whole person seems infested with civets.

Your worship is almost destroyed in church. One smell is before you, another behind you. The odors of sanctity are manifold abominations. If you repair to the concert-room, the air is polluted and waiting for you. Good manners forbid a gentleman to hold his nose while talking with a lady drenched with cologne or lavender. One may almost recognize his friends as dogs do game, by their peculiar odor. Every one affects a peculiar smell. We might almost name persons by their favorite odor. Miss Vanilla smiles yonder; next her the charming Miss Orris-root. There are several of the Lemon Verbena family present, and yet more of the Lemon family. Then there are the Bergamots, the Orange-blossoms, the Bitter Almonds, and other old and respectable families.

Once in a while comes a lady of transcendent good taste, wholly inodorous. She does not carry a sandal-wood fan. She wears nothing kept in a camphor-wood trunk. Her silks have neither been hung in a cedar closet, nor been smoked with French pastilles. Her gloves smell of kid leather — as they ought to. No myrrh, no incense, no nuts, blossoms, fruits, seeds, or leaves, have been crushed to yield for her any odor of offence. She is pure as water, and as inodorous; as bright as a pearl, and as scentless; witching as an opal, and as devoid of perfume. O, that she might live a thousand years, and be the ancestress of ten thousand just like her!

THE GOOD OF DISORDER.

MONG the superstitions of education are those in favor of order. It is not that there is no such thing as order, but that its advocates are bigoted, are narrow and exclusive. It is coolly taken for granted, that if order is good, disorder is bad. As if there might not be bad order and good disorder!

If order is Heaven's first law, disorder is at least

its second. What is order, as applied, I mean, to things? It is simply arrangement according to some notion, and disorder is simply arrangement according to some *other* notion. They might be called primary order and secondary order.

As practice almost always precedes philosophy, so already there is to be found the fact of disorder for the sake of benefits which cannot be had by despotic order. If a parlor is arranged with chairs in rows all around the walls, with everything in right lines, every one says, how stiff, how intolerable, how little taste is manifested! But swing round the lounge in the corner, carelessly; let the chairs be scattered about, just as they would be if persons had but now used them; shove the centre table a little out of the very middle of the medallion, so that it shall not be *set*, and then people say the parlor has a social and easy air. What is this but a disguised revolt against the despotism of order? The same is more remarkably true in gardens and pleasure-grounds. Formerly, grounds were arranged by geometric principles. Everything was squared and mated. Mathematical exactness ruled. Even the figures of geometry were copied. The French gardens might be said to be geometry in blossom. Against this has come up what is called the *Natural Style*. And what is the natural or picturesque style of landscape gardening? It aims to reproduce the beauty of nature, together with its negligence and graceful disorder. It is a system based upon the rejection of any absolute rule. It aims to arrange things just as they would be if they never had been arranged at all.

These instances are enough to show that the prejudices which lofty and virtuous housekeepers have against disorder are not founded in philosophy, and that order is often a mere nuisance. We don't believe it to be Heaven's first law; though we did not, for rhetorical effect, choose to say so earlier in this article. In so far as it can be made a foil, a background, a judicious contrast to disorder, we have no doubt it has a place and a function. But it is only a path to be trod on the way to graceful disorder.

The face of Nature is the most obvious and thorough refutation of the popular superstitions about order. Nothing is orderly till man takes hold of it. Everything in creation lies around loose, or is mixed up in the most inextricable disorder. Not in confusion. Disorder is never to be confounded with confusion. If our housekeepers had had the making of Nature, the world would have been a vast bureau, and every drawer would have had its appropriate specimens in lamentable regularity. Here we should have had Mineralogy, next Botany, next Zoölogy, and so on, in intolerable order. As it is, thank Nature! things are scattered about all over the world splendidly, and no housekeeper was ever created to put this world "to rights."

We spoke of bureaus. There is our own for instance. It is a moderately good one, with a movable top, and a looking-glass attached. *Our* way of arranging is, to put everything down on the top, just as it comes. *Hers* is just the other way.

We treat it as we should the globe, and leave things just as they dropped. Books, combs, and brushes, a fishing-reel, a pamphlet, matches, and lozenges, cologne, and troches, a battle-hymn and letters, watch-cases, and ribbons. Then one would know where to look if anything were missing. Alas! order steps up the moment we leave, and this beauteous disorder vanishes! It is distressing to every tender feeling of taste to open the first drawer. All is adjusted; nothing left to the imagination. Every lace smooth, every one folded, flat, regular. So it will be to-morrow, so next week, and to the end! The next drawer is *mine*. There repose the snow-white shirts, the pile of handkerchiefs; and they repose like Egyptian dead in rows and shelf-like order. Once in a while we thrust in a genuine touch of Nature, that is said to make all men kin; but a flatiron does not take a wrinkle out of linen quicker than the *order* does out of the drawer! And so it is with the next, and the next. So is it with the closet, with parlor, and entries. The same rectangular fate presides in parlor and dining-room. Nay, it stealthily creeps into the very study. Let us, in a moment rash with desperation, say our soul's faith (though it be heresy) that no housekeeper — foreordained housekeepeer — has any rights in a study. Here are we this morning, just returned after four days' absence. We left this room a Paradise, we find it a Purgatory. Our table was blossoming all over with a luxuriant and tangled abundance of letters, papers, scraps from newspapers, books, and books on books. It was a journal. Each day's deposit for weeks was there, almost with the regularity of geological strata. We could go back as in a register, and recall the topics of each several day, until memory failed, and the lower strata of papers, the very primitive formations, went back to dim and remote times inexplorable. Like an onion or tulip-bulb, the table was constructed in layers. Fatal absence! Misplaced confidence! We returned to find everything death-struck. All was order! Our articles sorted, our letters filed, our scraps classified, our pens collected and huddled like raw recruits in awkward squads, the scissors, the knife, the pins, the ink, the mucilage, standing round like officers dressed for a parade-day. A month will not suffice to bring back again the admired disorder, the graceful melange.

And then the books!

Mr. Bonner, — you have a kind nature, a genuine, sympathizing heart. Every one has seen how heartily you stand up for your friends, how heartily you thwack your adversaries. But even you cannot console us nor avenge us of our adversary! She steals in! She views the happy scene! There was Bayle lying on the floor, with Mape's Farmer in his lap, and an Atlas genially covering both. There was a squadron of Living Ages lying around, like a picket of cavalry at ease. In one corner was a thicket of newspapers, on the sofa a ream of paper, a shawl, an Affghan, a Concordance, a Bible, new books uncut, magazines, and various other treasures; near the window all the books that at various times for a month we had bought up, but had not put up, waiting till we had time to arrange; near the door a stack of portfolios, and here and there a picture, patiently waiting to be hung. The book-cases were in benevolent sympathy with the floor. Indeed, the book-case might be called a vertical floor, and the floor a horizontal book-case. Whichever way the eye turned it found unexpected contrasts. Nothing was tame. Everything was fitted to excite surprise in a well-regulated housekeeper's mind. It was a stimulating sight. No art could have designedly arranged it. It was the workmanship of distributive and gradual chance. Like frostwork on the window, it defied invention and challenged imitation.

The same remorseless hand that would rub out a windowful of frost etchings, for the sake of seeing vulgar things outside, has invaded our room and "put everything to rights." Two months of industrious carelessness will scarce suffice to bring back my paradise! And all the time that fatal fear will overhang us that, in an unguarded hour, the same calamity will sweep through the room again, and where it found all, everything in disorder and loneliness, leave everything blasted with regularity and order!

But ah, the days are coming! But seven days is it to Spring! Then in one more month, — and all our ills will be healed. We shall send everybody to the country. We shall be sole monarch. Then, descending, we shall overturn the despotism of the parlors, and bring to the solitude of the house the joyful boon of disorder! We will forget to put anything in its place. The sofa shall sprout with strange things. Every corner be planted with new commodities. The book-case door shall never be shut. The chairs shall never have less than half a dozen books. Engravings shall lie in heaps. Right in the midst of manuscripts shall be seen bread and cheese and apples that had begun to be eaten; the ashes shall heap itself in gray disorder; kindling-wood and waste paper shall ruffle the hearth; and everything see everything doing what it was never expected to do. Brooms we hate as we do a tyrant's rod. We will expel them! Dust-brushes are an utter abomination. We will drive them forth! At present we think it meet to submit. But we snuff the balmy air that tells us that the vernal days are coming. To us they mean more than to anybody else. To all they mean grass, leaves, lambs, birds, flowers, and odorous smell of soil and vegetation. But to us they mean also domestic liberty, the end of tyrannous order, the restoration of nature to the house, the undisturbed reign of joyous disorder!

Cambridge: Stereotyped and Printed by Welch, Bigelow, & Co.

☞ Any Books in this list will be sent free of postage, on receipt of price.

Boston, 135 Washington Street,
October, 1862.

A LIST OF BOOKS

PUBLISHED BY

TICKNOR AND FIELDS.

Sir Walter Scott.

Illustrated Household Edition of the Waverley Novels. 50 volumes. In portable size, 16mo. form. Now Complete. Price 75 cents a volume.

The paper is of fine quality; the stereotype plates are not old ones repaired, tho type having been cast expressly for this edition. The Novels are illustrated with capital steel plates engraved in the best manner, after drawings and paintings by the most eminent artists, among whom are Birket Foster, Darley, Billings, Landseer, Harvey, and Faed. This Edition contains all the latest notes and corrections of the author, a Glossary and Index; and some curious additions, especially in "Guy Mannering" and the "Bride of Lammermoor;" being the fullest edition of the Novels ever published. *The notes are at the foot of the page*,—a great convenience to the reader.

Any of the following Novels sold separate.

Waverley, 2 vols.
Guy Mannering, 2 vols.
The Antiquary, 2 vols.
Rob Roy, 2 vols.
Old Mortality, 2 vols.
Black Dwarf, Legend of Montrose, } 2 vols.
Heart of Mid Lothian, 2 vols.
Bride of Lammermoor, 2 vols.
Ivanhoe, 2 vols.
The Monastery, 2 vols.
The Abbot, 2 vols.
Kenilworth, 2 vols.
The Pirate, 2 vols.
The Fortunes of Nigel, 2 vols.
Peveril of the Peak, 2 vols.
Quentin Durward, 2 vols.
St. Ronan's Well, 2 vols.
Redgauntlet, 2 vols.
The Betrothed, The Highland Widow, } 2 vols.
The Talisman, Two Drovers, My Aunt Margaret's Mirror, The Tapestried Chamber, The Laird's Jock, } 2 vols.
Woodstock, 2 vols.
The Fair Maid of Perth, 2 vols.
Anne of Geierstein, 2 vols.
Count Robert of Paris, 2 vols.
The Surgeon's Daughter, Castle Dangerous, Index and Glossary, } 2 vols.

Tales of a Grandfather. Illustrated. 6 vols. $4.50.

Life. By J. G. Lockhart. Illustrated Edition. Uniform with Novels. 9 vols. Cloth. $6.75.

Thomas De Quincey.

Confessions of an English Opium-Eater, and Suspiria de Profundis. With Portrait. 75 cents.

Biographical Essays. 75 cents.

Miscellaneous Essays. 75 cents.

The Cæsars. 75 cents.

Literary Reminiscences. 2 vols. $1.50.

Narrative and Miscellaneous Papers. 2 vols. $1.50.

Essays on the Poets, &c. 1 vol. 16mo. 75 cents.

Historical and Critical Essays. 2 vols. $1.50.

Autobiographic Sketches. 1 vol. 75 cents.

Essays on Philosophical Writers, &c. 2 vols. 16mo. $1.50.

Letters to a Young Man, and other Papers. 1 vol. 75 cents.

Theological Essays and other Papers. 2 vols. $1.50.

The Note Book. 1 vol. 75 cents.

Memorials and other Papers. 2 vols. 16mo. $1.50.

The Avenger and other Papers. 1 vol. 75 cents.

Logic of Political Economy, and other Papers. 1 vol. 75 cents.

Beauties, selected from the writings of Thomas De Quincey. With an Introductory Notice and fine Portrait of the author. 1 vol. $1.25.

Alfred Tennyson.

Poetical Works. With Portrait. 2 vols. Cloth. $2.00.

Pocket Edition of Poems Complete. 2 vols. $1.50.

Poems. Complete in one volume. With Portrait. $1.00.

Poems. Cabinet Edition. Vellum cloth, elegant. 2 vols. $2.50.

The Princess. Cloth. 50 cents.

In Memoriam. Cloth. 75 cents.

The Same. Holiday Edition. With Portraits of Tennyson and Arthur Hallam, and Biographical Sketch. $2.50.

Maud, and other Poems. Cloth. 50 cents.

Idylls of the King. Cloth. 75 cents.

Thomas Hood.

MEMORIALS. Edited by his Children. 2 vols. $1.75.

Charles Dickens.

[ENGLISH EDITION.]

THE COMPLETE WORKS OF CHARLES DICKENS. Fine Library Edition. Published simultaneously in London and Boston. English print, fine cloth binding, 22 vols. 12mo. $27.50.

Henry W. Longfellow.

POETICAL WORKS. 2 vols. Boards, $2.00. Cloth, $2.25.

POETICAL WORKS. Cabinet Edition. Vellum cloth, elegant. 2 vols. $2.50.

POCKET EDITION OF POETICAL WORKS. In two volumes. Blue and gold. $1.75.

POCKET EDITION OF PROSE WORKS COMPLETE. In two volumes. Blue and gold, $1.75.

THE SONG OF HIAWATHA. $1.00.

EVANGELINE: A Tale of Acadia. 75 cents.

THE GOLDEN LEGEND. A Poem. $1.00.

HYPERION. A Romance. $1.00.

OUTRE-MER. A Pilgrimage. $1.00.

KAVANAGH. A Tale. 75 cents.

THE COURTSHIP OF MILES STANDISH. 1 vol. 16mo. 75 cents.

Illustrated editions of EVANGELINE, POEMS, HYPERION, THE GOLDEN LEGEND, and MILES STANDISH.

Charles Reade.

PEG WOFFINGTON. A Novel. 75 cents.

CHRISTIE JOHNSTONE. A Novel. 75 cents.

CLOUDS AND SUNSHINE. A Novel. 75 cents.

"NEVER TOO LATE TO MEND." 2 vols. $1.50.

WHITE LIES. A Novel. 1 vol. $1.25.

PROPRIA QUÆ MARIBUS and THE BOX TUNNEL. 25 cts.

THE EIGHTH COMMANDMENT. 75 cents.

James Russell Lowell.

Complete Poetical Works. In Blue and Gold. 2 vols. $1.50.

Poetical Works. 2 vols. 16mo. Cloth. $1.50.

Sir Launfal. New Edition. 25 cents.

A Fable for Critics. New Edition. 50 cents.

The Biglow Papers. New Edition. 63 cents.

Conversations on the Old Poets. 3d edition. 75 cts.

Fireside Travels. *In Press.*

Nathaniel Hawthorne.

Twice-Told Tales. Two volumes. $1.50.

The Scarlet Letter. 75 cents.

The House of the Seven Gables. $1.00.

The Snow Image, and other Tales. 75 cents.

The Blithedale Romance. 75 cents.

Mosses from an Old Manse. 2 vols. $1.50.

The Marble Faun. 2 vols. $1.50.

True Stories. 75 cents.

A Wonder-Book for Girls and Boys. 75 cents.

Tanglewood Tales. 88 cents.

Edwin P. Whipple.

Essays and Reviews. 2 vols. $2.00.

Lectures on Literature and Life. 63 cents.

Washington and the Revolution. 20 cents.

Charles Kingsley.

Two Years Ago. A New Novel. $1.25.

Amyas Leigh. A Novel. $1.25.

Glaucus; or, the Wonders of the Shore. 50 cts.

Poetical Works. 75 cents.

The Heroes; or, Greek Fairy Tales. 75 cents.

Andromeda and other Poems. 50 cents.

Sir Walter Raleigh and his Time, &c. $1.25.

New Miscellanies. 1 vol. $1.00.

Mrs. Howe.

Passion Flowers. 75 cents.
Words for the Hour. 75 cents.
The World's Own. 50 cents.
A Trip to Cuba. 1 vol. 16mo. 75 cents.

George S. Hillard.

Six Months in Italy. 1 vol. 16mo. $1.50.
Dangers and Duties of the Mercantile Profession. 25 cents.
Selections from the Writings of Walter Savage Landor. 1 vol. 16mo. 75 cents.

Oliver Wendell Holmes.

Elsie Venner: a Romance of Destiny. 2 vols. Cloth. $1.75.
Poems. With fine Portrait. Cloth. $1.00.
Poems. Blue and Gold. With new Portrait. 1 vol. Cloth. 88 cents.
Astræa. Fancy paper. 25 cents.
The Autocrat of the Breakfast Table. With Illustrations by Hoppin. 16mo. $1.00.
The Same. Large Paper Edition. 8vo. Tinted paper. $3.00.
The Professor at the Breakfast Table. 16mo. $1.00.
The Same. Large Paper Edition. 8vo. Tinted paper. $3.00.
Songs in Many Keys. A new volume. $1.25.
Currents and Counter-Currents, and other Medical Essays. 1 vol. Cloth. $1.25.
Border Lines in some Provinces of Medical Science. 1 vol. Cloth. 50 cents.

Ralph Waldo Emerson.

Essays. 1st Series. 1 vol. $1.00.
Essays. 2d Series. 1 vol. $1.00.
Miscellanies. 1 vol. $1.00.
Representative Men. 1 vol. $1.00.
English Traits. 1 vol. $1.00.
Poems. 1 vol. $1.00.
Conduct of Life. 1 vol. $1.00.

Goethe.

Wilhelm Meister. Translated by *Carlyle.* 2 vols. $2.50
Faust. Translated by *Hayward.* 75 cents.
Faust. Translated by *Charles T. Brooks.* $1.00.
Correspondence with a Child. *Bettina.* 1 vol. 12mo. $1.25.

Henry Giles.

Lectures, Essays, &c. 2 vols. $1.50.
Discourses on Life. 75 cents.
Illustrations of Genius. Cloth. $1.00.

John G. Whittier.

Pocket Edition of Poetical Works. 2 vols. $1.50.
Old Portraits and Modern Sketches. 75 cents.
Margaret Smith's Journal. 75 cents.
Songs of Labor, and other Poems. Boards. 50 cts.
The Chapel of the Hermits. Cloth. 50 cents.
Literary Recreations, &c. Cloth. $1.00.
The Panorama, and other Poems. Cloth. 50 cents.
Home Ballads and Poems. A new volume. 75 cents.

Capt. Mayne Reid.

The Plant Hunters. With Plates. 75 cents.
The Desert Home: or, The Adventures of a Lost Family in the Wilderness. With fine Plates. $1.00.
The Boy Hunters. With fine Plates. 75 cents.
The Young Voyageurs: or, The Boy Hunters in the North. With Plates. 75 cents.
The Forest Exiles. With fine Plates. 75 cents.
The Bush Boys. With fine Plates. 75 cents.
The Young Yagers. With fine Plates. 75 cents.
Ran Away to Sea: An Autobiography for Boys. With fine Plates. 75 cents.
The Boy Tar: A Voyage in the Dark. A New Book. With fine Plates. 75 cents.
Odd People. With Plates. 75 cents.
The Same. Cheap Edition. With Plates. 50 cents.
Bruin: or, The Grand Bear Hunt. With Plates. 75 cts.

Rev. F. W. Robertson.

SERMONS. First Series, $1.00.
" Second " $1.00.
" Third " $1.00.
" Fourth " $1.00.
LECTURES AND ADDRESSES ON LITERARY AND SOCIAL TOPICS. $1.00.

Mrs. Jameson.

CHARACTERISTICS OF WOMEN. Blue and Gold. 75 cents.
LOVES OF THE POETS. " " 75 cents.
DIARY OF AN ENNUYÉE. " " 75 cents.
SKETCHES OF ART, &c. " " 75 cents.
STUDIES AND STORIES. " " 75 cents.
ITALIAN PAINTERS. " " 75 cents.
LEGENDS OF THE MADONNA. " " 75 cents.
SISTERS OF CHARITY. 1 vol. 16mo. 75 cents.

Grace Greenwood.

GREENWOOD LEAVES. 1st and 2d Series. $1.25 each.
POETICAL WORKS. With fine Portrait. 75 cents.
HISTORY OF MY PETS. With six fine Engravings. Scarlet cloth. 50 cents.
RECOLLECTIONS OF MY CHILDHOOD. With six fine Engravings. Scarlet cloth. 50 cents.
HAPS AND MISHAPS OF A TOUR IN EUROPE. $1.25.
MERRIE ENGLAND. 75 cents.
A FOREST TRAGEDY, AND OTHER TALES. $1.00.
STORIES AND LEGENDS. 75 cents.
STORIES FROM FAMOUS BALLADS. Illustrated. 50 cents.
BONNIE SCOTLAND. Illustrated. 75 cents.

Henry D. Thoreau.

WALDEN. 1 vol. 16mo. $1.00.
A WEEK ON THE CONCORD AND MERRIMACK RIVERS. 1 vol. 12mo. $1.25.

Mrs. Harriet Beecher Stowe.

THE PEARL OF ORR'S ISLAND. 1 vol. $1.25.

AGNES OF SORRENTO. 1 vol. $1.25.

Samuel Smiles.

LIFE OF GEORGE STEPHENSON, ENGINEER. $1.00.

SELF HELP; WITH ILLUSTRATIONS OF CHARACTER AND CONDUCT. With Portrait. 1 vol. 75 cents.

BRIEF BIOGRAPHIES. With Plates. $1.25.

Theodore Winthrop.

CECIL DREEME. 1 vol. Cloth. $1.00.

JOHN BRENT. 1 vol. Cloth. $1.00.

EDWIN BROTHERTOFT. 1 vol. Cloth. $1.00.

Miss Cummins.

EL FUREIDIS. By the Author of "The Lamplighter," &c. $1.00.

Thomas Hughes.

SCHOOL DAYS AT RUGBY. By *An Old Boy.* 1 vol. 16mo. $1.00.

The Same. Illustrated edition. $1.50.

THE SCOURING OF THE WHITE HORSE, OR THE LONG VACATION HOLIDAY OF A LONDON CLERK. By *The Author of "School Days at Rugby."* 1 vol. 16mo. $1.00.

TOM BROWN AT OXFORD. A Sequel to School Days at Rugby. 2 vols. 16mo. With fine Steel Portrait of the Author. $2.00.

Mrs. Mowatt.

AUTOBIOGRAPHY OF AN ACTRESS. $1.25.

PLAYS. ARMAND AND FASHION. 50 cents.

MIMIC LIFE. 1 vol. $1.25.

THE TWIN ROSES. 1 vol. 75 cents.

Bayard Taylor.

POEMS OF HOME AND TRAVEL. Cloth. 75 cents.

POEMS OF THE ORIENT. Cloth. 75 cents.

A POET'S JOURNAL. *In Press.*

R. H. Dana, Jr.

TO CUBA AND BACK, a Vacation Voyage, by the Author of "Two Years before the Mast." 75 cents.

Miscellaneous Works.

[POETRY.]

ALFORD'S (HENRY) POEMS. 1 vol. 16mo. Cloth. $1.00.
ANGEL IN THE HOUSE: THE BETROTHAL. 1 vol. 16mo. Cloth. 75 cents.
" " THE ESPOUSALS. 1 vol. 16mo. Cloth. 75 cents.
ARNOLD'S (MATTHEW) POEMS. 1 vol. 75 cents.
AYTOUN'S BOTHWELL. A Narrative Poem. 1 vol. 75 cents.
BAILEY'S (P. J.) THE MYSTIC. 1 vol. 16mo. Cloth. 50 cents.
" " THE AGE. 1 vol. 16mo. Cloth. 75 cents.
BARRY CORNWALL'S ENGLISH SONGS AND OTHER POEMS. 1 vol. $1.00.
" " DRAMATIC POEMS. 1 vol. $1.00.
BOKER'S PLAYS AND POEMS. 2 vols. 16mo. Cloth. $2.00.
BROOKS'S GERMAN LYRICS. 1 vol. $1.00.
" FAUST. A new Translation. 1 vol. $1.00.
BROWNING'S (ROBERT) POEMS. 2 vols. $2.00.
" " MEN AND WOMEN. 1 vol. $1.00.
CARY'S (PHŒBE) POEMS AND PARODIES. 1 vol. 75 cts.
CLOUGH'S (ARTHUR HUGH) POEMS. Blue and gold. 75 cents.
FRESH HEARTS THAT FAILED. By the Author of "The New Priest." 1 vol. 50 cents.
HAYNE'S POEMS. 1 vol. 63 cents.
" AVOLIO AND OTHER POEMS. 1 vol. 16mo. Cloth. 75 cents.
HUNT'S (LEIGH) POEMS. 2 vols. Blue and Gold. $1.50.
" " RIMINI. 1 vol. 50 cents.
HYMNS OF THE AGES. 1 vol. Enlarged edition. $1.25.
HYMNS OF THE AGES. 2d Series. 1 vol. $1.25.
The Same. 8vo. Bevelled boards. Each volume, $3.00.
JOHNSON'S (ROSA V.) POEMS. 1 vol. $1.00.
KEMBLE'S (MRS.) POEMS. 1 vol. $1.00.
LUNT'S (GEO.) LYRIC POEMS. 1 vol. 16mo. Cloth. 63 cents.
" " JULIA. 1 vol. 50 cents.

LOCKHART'S (J. G.) SPANISH BALLADS. With Portrait. 1 vol. 75 cents.
MACKAY'S POEMS. 1 vol. $1.00.
MASSEY'S (GERALD) POEMS. 1 vol. Blue and Gold. 75 cents.
MEMORY AND HOPE. A Collection of Consolatory Pieces. 1 vol. $2.00.
MOTHERWELL'S POEMS. 1 vol. Blue and Gold. 75 cts.
" MINSTRELSY, ANCIENT AND MODERN. 2 vols. $1.50.
MULOCH'S (MISS) POEMS. (By Author of "John Halifax.") 1 vol. 75 cents.
OWEN MEREDITH'S POEMS. 1 vol. Blue and Gold. 75 cts.
PARSONS'S POEMS. 1 vol. $1.00.
" DANTE'S INFERNO. Translated. *In Press.*
PERCIVAL'S POEMS. 2 vols. Blue and Gold. $1.75.
QUINCY'S (J. P.) CHARICLES. A Dramatic Poem. 1 vol. 50 cents.
" " LYTERIA: A Dramatic Poem. 50 cents.
READ'S (T. BUCHANAN) POEMS. New and complete edition. 2 vols. $2.00.
REJECTED ADDRESSES. By Horace and James Smith. New edition. 1 vol. 63 cents.
SAXE'S (J. G.) POEMS. With Portrait. 1 vol. 75 cents.
" " THE MONEY KING AND OTHER POEMS. With new Portrait. 1 vol. 75 cents.
" " POEMS — the two foregoing vols. in one. $1.25.
" " POEMS. Complete in Blue and Gold. With Portrait. 75 cents.
SMITH'S (ALEXANDER) LIFE DRAMA. 1 vol. 50 cents.
" " CITY POEMS. 1 vol. 63 cents.
" " EDWIN OF DEIRA. With Portrait. 75 cents.
STODDARD'S (R. H.) POEMS. 1 vol. 63 cents.
" " SONGS OF SUMMER. 1 vol. 75 cts.
SPRAGUE'S (CHARLES) POETICAL AND PROSE WORKS. With Portrait. 1 vol. 88 cents.
THACKERAY'S BALLADS. 1 vol. 75 cents.
THALATTA. A Book for the Seaside. 1 vol. 75 cents.
TUCKERMAN'S (H. T.) POEMS. 1 vol. 75 cents.
WARRENIANA. 1 vol. 63 cents.

[PROSE.]

ALLSTON'S MONALDI. A Tale. 1 vol. 16mo. 75 cents.
ARAGO'S (FRANCOIS) BIOGRAPHIES OF DISTINGUISHED SCIENTIFIC MEN. 2 vols. 16mo. $2.00.
ARNOLD'S (DR. THOMAS) LIFE AND CORRESPONDENCE. Edited by A. P. Stanley. 2 vols. 12mo. Cloth. $2.00.

ARNOLD'S (W. D.) OAKFIELD. A Novel. 1 vol. 16mo. Cloth. $1.00.

ALMOST A HEROINE. By the Author of "Charles Auchester." 1 vol. 16mo. Cloth. $1.00.

ARABIAN DAYS' ENTERTAINMENT. Translated from the German, by H. P. Curtis. Illustrated. 1 vol. $1.25.

ADDISON'S SIR ROGER DE COVERLEY. From the "Spectator." 1 vol. 16mo. Cloth. 75 cents.

The Same. 1 vol. 16mo. Cloth, gilt edge. $1.25.

ANGEL VOICES; OR, WORDS OF COUNSEL FOR OVERCOMING THE WORLD. 1 vol. 16mo. Cloth, gilt, 38; gilt edge, 50; full gilt, 63 cents.

The Same. Holiday Edition. Tinted paper. 50 cents.

AMERICAN INSTITUTE OF INSTRUCTION. Lectures delivered before the Institute in 1840–41–42–43–44–45–46–47–48–49–50–51–52–53–54–55–56–57–58–59–60–61. 22 vols. 12mo. Sold in separate volumes, each 50 cents.

BACON'S (DELIA) THE SHAKSPERIAN PROBLEM SOLVED. With an Introduction by Nathaniel Hawthorne. 1 vol. 8vo. Cloth. $3.00.

BARTOL'S CHURCH AND CONGREGATION. 1 vol. 16mo. Cloth. $1.00.

BAILEY'S ESSAYS ON OPINIONS AND TRUTH. 1 vol. 16mo. Cloth. $1.00.

BARRY CORNWALL'S ESSAYS AND TALES IN PROSE. 2 vols. $1.50.

BOSTON BOOK. Being Specimens of Metropolitan Literature. Cloth, $1.25; gilt edge, $1.75; full gilt, $2.00.

BUCKINGHAM'S (J. T.) PERSONAL MEMOIRS. With Portrait. 2 vols. 16mo. Cloth. $1.50.

CHANNING'S (E. T.) LECTURES ON RHETORIC AND ORATORY. 1 vol. 16mo. Cloth. 75 cents.

CHANNING'S (DR. WALTER) PHYSICIAN'S VACATION. 1 vol. 12mo. Cloth. $1.50.

COALE'S (DR. W. E.) HINTS ON HEALTH. 1 vol. 16mo. Cloth. 63 cents.

COMBE ON THE CONSTITUTION OF MAN. 30th edition. 12mo. Cloth. 75 cents.

CHAPEL LITURGY. Book of Common Prayer, according to the use of King's Chapel, Boston. 1 vol. 8vo. Sheep, $2.00; sheep, extra, $2.50; sheep, extra, gilt edge, $3.00; morocco, $3.50; do. gilt edge, $4.00; do. extra gilt edge, $4.50.

The Same. Cheaper edition. 1 vol. 12mo. Sheep, $1.50.

CROSLAND'S (MRS.) LYDIA: A WOMAN'S BOOK. 1 vol. 75 cents.

" " ENGLISH TALES AND SKETCHES. 1 vol. $1.00.

CROSLAND'S (MRS.) MEMORABLE WOMEN. Illustrated. 1 vol. $1.00.

DANA'S (R. H.) TO CUBA AND BACK. 1 vol. 16mo. Cloth. 75 cents.

Dufferin's (Lord) Yacht Voyage. 1 vol. $1.00.

El Fureidis. By the author of "The Lamplighter." 1 vol. 16mo. Cloth. $1.00.

Ernest Carroll; or, Artist-Life in Italy. 1 vol. 16mo. Cloth. 88 cents.

Favorite Authors: A Companion Book of Prose and Poetry. With 26 fine Steel Portraits. $2.50.

Fremont's Life, Explorations, and Public Services. By C. W. Upham. With Illustrations. 75 cents.

Gaskell's (Mrs.) Ruth. A Novel. 8vo. Paper. 38 cts.

Guesses at Truth. By Two Brothers. 1 vol. 12mo. $1.50.

Greenwood's (F. W. P.) Sermons of Consolation. 16mo. Cloth, $1.00; cloth, gilt edge, $1.50; morocco, plain gilt edge, $2.00; morocco, extra gilt edge, $2.50.

" History of the King's Chapel, Boston. 12mo. Cloth. 50 cents.

Heroes of Europe. A capital Boy's Book. With 16 Illustrations. 1 vol. 16mo. $1.00.

Hodson's Soldier's Life in India. 1 vol. Cloth. $1.00.

Howitt's (William) Land, Labor, and Gold. 2 vols. $2.00.

" " A Boy's Adventures in Australia. 75 cents.

Howitt's (Anna Mary) An Art Student in Munich. $1.25.

" " A School of Life. A Story. 75 cents.

Hufeland's Art of Prolonging Life. 1 vol. 16mo. Cloth. 75 cents.

Jerrold's (Douglas) Life. By his Son. 1 vol. 16mo. Cloth. $1.00.

" " Wit. By his Son. 1 vol. 16mo. Cloth. 75 cents.

Judson's (Mrs. E. C.) Alderbrook. By Fanny Forrester. 2 vols. $1.75.

" " The Kathayan Slave, and other Papers. 1 vol. 63 cents.

" " My two Sisters: A Sketch from Memory. 50 cents.

Kavanagh's (Julia) Seven Years. 8vo. 30 cents.

Kingsley's (Henry) Geoffry Hamlyn. 1 vol. 12mo. Cloth. $1.25.

" " Ravenshoe. 1 vol. 12mo. $1.25.

Krapf's Travels and Researches in Eastern Africa. 1 vol. 12mo. Cloth. $1.25.

Leslie's (C. R.) Autobiographical Recollections. Edited by Tom Taylor. With Portrait. 1 vol. 12mo. Cloth. $1.25.

Lake House. From the German of Fanny Lewald. 1 vol. 16mo. Cloth. 75 cents.

LOWELL'S (REV. DR. CHARLES) PRACTICAL SERMONS. 1 vol. 12mo. Cloth. $1.25.

" " OCCASIONAL SERMONS. With fine Portrait. 1 vol. 12mo. Cloth. $1.25.

LIGHT ON THE DARK RIVER; OR, MEMOIRS OF MRS. HAMLIN. 1 vol. 16mo. Cloth. $1.00.

The Same. 16mo. Cloth, gilt edge. $1.50.

LONGFELLOW (REV. S.) AND JOHNSON (REV. S.) A book of Hymns for Public and Private Devotion. 6th edition. 63 cents.

LABOR AND LOVE. A Tale of English Life. 1 vol. 16mo. Cloth. 50 cents.

LEE'S (MRS. E. B.) MEMOIR OF THE BUCKMINSTERS. $1.25.

" " FLORENCE, THE PARISH ORPHAN. 50 cents.

" " PARTHENIA. 1 vol. 16mo. $1.00.

LUNT'S (GEORGE) THREE ERAS IN THE HISTORY OF NEW ENGLAND. 1 vol. $1.00.

MADEMOISELLE MORI: A Tale of Modern Rome. 1 vol. 12mo. Cloth. $1.25.

M'CLINTOCK'S NARRATIVE OF THE SEARCH FOR SIR JOHN FRANKLIN. Library edition. With Maps and Illustrations. 1 vol. small 8vo. $1.50.

The Same. Popular Edition. 1 vol. 12mo. 75 cents.

MANN'S (HORACE) THOUGHTS FOR A YOUNG MAN. 1 vol. 25 cents.

" " SERMONS. 1 vol. $1.00.

MANN'S (MRS. HORACE) PHYSIOLOGICAL COOKERY-BOOK. 1 vol. 16mo. Cloth. 63 cents.

" " THE FLOWER PEOPLE. 1 vol. Illustrated. 63 cents.

MELVILLE'S HOLMBY HOUSE. A Novel. 8vo. Paper. 50 cts.

MITFORD'S (MISS) OUR VILLAGE. Illustrated. 2 vols. 16mo. $2.50.

" " ATHERTON, AND OTHER STORIES. 1 vol. 16mo. $1.25.

MORLEY'S LIFE OF PALISSY THE POTTER. 2 vols. 16mo. Cloth. $1.50.

MOUNTFORD'S THORPE. 1 vol. 16mo. Cloth. $1.00.

NORTON'S (C. E.) TRAVEL AND STUDY IN ITALY. 1 vol. 16mo. Cloth. 75 cents.

NEW TESTAMENT. A very handsome edition, fine paper and clear type. 12mo. Sheep binding, plain, $1.00; roan, plain, $1.50; calf, plain, $1.75; calf, gilt edge, $2.00; Turkey morocco, plain, $2.50; do. gilt edge, $3.00.

OTIS'S (MRS. H. G.) THE BARCLAYS OF BOSTON. 1 vol. Cloth. $1.25.

PARSONS'S (THEOPHILUS) LIFE. By his Son. 1 vol. 12mo Cloth. $1.50.

PRESCOTT'S HISTORY OF THE ELECTRIC TELEGRAPH. Illustrated. 1 vol. 12mo. Cloth. $1.75.

POORE'S (BEN PERLEY) LOUIS PHILIPPE. 1 vol. $1.00.

PHILLIPS'S ELEMENTARY TREATISE ON MINERALOGY. With numerous additions to the Introduction. By Francis Alger. With numerous Engravings. 1 vol. New edition in press.

PRIOR'S LIFE OF EDMUND BURKE. 2 vols. 16mo. $2.00.

RAB AND HIS FRIENDS. By John Brown, M. D. Illustrated. 15 cents.

SALA'S JOURNEY DUE NORTH. 1 vol. 16mo. Cloth. $1.00.

SCOTT'S (SIR WALTER) IVANHOE. In one handsome volume. $1.75.

SIDNEY'S (SIR PHILIP) LIFE. By Mrs. Davis. 1 vol. Cloth. $1.00.

SHELLEY MEMORIALS. Edited by the Daughter-in-law of the Poet. 1 vol. 16mo. 75 cents.

SWORD AND GOWN. By the Author of "Guy Livingstone." 1 vol. 16mo. Cloth. 75 cents.

SHAKSPEAR'S (CAPTAIN H.) WILD SPORTS OF INDIA. 1 vol. 16mo. Cloth. 75 cents.

SEMI-DETACHED HOUSE. A Novel. 1 vol. 75 cents.

SMITH'S (WILLIAM) THORNDALE; OR, THE CONFLICT OF OPINIONS. 1 vol. 12mo. Cloth. $1.25.

SUMNER'S (CHARLES) ORATIONS AND SPEECHES. 2 vols. 16mo. Cloth. $2.50.

ST. JOHN'S (BAYLE) VILLAGE LIFE IN EGYPT. 2 vols. 16mo. Cloth. $1.25.

TYNDALL'S (PROFESSOR) GLACIERS OF THE ALPS. With Illustrations. 1 vol. Cloth. $1.50.

TYLL OWLGLASS'S ADVENTURES. With Illustrations by Crowquill. 1 vol. Cloth, gilt. $2.50.

THE SAND-HILLS OF JUTLAND. By Hans Christian Andersen. 1 vol. 16mo. 75 cents.

THE SEVEN LITTLE SISTERS, who live in the Round Ball that floats in the Air. Illustrated. 63 cents.

THE SOLITARY OF JUAN FERNANDEZ. By the Author of "Picciola." 1 vol. 16mo. Cloth. 50 cents.

TRUE WOMANHOOD. A Novel. By John Neal. $1.25.

TAYLOR'S (HENRY) NOTES FROM LIFE. 1 vol. 16mo. Cloth. 50 cents.

TRELAWNY'S RECOLLECTIONS OF SHELLEY AND BYRON. 1 vol. 16mo. Cloth. 75 cents.

WARREN'S (DR. JOHN C.) LIFE. By Edward Warren, M. D. 2 vols. 8vo. $3.50.

" THE PRESERVATION OF HEALTH. 1 vol. 38 cents.

WALLIS'S (S. T.) SPAIN AND HER INSTITUTIONS. 1 vol. 6mo. Cloth. $1.00

WILLIAMS'S (DR. H. W.) DISEASES OF THE EYE. 1 vol. $1.50.

WORDSWORTH'S (WILLIAM) BIOGRAPHY. By Dr. Christopher Wordsworth. 2 vols. 16mo. Cloth. $2.50.

WENSLEY: A STORY WITHOUT A MORAL. 1 vol. 16mo. Paper. 50 cents. Cloth. 75 cents.

WHEATON'S (ROBERT) MEMOIRS. 1 vol. 16mo. Cloth. $1.00.

In Blue and Gold.

LONGFELLOW'S POETICAL WORKS. 2 vols. $1.75.
" PROSE WORKS. 2 vols. $1.75.
TENNYSON'S POETICAL WORKS. 2 vols. $1.50.
WHITTIER'S POETICAL WORKS. 2 vols. $1.50.
LEIGH HUNT'S POETICAL WORKS. 2 vols. $1.50.
GERALD MASSEY'S POETICAL WORKS. 1 vol. 75 cents.
MRS. JAMESON'S CHARACTERISTICS OF WOMEN. 75 cts.
" DIARY OF AN ENNUYÉE. 1 vol. 75 cts.
" LOVES OF THE POETS. 1 vol. 75 cts.
" SKETCHES OF ART, &c. 1 vol. 75 cts.
" STUDIES AND STORIES. 1 vol. 75 cts.
" ITALIAN PAINTERS. 1 vol. 75 cents.
" LEGENDS OF THE MADONNA. 1 vol 75 cents.
OWEN MEREDITH'S POEMS. 1 vol. 75 cents.
" LUCILE: A Poem. 1 vol. 75 cents.
BOWRING'S MATINS AND VESPERS. 1 vol. 75 cents.
LOWELL'S (J. RUSSELL) POETICAL WORKS. 2 vols. $1.50.
PERCIVAL'S POETICAL WORKS. 2 vols. $1.75.
MOTHERWELL'S POEMS. 1 vol. 75 cents.
SYDNEY DOBELL'S POEMS. 1 vol. 75 cents.
WILLIAM ALLINGHAM'S POEMS. 1 vol. 75 cents.
HORACE. Translated by Theodore Martin. 1 vol. 75 cts.
SAXE'S POETICAL WORKS. With Portrait. 1 vol. 75 cents.
CLOUGH'S POETICAL WORKS. 1 vol. 75 cents.
HOLMES' POETICAL WORKS. With new Portrait. 1 vol. 88 cents.

Works Lately Published.

SIR THOMAS BROWNE'S WRITINGS. A New and Elegant Edition, comprising "Religio Medici," "Urn-Burial," "Christian Morals," &c. With fine Portrait. 1 vol. $1.50.

SPARE HOURS. By John Brown, M. D. 1 vol. $1.50.

MEMOIRS, LETTERS AND REMAINS OF ALEXIS DE TOCQUEVILLE, Author of "Democracy in America." 2 vols. $2.50.

MARGRET HOWTH: A story of To-Day. 1 vol. 16mo. 75 cents.

Works Lately Published.

EYES AND EARS. By Henry Ward Beecher. 1 vol. 12mo. $1.25.

COUNTRY LIVING AND COUNTRY THINKING. By Gail Hamilton. 1 vol. 16mo. $1.25.

THE PATIENCE OF HOPE. With an Introduction by John G. Whittier. 1 vol. 16mo. 75 cents.

THE NEW GYMNASTICS. By Dio Lewis, M. D. With 300 Illustrations. 1 vol. $1.00.

THE GOLDEN HOUR. By M. D. Conway, Author of "The Rejected Stone." 1 vol. 63 cents.

SERMONS Preached in Harvard Chapel. By James Walker, D. D. 1 vol. $1.50.

EDWIN OF DEIRA. By Alexander Smith, Author of "A Life Drama," &c. 1 vol. With fine Portrait of the Author. 75 cents.

THE AUTOBIOGRAPHY, LETTERS, AND LITERARY REMAINS OF MRS. THRALE PIOZZI. Edited by A. Hayward, Esq. 1 vol. $1.50.

THE LIFE AND CAREER OF MAJOR JOHN ANDRE. By Winthrop Sargent. 1 vol. $1.50.

THE SABLE CLOUD. By Nehemiah Adams, D. D., Author of "A South-Side View of Slavery." 1 vol. 75 cents.

FAITHFUL FOREVER. By Coventry Patmore, Author of "The Angel in the House." 1 vol. $1.00.

OVER THE CLIFFS: A Novel. By Charlotte Chanter, (a sister of Rev. Charles Kingsley.) 1 vol. $1.00.

THE RECREATIONS OF A COUNTRY PARSON. 2 vols. $1.25 each. Sold together or separately.

LEISURE HOURS IN TOWN. By the "Country Parson." 1 vol. $1.25.

REMINISCENCES OF SCOTTISH LIFE AND CHARACTER. By Dean Ramsay. From the Seventh Enlarged Edinburgh Edition. With an American Preface. 1 vol. 16mo. $1.00.

POEMS BY REV. WM. CROSWELL, D. D. Edited, with a Memoir, by Rev. Arthur Cleveland Coxe, D. D. 1 vol. $1.00.

PERSONAL HISTORY OF LORD BACON. From Original Letters and Documents. By Hepworth Dixon. 1 vol. $1.25.

POEMS. By Rose Terry. 1 vol. 16mo. 75 cents.

THE AUTOBIOGRAPHY OF THE REV. DR. ALEXANDER CARLYLE. Containing Memorials of the Men and Events of his Times. Edited by John Hill Burton. 1 vol. $1.50.